THE MAGIC HOUR

A VERY PERSONAL HISTORY
OF STATE STREET

JANICE DURAND

LITTLE CREEK PRESS
AND BOOK DESIGN
MINERAL POINT, WISCONSIN

Little Creek Press
5341 Sunny Ridge Road
Mineral Point, WI 53565

ORDERING INFORMATION
Quantity sales. Special discounts are available on quantity purchases by corporations, associations, and others. For details, contact info@littlecreekpress.com

Orders by US trade bookstores and wholesalers.
Please contact Little Creek Press or Ingram for details.

Printed in the United States of America

Cataloging-in-Publication Data
Names: Durand, Janice, author
Title: The Magic Hour. A Very Personal History of State Sreet
Description: Mineral Point, WI: Little Creek Press, 2023
Identifiers: LCCN: 2023905515 | ISBN: 978-1-955656-50-4
Subjects: Biography and Autobiography / General

Cover art by John Ribble
Book design by Mimi Bark and Little Creek Press

To see what is in front of one's nose
needs a constant struggle.

—GEORGE ORWELL

It's hard to walk down State Street in Madison, Wisconsin, without realizing it is one of the great streets in America. Just over half a mile long, a 12-minute walk from end to end, it links two great landmarks: the University of Wisconsin and the state Capitol. Its sidewalks are lined with stores, art displays, restaurants and bars that make it feel like a longer piece of territory than it really is.

—ALAN EHRENHALT, Senior Editor, *Governing Magazine*

1987

I stepped out of the sleek, black limo into an electric din of taxi horns and pulsating music. Neon signs flashed: *Peep Show! Private Booths! Sexual Frenzy!* Across the street, a theatre marquee blazed *Hot, Horny, Lusty Nymphs*. A middle-aged man in a white shirt and tie stood in front of a wall plastered with CATS posters, shouting through a megaphone: “Jesus is coming: Repent!” Sure, it had gone seedy, but it was still Times Square.

My two top managers and I had splurged on a limo to get us here, after a lavish banquet on the top floor of a 6th Avenue skyscraper, where I'd accepted a national award for the Puzzlebox from *Playthings* magazine for best toy store design. Mary Ann, Laura, and I stood together, looking across the intersection at the electric news ticker that raced across the facade of a tall building. Our award would be announced on the ticker at 11:00 p.m., and we weren't going to miss it.

I felt a little dizzy with my own success, which I sometimes thought had come unbidden. When I'd opened my first store in 1979, the Vietnam war was over, but its effects lingered. The anti-war protests had gone violent, alarming the older generation. Tired of the ruckus, they elected mostly Republicans for the next dozen years, including Ronald Reagan in 1982.

The U.S. economy loved Reagan's tax cuts, and by the middle of the eighties, money and energy and optimism flooded the country. People just wanted to forget the war, wanted to feel good again. They wanted pleasure, fun, and shopping, and they loved the toys and games the Puzzlebox sold.

In a spot of good luck and timing, I had landed on one of the best retail streets in the country during a decade when small specialty stores that sold a single product, like soap or beads or paper products, boomed. The Puzzlebox, with its imported European toys, fit the era perfectly. In the flush of my success, I expanded, improbably ending up with three stores in three cities.

It seemed I now had everything I could want. I'd ridden the crest of the second feminist wave in the late seventies. My smart, plucky mother, who raised eight children during the depression years, had settled for a job selling beauty products at home parties after her last child was out of the house. She marveled at my stores, which were not only successful but beloved.

At 48, I was single and self-sufficient, with two sons almost grown, and for the first time since my divorce four years earlier, I had a man in my life—a smart, good-looking guy who seemed to adore me.

I'd had some reservations about expanding. Business wasn't something I'd pursued as a career. It was more like a job, until I found my vocation. But I couldn't ignore the fact that the stores did remarkably well, and I liked the praise.

Now, as I watched the message crawl across the ticker—*1987 winner of best toy store design, The Puzzlebox, Madison, Wisconsin*—all my doubts dissipated. The future was there to grab, so why not go for it?

TEN MONTHS LATER we opened a fourth store in a suburb of Milwaukee. A week after the opening, I sat across from Jennifer Riddle, a business reporter from the *Wisconsin State Journal*, in our spiffy new offices above the Madison store.

I was good with reporters. A story in the local paper provided publicity that couldn't be bought. I loved talking about toys, and it was easy to be candid with the press when our sales were so good.

Today, however, was different. I hadn't slept well in a week. I felt haggard, and I wondered if it showed. The Milwaukee opening had been riddled with delays. I still needed another store in Madison to make the finances work, and I couldn't find a good location.

Across from me, Jennifer put down her notes. "With this fourth store, you're making it look easy, Janice."

Whoa, I thought. She'd caught me unawares, and I spoke without thinking it through. "There's too much competition now for it to be easy. When I started in retail, nobody was selling the European toys we carried. Now you see them in chain toy stores and even department stores. It's harder to keep our shelves filled with the special things customers have come to expect from us."

She looked up sharply from her notebook. "How do you deal with that?"

How indeed? With every passing year, it was more challenging to come up with new stuff. Sometimes I just had to hold my nose and order something I didn't like. But I wouldn't admit that to Jennifer. And I wouldn't talk about the other pesky problems that had surfaced recently, like the monthly declines in the St. Louis store or the erratic sales at the Grand Avenue store. Instead, I shifted gears and accentuated the positive: the beautiful new location, our exceptional customer service. And I did it well enough that a few days later the paper ran a story with a full-color photo of the new store, under the headline No Longer a Puzzle.

Just days after the interview, October 18, 1987, the stock market crashed. It turned out to be the largest one-day market crash in history. In the weeks afterwards, in bed in the morning with coffee and the papers, I read everything I could find to explain it. Most analysts linked the crash to the bull market that began in 1982, fueled by low interest rates, hostile takeovers, and merger mania. They were calling 1986 and 1987 banner years. Later, I would remember how during that period we could sell just about anything.

I felt a little sick. I'd bought a new car to celebrate my success, a bright red Nissan with a removable T-bar roof, the closest I'd ever come to a convertible. Was the party over?

It would be six more months before I faced the reality that I had to reform and repair my business or lose it altogether. But it would take longer than that to come to understand the early eighties as a kind of magic hour when it seemed I could do nothing wrong. But apparently, I had.

In retrospect, my business was like the stock market, relentlessly climbing—soaring even—then tumbling down. Maybe it was a microcosm of the country. At some point in the eighties, I noticed a business culture developing that assumed making money justified any tactics. Ethics slipped—locally, nationally. Starbucks introduced a smart strategy of opening new stores near established ones. New stores opened on State Street that competed directly with neighbors, which I found shocking. All of a sudden, it was good business now, even smart, to take out the other guy.

In a boom era, greed sets in—for money, for wins, for kudos—and when that happens, it's easy for a person or a business or even a country to lose sight of its vision for itself. But I felt confident that I wasn't like that. My original operating principles held.

I'd opened my first store with no thought of profit or fame, only good work. I'd been home with children for almost ten years and was ready to fly. I'd found my power and had been rewarded with success. I guess I'd thought it would go on forever.

Now I felt a need to go back to the time and place where it all started. I wanted to revisit my original vision for myself and my business. The truth was, I had no idea where I had gone off course.

BUT IT WAS TOO early then, at the end of the eighties, to see the past decade with clarity, too soon to have a sense of the seismic changes to come. While most of us thought we were paying attention, anti-trust law was being interpreted in a new way that would create huge new monopolies, transforming the economy, transforming the retail trade, radically changing where and how people shopped. At the same time, technology was leading us into the third industrial revolution, and a new Gilded Age would emerge, one as cruel to the middle and lower classes as the one that had wreaked similar havoc at the end of the nineteenth century.

When I opened my first store in 1979, the U.S. was at a high mark of income equality. My dad hadn't gone past seventh grade, and yet he'd built a respected career as an electrical worker with good pay and benefits, including a pension. But by the late nineties, with more than 300 free-trade agreements signed by President Bill Clinton, most factories had moved abroad. Blue-collar workers took the hit for the country, as jobs dried up and never returned. The rest of us liked globalization, liked the shiny, cheap imported products. My stores had grown more and more profitable selling these products during the national shopping spree of the late twentieth century.

But gradual changes in retail presaged the future economy for anyone looking closely. By 2020, big-box stores had decimated small shops and even taken out many national chains. High rents on city streets would shut out all but the most successful small businesses. Shopping malls emptied out while the big boxes got even bigger, leaving Walmart, Costco, and Amazon dominating the retail market. In a stunning reversal, the U.S. would become the world's most enthusiastic consumer of things made mostly in Asia. Luckily, the tech industry grew rapidly, but it required far fewer workers than the factories, and other than the top-tier tech sector, offered mostly low-paying service jobs to feed the workers and keep their spaces clean.

In 2020, at a town hall in Wisconsin, when asked if the loss of small farms was inevitable, Sonny Perdue, President Trump's Agriculture Secretary, replied: "In America, the big get bigger, and the small will go out," as if that were always true. But it wasn't. It was only in the last few decades of the twentieth century that seventy-five years of anti-trust legislation was upended. As long as corporations could show their monopoly did not raise consumer prices, they could get as big as they liked. An original requirement of community good disappeared, and the suffocating effect of monopolies on competition spread.

And the people began to grow more and more divided by income, politics, and culture, step by step, in changes hardly noticed by most of us, until the pandemic of 2020 revealed everything, in slow motion at first, then in a cascade of turbulent economic, political, and cultural change. In New York, new billionaires chose to dwell high above the city streets in the tallest skyscraper condos ever, marvels of engineering but bereft of beauty to those below and perfectly designed to hide great wealth. The gig economy grew, with plentiful but low-paying jobs in the cities, which were now unaffordable for the working class. Huddled together in New York's outer boroughs, they took the subway daily to service jobs in the city and became the first victims of the pandemic.

The detailed graphs published in the *New York Times* that year revealed that the wealthy heart of Manhattan sustained far fewer deaths from the virus, blowing apart any remaining belief that the U.S. was still the land of equal opportunity.

The clues to the change were there in the early years of my business, in the shopping mania that swept the eighties after the rapid incursion of imports, in the shift from shopping for fun to shopping cheap, even in the changing nature of customers on State Street over the decades. Indeed, the change had happened before my eyes, and I wish I could say I'd seen it coming, but I hadn't.

The Spanish philosopher George Santayana famously said that those who cannot remember the past are condemned to repeat it. When I opened my store in 1979, there were no signs that I would be witness to a 35-year period of momentous national change, but I was. And it didn't happen with one big boom. We got there step by step, in changes hardly noticed by most of us.

ONE

1969

State Street stretched out in front of me, its seven lively blocks pointing the way to the splendid Capitol building on the Square. My small sons stood on either side of me, tiny hands curled in mine, faces bright with excitement. Cars and delivery trucks jammed the narrow street, motors humming, horns beeping. A city bus idled loudly at a stop light. The urban noise was a sweet symphony after the deadly quiet of our last neighborhood. We were back in Madison, permanently released from the small log cabin back in exurban Long Island. I breathed in deeply, relishing the fresh Wisconsin air, tinged with motor oil but full of energy and promise.

This is where I belong, I thought.

As we walked, I smiled at the faint sound of band music floating across the lake from the west campus. I squeezed the boys' hands. "That's the Badger marching band, guys, practicing for a football game."

We crossed the street toward Memorial Library. Students loaded with books rushed by. The women wore their hair long and straight, like mine, parted in the middle; the men's hair hung longish and unkempt, bangs crowding their eyes, kind of like the cuts my little boys wore.

As we passed the library, I heard the sound of a crowd, then shouting, but couldn't hear the words. We turned the corner to the mall, and I stopped, holding back the boys. Ahead of us, a swirling group of students held signs that read STOP THE WAR. I was startled but kind of excited, too. I held the boys tight and took a good look. The protesters were mostly men, with a sprinkling of women, dressed in baggy jeans and long, untucked shirts. A man with scraggly, shoulder-length hair was shaking his fist at a group of helmeted police who stood about twenty feet away. I felt like we were in a newsreel, but I wasn't afraid. From the year we'd spent here in 1964, I knew this was a liberal community, the seat of state government and the University of Wisconsin. Just about everybody in Madison was sympathetic to the anti-Vietnam war protests. "It's OK, kids," I said.

But then, one of the police threw something, and a cloud of smoke broke up the crowd. The protestors started running, the police following closely. One of the students ran close to us, rubbing his eyes frantically. I had a vision of my boys screaming as the acrid tear gas attacked their innocent eyes. I grabbed Peter in my arms, made sure Johnny's hand was tight in mine, and ran in the other direction, my heart thumping. What the hell was going on in Madison?

The sixties were a turbulent decade in the U.S., a crazy quilt of increasingly violent anti-war protests, grotesque political assassinations, and a steady stream of race riots in central cities, beginning with the Harlem riots in 1964, the Watts riots in Los Angeles in 1965, and in Newark and Detroit in 1967. That was the year I wrote my senators to advocate a Marshall plan for the inner cities. But the decade didn't start that way. John Kennedy's short presidency was glamorous and inspiring all at once, full of youthful energy and great hope. Even after he was killed, Lyndon Johnson put in place revolutionary social programs designed to eradicate racism and poverty: Medicare, Medicaid, the War on Poverty, the Voting Rights and Civil Rights bills, Head Start. It was the most ambitious legislation since FDR's New Deal.

And the American economy boomed. Europe had been physically devastated by World War II, but the U.S. infrastructure escaped untouched, with a lot of now-idle munitions factories primed to make consumer products. The Marshall Plan, which sent billions to the continent to help rebuild our allies' cities, proved a great investment.

As Europe recovered, they sent most of the money back for goods made in the U.S. The economic boom gave strength to the American Century and would last well into the eighties, making heroes of industrialists.

But Lyndon Johnson's legacy turned sour when he couldn't win the Vietnam War and refused to end it in defeat. After 1966, dissent grew stronger, protests were frequent and more violent. The assassinations of Malcolm X, Martin Luther King, and finally Bobby Kennedy ignited more protests and riots. It felt a terrible time to me, as if everything familiar were turning bad, and so quickly. It was a bad time for Lyndon Johnson too, who had started as a liberal hero and ended as a villain. When he realized he couldn't be reelected, LBJ decided not to run for a second term. By the time we moved back to Madison in 1969, Richard Nixon had been president for a year, elected handily on a platform of law and order.

MY HUSBAND JOHN and I had joined the Peace Corps in 1962, recent college graduates, sure that our country was the good guy. We'd come home to Wisconsin from our tour in the Philippines just weeks after Kennedy was shot, bereft by the loss of the man who'd inspired us to action, but still believing in a heroic version of America. Seven years later, our country seemed to be in the hands of the bad guys. Sometimes I felt angry about it, but mostly I was sad.

We'd lived in Boston and Long Island during the contentious late sixties. By 1967, I'd come to dread the racketing drone of helicopters on the evening news, returning from the jungles and deltas to unload bodies.

That day in Madison in 1969 when we encountered the protests, Peter was too young at two to register alarm at the police action. He was at the stage where he watched, listened, absorbed, and often popped out a new word. But Johnny at five was articulate and curious.

"Why were the police chasing those students, Mom?" he said as we walked to the housing office. "Did they do something bad?"

I struggled for objectivity. "No, I don't think so. They don't like the war and are trying to get it stopped. It makes the police nervous when they get loud, I think, so they try to break them up."

He knew about the war, had watched the helicopters on the news, had heard us discussing it. But now he was more intrigued by the tear gas than the politics. Shivering at how close he'd come to experiencing it personally, I told him it stung your eyes and made your stomach sick. He nodded, digesting this new fact.

After I got a few listings for apartments, we headed back to State Street. I was surprised to see another group of police milling around at Lake Street and State, the very foot of the long street. Johnny stopped, confused.

"Why are the police here now," he asked, "when nothing's going on?"

Good question, I thought. The danger, if any, had passed quickly. I checked the hostility I instinctively felt toward the police, part of the times for those of us who opposed the war.

"They're probably making sure the students don't get on State Street," I said. I wanted my kids to respect the police, so I didn't let my voice reflect my feeling that the response felt way out of proportion in this safe city. "I know some demonstrators have broken store windows there."

State Street in 1969, Courtesy of Wisconsin Historical Society

I was anxious to put the war behind us and show State Street to my children. The street was seven short, supremely walkable blocks lined with more than a hundred small local stores selling products ranging from typewriters to sheet music to lingerie and fancy dresses. Now, the sweeping view of the hundred-year-old brick commercial buildings made me completely forget the police presence behind us. I was grateful that State Street was the same as when I'd left it.

"The Capitol is huge," Johnny said, pointing up the street where the large white granite building overlooked State Street.

"Cars," Peter said, walking up to a long, bright orange Pontiac, one of dozens of cars parked bumper-to-bumper on the street.

Rennebohms drugstore was on the corner in front of us. The hot, sweet smell of its signature grilled Danish pastries wafted out the open door from the lunch counter. But Johnny had spotted something else. "Mom, look, the windows have boards on them!" Sure enough, half of the front window of the store was covered with plywood. He was getting an education today.

State Street was originally residential, and in some cases, the old houses were still there, nestled behind storefronts. The street was mostly two- and three-story brick buildings, designed for retail on the ground with apartments above. The boys squealed with pleasure at the changing window displays. A song from Hair blasted out of a record store: *"This is the dawning of the age of Aquarius..."*

A heavy, spicy smell of fat and pork came in waves from the Brat House across the street. We passed barber shops and hair salons, shops selling perfume, tobacco, wire-rimmed eyeglasses, typewriters, oil paints and easels, Chinese rice bowls, colored yarns, and tennis rackets.

I'd promised the kids ice cream at the Chocolate House, and after they picked their flavors, we sat licking our cones at a small, round table by the window. Watching the scene outside, I felt a strong sense of change. Five years ago, when we'd lived here, students wanted to look grown-up. Boys had worn trousers and sport jackets, girls pleated skirts and cardigan sweaters. Now the counter-culture that emerged from the Vietnam protests wore jeans, plaid shirts that hung past the hips, mini-skirts and long beads, with peace signs plastered on notebooks, backpacks, and jackets.

It had never occurred to me at their age to question my elders or to dress differently from them. I was a little in awe at the self-assurance of these students. I, too, felt part of the political and cultural change, but it had taken me longer. In the recent past, as a young mother, I'd have worn a dress or skirt. Today, I wore a favorite pair of bright, multi-striped, green pants.

We'd passed a few traditional stores as we walked—Redwood and Ross with a stack of button-down shirts in the window; Antoine's, an expensive women's clothing store where many of the dresses remained in the back, brought out for special customers. But Hershleder's Furs felt way out of place in the new, politicized environment.

The closest store to our house on Long Island had been in a strip mall thirty minutes away, so State Street's stimulating urban environment, broken windows and all, was a breathtaking change. For almost a year, we'd lived in a place far from public spaces and visible political action. We'd had no good public library near us, no city hall, no central gathering space for art or pleasure, and hardly any local stores. Now we were in a city that had all of that and more. Both boys were all attention, faces turned eagerly to the shiny storefronts.

We wouldn't walk to the Capitol Square that day, but when we did, we'd be in the center of both local and state government, a large and excellent public library, five churches, three movie theaters, and a big, beautiful public park. Before the war was finally over four years later, thousands of demonstrators would wend their way from campus up State Street to the steps of the Capitol building, my husband and I among them.

In 1948, *Life* magazine had done a cover story on "The Good Life in Madison, Wisconsin," with a photo of a beaming woman holding a laughing baby high. *Life* had lauded the city for its beauty, clean lakes, and lively, youthful culture. I wondered what it would make of the city now.

I'd been on the sidelines most of my adult life, raising my sons. I loved having children and hoped to give them the good life the magazine had described twenty years earlier. But I was also listening to the new voices championing women's rights. I was eager for work of my own, something challenging that would allow me to find out just what I had in me.

My work would have to fit into this troubling, stimulating new era. I had no idea how I'd make that happen, but I had immediately reconnected with State Street. It was the beating heart of the city, and one way or the other, I wanted it in my life.

TWO

As the eighth child of working-class parents, I had no business going to college at all. Most of my siblings got a job right out of high school, and if they continued to live at home, they paid room and board. But I was put on a more privileged path by my senior English teacher, a brilliant nun named Sister Kathleen. Despite her near-reclusive life in a convent in Chippewa Falls, Wisconsin, this thin-faced, middle-aged woman in a habit that covered everything but her face and hands was hardly provincial. In the course of a month, I'd barely finished memorizing the 'tomorrow and tomorrow' soliloquy from Macbeth when she moved the class on to Paddy Chayevsky's play, *Marty*, about a lonely, Italian-American butcher from the Bronx.

It was Sister Kathleen who convinced my parents to send me to the state teachers' college in nearby Eau Claire. Initially resistant, Mom agreed when she realized it would be good for me to have a teaching degree in case something happened to my husband.

I was a late academic bloomer, just getting by during my first two years of college, until I scored an A in an American history class taught by another brilliant teacher. I still remember the look of passion on Prof. Laura Sutherland's face as she raised her voice over the sound of the closing bell and repeated the sentence she'd opened the class with: "The railroad cut the buffalo in half." That sentence stayed with me all my life, resurfacing at every news story delineating another chapter in the declining fortunes of Native Americans. After that, I started taking a lot of history and literature courses. Eventually, an English professor named John Morris, whose classes in Romantic Poetry and the English novel had opened yet more vistas to me, was assigned to be my adviser.

One day, standing in front of the class, his trim form dapper in a checked sport jacket, Dr. Morris took off his horn-rimmed glasses, propped them on his head, and shocked his small-town students with the statement that if he had been an educated woman in Jane Austen's time, faced with the limited choice of getting married or working as a governess, he might well have turned to prostitution. In 1959, at twenty, I took the restricted role of women as part of the natural order of things. John Morris woke me to the possibility of something different.

I loved all my classes, worked hard in them, and my grade point rose rapidly, and yet I was astonished when in my senior year Dr. Morris recommended me for a teaching fellowship at his alma mater, the University of Tennessee. At the same time, my boyfriend John, whom I'd been dating for a year, received a similar post at another university.

The world opened up to me with infinite possibilities in a field of work I loved. My college years had been the happiest of my life, and the idea of a teaching career modeled on my adviser's was thrilling. But my first real boyfriend and I had gotten serious.

John Durand had grown up in Spooner, a northern Wisconsin town even smaller than mine. I fell in love with his mind, and we both fell in love with our shared desire to escape our origins. He wrote opinion columns for the school paper and aspired to write great novels, which for me evoked Paris or at least New York. I felt John could be a life companion who wouldn't tie me down, a like-minded soul with whom I would share an adventuresome life.

The attraction between us was more mental than physical at first, but when our hormones kicked in, my plans went awry. Long years of Catholic schooling had made sex synonymous with marriage for me. Convinced ours could be a unique wedding of true partners, I came up with a solution: I would forego my fellowship to support him while he got his PhD. When he was done and had a teaching job, I'd get mine.

When I went to my adviser's office to tell him my new plans, Dr. Morris listened silently, his brow furrowed, his clear, blue eyes piercing behind his glasses. For some reason, I'd thought he would understand. He liked John, and my solution seemed reasonable. I hastened to reassure him.

"I will get to graduate school, Dr. Morris. You know I love the field and want to be a great teacher like you."

His face was serious, his eyes unblinking. "This is a mistake, Janice. It'll be three years or more before John finishes his PhD. Your best chance of getting a position like the one you've been offered comes at the end of your undergraduate work."

I shifted in my seat, uncertain. I was only used to approval and praise from Dr. Morris. I struggled for words.

"I'm sorry," I said. "I do appreciate everything you've done for me. But I can't go back now. John and I are engaged."

"John will be in Kentucky, just across the border. You can see each other easily." His face was expressionless, but he sounded annoyed.

"We don't want to be separated," I explained. "We feel we'll be stronger together as a team."

Now he was frowning. He said nothing for a long five seconds. Then: "Are you absolutely sure about this?" His tone was dry and resigned.

I hesitated but held my ground. "Yes. In fact, we're planning to get married next summer."

Looking away from me, he turned back to his papers. His voice was cool. "All right. I'll withdraw your name."

When I left, my stomach hurt, as though my intestines had been squeezed into a ball. Had I just thrown away my big opportunity? But that wasn't to be the worst of it. Two days later, Dr. Morris called John into his office and offered him the fellowship I had rejected. It seemed mine was quite a bit better than his, which would now go to another student.

I felt this like a body blow. I'd let down the man I'd most admired in my short life. He had believed in me, offered me a way to a life I'd never dreamed I could have. And I had not kept faith with his expectations. But I'd made my decision, and I had to tell myself that on this one thing, he was wrong.

Graduation, 1960, with Anna, Ed & Bertha

JOHN MORRIS WAS the first feminist I'd ever met. And, of course, he was right about me. I never did get to graduate school. John struggled in academia, abandoning one thesis he'd been well into before finding another that worked. He finally got the degree, but his fellowship had run out, and my salary as an office manager was meager. That was when I suggested we join the Peace Corps. Jack Kennedy, whom we both admired, had just created the program. The idea of living and working in a village in a third-world country suited our young idealism. For two small-town Wisconsin kids, just the adventure of it was thrilling.

We applied and were quickly accepted for a program in the Philippines. After intensive training, we taught English as a Second Language in rural barrios for eighteen months. We lived in nipa huts with no electricity or running water, adapting as only kids can do. We came to accept our limitations as change agents, and in the end, I valued most the close friendships I forged with fellow teachers and village neighbors. When we were near the end of our tour, I learned that Harvard was offering master's degrees in an innovative teaching program, with generous financial aid to returning Peace Corps volunteers. I would have loved that, but I'd just become pregnant, and John had become politically ambitious.

Back in Madison, he landed a job as field director of the state Democratic party, a position that would ease him into state politics.

The plan was to move north in a year to run for a State Senate seat near our hometowns. The new job was demanding and kept him on the road four days a week.

My infant son, named John after his father, was an angel, and his care made few demands on my time. It was a lonely year for me, with no car and no family or friends nearby. Luckily, there was an excellent library within walking distance, next door to a good bakery. One day I brought home Betty Friedan's *The Feminine Mystique*, a new book about the restricted role of women since the 1940s, when heroines in the women's magazines were adventurous career women.

Dipping into my bag of jelly doughnuts, I read Friedan's theory of the post-World War II feminine mystique, which asserted that women had no greater destiny than to glory in their own femininity. Women's magazines told women how to catch a man and keep him, how to breastfeed their babies, buy a dishwasher, bake bread. How to dress, look, and act more feminine and make marriage more exciting. The feminine mystique maintained that truly feminine women did not want careers, advanced degrees, and the political rights the old-fashioned feminists fought for.

But I knew I was different. I'd had career aspirations all my adult life. My mother was a housewife, but an amazingly strong one, bringing up eight children on a working-class salary, running the family farm when my dad took a job in town.

Still, she had expected me to put my marriage first. When I was honest, I saw just how well I'd fashioned my own destiny. It was my idea to turn down my teaching fellowship and support my husband. When graduate school didn't work out and we were out of money, I solved that problem by getting us into the Peace Corps. Later, when I understood our partnership was weak, I got pregnant to strengthen it.

The dominant culture of the times was telling both of us that John came first. We were products of our upbringing, and I'd set the pattern with my own decisions. And as my mother loved to say, if you made your bed, you had to lie in it. I knew I would need good work in the future, but, in truth, I wanted a family, too. I'd do that now and figure out the rest later.

We moved five times in the next five years. First, John lost the State Senate election to the incumbent. I had gotten pregnant again, and

With Johnny & Peter in Boston, 1967

out of money, with slim prospects for jobs in northern Wisconsin, we moved to Boston, where John got a good job training Peace Corps volunteers. Our second son, Peter, was born there.

THE VIETNAM WAR had morphed into a virus that followed us from state to state, fading for a while, and then resurfacing, meaner than before. In 1965, when more soldiers were needed to replace the thousands who had died or been wounded, college students lost their deferments, and the war came closer for many people we knew. Up to this time, the fighting army had been made up of working-class white and black men.

Knowing his reelection was doomed, Lyndon Johnson resigned from the Presidency in March of 1968. Eugene McCarthy announced his Democratic candidacy, followed by Bobby Kennedy. That spring, Martin Luther King was shot in Memphis, and Kennedy was killed while campaigning in Los Angeles. I was numb, then outraged. Race riots erupted in major cities that summer, including Boston, where we were living. It all felt hopeless.

I remember sitting at the little desk on the screened porch of our second-floor apartment in Belmont, just miles away from the site of the Boston Tea Party, writing my senators to ask them to sponsor a bill similar to the Marshall Plan to rebuild the burned-out black neighborhoods. The situation felt desperate, but in the end little changed.

After a year and a half, we moved again, to a new job at Stony Brook State University on Long Island. We found a small log cabin to rent just a few blocks from the Sound. That fall I enjoyed walking the beach with the kids, collecting horseshoe crabs, but in winter, the wind blew hard and cold across the water, and the tiny cabin became a jail.

Thankfully, after a scant year there, we moved back to Madison, yearning for the proximity of home amid the growing turmoil. And so

I found myself, on our first day in Madison, running from tear gas on the UW campus, the boys in hand.

We found an apartment in University Heights, a lovely old neighborhood of early twentieth-century houses that had been home to college professors for over a century. It felt reassuringly stable, despite the tear gas that occasionally drifted in from the campus half a mile away.

Both boys loved their new neighborhood. They looked healthy and happy now, with shiny caps of blond hair, blue eyes, and fair skin. Their distinct personalities were emerging clearly. Johnny was brainy, interested in toys that did things—planes, cars. He dug deeper, read early and quickly, loved books. Peter was more outgoing, loving and lovable, blindly adoring of his big brother.

My own youth had been happy despite spatting parents, simply because so much love flowed to me from my seven older brothers and sisters. My children had just the two of us and each other. Except for the brief time when John ran for political office up north, we'd never lived near our families. We'd always been by ourselves, a super-nuclear unit.

There had been many nights in those early years when I lay awake in bed worrying the boys didn't have enough people in their lives, enough love. That ended in University Heights, where we found a great school and plenty of friends, which explains why in the future I would have such a hard time leaving it.

A MONTH AFTER we moved back, we learned along with our fellow citizens that hundreds of Vietnamese civilians who lived in a small hamlet called My Lai had been murdered by American soldiers. Up to that time, I would not have believed American soldiers were capable of such brutality.

Six months later, at a Kent State University anti-war demonstration, Ohio National Guard soldiers shot and killed four students, including a girl who was simply walking to class.

A poll taken soon after showed that 58% of Americans felt the shooting was justified. In the past, a majority had supported the protests. But when they turned violent, with looting and destruction, public opinion turned against the peace movement. For the first time in my life, I felt estranged from the majority of my countrymen and from my parents, who still believed the war was necessary. It was a terrible feeling, like I'd lost my country and my moorings.

In that chaotic period, families couldn't get together without fighting. We visited my parents in Chippewa Falls right after the volatile 1968 Democratic convention in Chicago, with its huge antiwar protests and violence. One day my dad was showing John the latest issue of *Life*, full of photos of the Chicago convention. My dad was a union man, with a good salary and benefits, so he automatically backed the Democratic party's candidate, Hubert Humphrey. I'd warned John not to speak up for Eugene McCarthy, the anti-war candidate we supported in the primary. John passed the magazine to my mother, and I stood with her looking at a photo of a girl in a hospital bed, with bandages on her forehead, arms, and legs. I sucked in my breath, shocked that someone who looked a lot like me would have been attacked by police. But my mother's eyes were riveted on the short skirt of the girl who was standing next to her friend's bed. Mom was a kind person, but now her face was harsh in judgment as she spoke: "Her skirt barely covers her backside. Disgusting!"

"How can you focus on her skirt when her friend's been beat up by police?" I couldn't hide my outrage. She looked surprised.

"Any girl who dresses like this shouldn't be surprised when she gets a reaction. Why would such young girls think they know better than the President?"

My mother's uneasiness with the short skirt was a clue I ignored, but also a warning shot across a decade, which Ronald Reagan would hear when he ran for President in 1982. It was the sound of a nation tired of strife and violence, yes, but also of social change that threatened the order of many people's lives, especially those over thirty or those who practiced traditional religion. A girl who *dressed like that* would not care if a boy thought of sex when he saw her, might like it, might indignantly assert a woman's right to dress as she liked without considering a man's response. She might think sex without marriage was just fine. In fact, maybe marriage was outdated. And what, my mother thought, would happen to children then, and to the community and the country, and the unwritten laws that bound it all together and kept everyone safe?

Fifty years later, walking down a corridor full of adolescents at the middle school where I tutored, I would notice an assistant principal ahead of me. She was wearing a black and white striped, ankle-length jersey knit skirt, and I couldn't help noticing it clung to her hips like water to a wet T-shirt. Just behind her, a teen-aged boy with curly brown hair couldn't take his eyes off the sinuous movement of her buttocks.

What? I thought. Why would a teacher wear an outfit like that in a school full of testosterone-loaded adolescents? Does she have no inkling the effect she was having on that kid? I was seeing girls on the streets of Madison now wearing shorts cut so high on the thigh they seemed to be an invitation to sex. And I tried to remember when being a sex object felt desirable, when premarital sex became common. And then my mind flashed back to Mom and the short skirt in 1968. Had what she feared come true? Was this why women were marrying at an older age, if at all, and divorce was normalizing? With a little jolt, I remembered that day at my parents' home fifty years earlier. I was pretty sure I hadn't turned into my mother, but I was starting to see her point.

IN 1970, in the early hours of the morning, we woke to a loud explosion. The ominous sound of sirens followed, but it wasn't until morning that we learned a radical group had bombed Sterling Hall, the campus physics building that housed a research center funded by the U.S. Army. The bomb inadvertently killed Robert Fassnacht, a research physicist with no connection to the target, who just happened to be working late.

Sterling Hall was a turning point for Madison. The public tolerated the protests but overwhelmingly opposed them when they turned violent and destructive. The extremists had gone too far, and student demonstrations died down, although the war would not formally end for three more years.

But the political and cultural gap that had grown through the sixties was here to stay. In fact, the next decade would bring even more change to up the game.

THREE

One day in 1972, almost three years after our return to Madison, John came home from work eager to talk. He was looking good, wearing the dress slacks and white shirt and tie his state government job called for. He had thick, lustrous hair and he wore it longish, covering his ears, in the style of the day. He paced the living room, avoiding my eyes.

"I think we should have an open marriage," he blurted.

"What?" I bolted out of the chair. *Open Marriage*, a book that had come out that year, had advocated the acceptance of extramarital affairs.

"It's silly that people should be confined to just one partner," he said, chin rising.

"Do you have someone in mind?" I was recovering fast, shock changing to quiet anger.

He was walking around as he talked. The kids were playing in their rooms at the back of the apartment. I sat back down, one leg crossed over the other, arms folded against my chest. I knew he was attracted to a co-worker, a slightly younger blonde woman who'd presented a cool face to me at staff parties. She had a vaguely Nordic air and rarely smiled. But apparently he hadn't taken things further—not without my permission, it seemed.

"You know I like Ingrid. A lot. She's different than anyone I know. But that's not the point. What reason is there for two people to have only one partner forever?"

My heart was constricting. My pride was wounded. But mostly, I found myself irritated that he had the bad taste to tell me about his crush. Why couldn't he have just suffered silently? I myself had been seriously attracted to several men during my married years, men who had frankly admired me and seemed to see things in me my husband didn't. But it had never occurred to me to act on my feelings. And certainly, there had been no reason to mention it to John.

This conversation opened up many thoughts that I had repressed: John and I had married too young, attracted to each other's politics and ambitions rather than bodies and spirits. Inadvertently, John had cracked the facade of our cool marriage. Still, we'd made a deal, had children now. I was sticking with it and expected him to as well.

I insisted we see a counselor, and John reluctantly agreed. But after a few sessions, he backed off his expressed wish for more freedom, refusing more therapy. I knew he was avoiding a close inspection of our relationship, but still I felt relief when the marriage resumed its surface normality. We'd settled into a lovely, friendly neighborhood, and my children had steady friends for the first time in their lives. They needed an intact family, and I needed the marriage to stay together for them. Someday when they were grown it would be different, but I wouldn't think about that now.

Open marriage never caught on in the mainstream culture. It was part of the experimentation going on then, part of the "question everything" mood. Values were shifting. But while many people, mostly younger then, embraced a new sexual permissiveness, others saw it as an attack on life as they knew it. The idea of open marriage was the tip of a cultural iceberg that would emerge later in the decade, when morality itself would be redefined.

And there was something distinctly different about the value shift in the seventies. In another era, values might change, but only temporarily. The roaring twenties, for instance, were decidedly decadent, with prohibition making criminals out of ordinary people. But when the depression hit, followed by the attack on Pearl Harbor, there was scant time or money for dissipation.

It was the charged atmosphere of the seventies, the resistance to an immoral war waged by our government, that made the new values stick. Many in the younger generation were now in open rebellion against the conventions of their elders.

Not coincidentally, a movement among social scientists in university circles was redefining right and wrong. The new thinkers maintained that morality was about treating people well. It was about harm and fairness—not loyalty, patriotism, respect, duty, tradition. Breaking social conventions that had been in place for decades—whom you slept with, what you smoked—were OK as long as you didn't harm anyone. These new values were absorbed by many boomers in college in the late seventies, who were suspicious of hierarchy and authority. *(Don't trust anyone over 30*! was a familiar cry.) Everyone had the right to question authority, and many schools would eventually embody progressive principles.

Of course, not everyone bought into the new thinking. Religious people and conservatives found the new morality incompatible with their faith and convictions, many of which were centered in the welfare of children and the family. In general, those resisting the changes lined up with the Republican party. Those who liked the new morality tended to line up as liberal Democrats. Political rigidity on each side grew as the nation found another reason to be divided.

And yet, for most people on the planet, morality was still defined conventionally in cultures that were more centered in the good of the community rather than the freedom of the individual. And so, we agreed less and less about what was moral.

I was raised in the fifties, in a town where community came first, and I never questioned the way things were. People's roles were clear, designed to keep the community intact. A woman's role was to bear and raise children. It was OK to work if you had to, and only if you could still take good care of your children. And divorce was rare; it was harmful to kids. My parents had such a stormy relationship that my mother often threatened divorce, but they lived together for better and for worse until Mom died at 82. The new morality would eventually sanction premarital sex, living together without marriage, having children without marriage or a spouse, abortion, and divorce. Many values of previous generations were rejected. We could have casual sex and not go to hell, use drugs in general company. I remember a party in the seventies when I got high on hashish someone's brother brought back from Vietnam, then vomited all night. But who did that harm? In time, we'd all be free to live together without marriage and divorce and without shame, and it all started in the seventies. And why not? After all, our elders had sanctioned a war that killed a lot of innocent people, even putting their own children in peril to defend a morally questionable cause. That was real harm.

With all that permission, the decade was an exciting one—but it was not a nice time. People on both sides were angry, brittle, defiant, intolerant, edgy. There was social pressure to adopt the changes, even if you had reservations. I wanted to be hip, to be part of the movement. I grew my straight hair long, and my oval plastic glasses gave way to round, yellow-tinted, wire-rimmed ones. I favored turtleneck sweaters with long beaded necklaces and dangly earrings that made me feel sexy.

Janice, 1972

Soon, all of this cultural change got personal. I began to think more about my own perception of what I could be rather than what my upbringing had dictated. I loved the idea of a teaching career, but with new eyes, I saw it was one of two professional paths encouraged for women in my era; the other was nursing. I read an article by Judy Brandy called "I Want a Wife" in *Ms. Magazine*; Brandy argued that if women had wives as men do, they could achieve as much. I thought back to the years I'd traveled with John, putting my career aside as he searched for his.

The women's movement would pick up full steam in the late seventies, but a few icons had emerged earlier. Gloria Steinem's combination of beauty, brains, and grit was irresistible. Mary Tyler Moore, whose charming, friendly, socially inept character debuted on TV in 1970, seemed most like me, but better, a nice Minnesota girl brought up to know her place. She lived alone, worked in a field dominated by men, and screwed up her courage regularly to ask for what she deserved. Despite her ambition, she was feminine, with long hair made a little wild for the seventies.

For young people, the seventies felt like a fresh start. One generation was leaving, and a new one was taking its place. But I was between the old and the new, and it wasn't so easy for me to change. No one I grew up with had divorced parents. Divorce felt wrong, awful even. But as I absorbed the new culture, I started to think maybe an unhappy marriage was as bad for kids as divorce.

In time, I saw how in his open-marriage gambit, John had been more honest than I. He had admitted a lack of passion between us, a lack I would admit to myself but to no one else. The last thing I would do at this stage of my sons' development was to give them warring parents, not to mention divorce. I had settled into a new version of my marriage, based on the best interests of the children.

My turn would come, soon.

FOUR

I stood paralyzed with confusion behind the cash register, wondering what I was supposed to do with the twenty-dollar bill in my hand. The customer who'd given it to me was waiting, a frown on her face, while behind me my sister yammered in my ear.

"Jesus, Janice, you were supposed to have your crew finished with lunch breaks a half hour ago. What are you thinking?"

Well, that woke me up. I made change for the customer while I hissed over my shoulder: "They've been shoving money at us for an hour, and I don't have enough people to cover."

Joan was driving me crazy. It was bad enough I was standing on concrete twelve hours a day without her critiquing my performance. She'd known I'd never even worked in a store. And it was only the second day of the ten-day fair.

I hadn't worked at all when the kids were small, but each year for three years after we settled in Madison, I left them with John for twelve days in August to run a sixties boutique called Mother Earth for my brother-in-law Ed at the state fair in Minneapolis. Ed had originally opened a stand called Eddie's Teddyland. Set up next to encyclopedia salesmen and ginzo knife pitchmen, he sold stuffed toys to all the poor guys who'd failed to win a prize for their girlfriends at the rigged midway games. The store did so well he expanded to other temporary stands, including Mother Earth, which my sister set up for him and recruited me to run.

It was an exhausting job, but I got better quickly. Managing employees was the hardest part, but deterring shoplifters was a close second.

Thieves loved the Mexican silver jewelry, the patchouli incense, the leather headbands, and the rolled-up posters of rock bands. Once at the end of the day we discovered that a large spinning display of earrings had simply disappeared from the counter.

For three summer seasons, I ran Mother Earth for fun, but it turned out to be excellent training for a retail career, involving as it did massive crowds, long hours, volume sales, and a bunch of employees to oversee. The ten-day fair was as compressed as the retail Christmas season, and learning happens fast under that kind of pressure. I also learned at the fair that I loved the sheer physicality of the work and the stimulation of being close to the action.

As for meal breaks, I preferred taking mine later, when everyone else was done. I loved it then, when the midway was getting dark, the neon flashing, the carnies hawking the games and rides, cigarettes dangling from their mouths as they flirted with the teenage girls. The sugary and deep-fried-fat smells of fair food flooded my senses. I wolfed down a Pronto Pup, a superior Minnesota version of the corn dog, as I strolled blissfully, stopping to watch the screaming teens braced against the wall of the Round Up, an insane ride based on centrifugal force. I was never happier in the moment than on those nights on the midway of the Minnesota State Fair.

JOHN AND I DIDN'T have much money in those days, but neither of us worried about it. Our minds were elsewhere, and the truth is it was much easier to live on a small salary then. The sixties and seventies were good for working-class people like my parents, too. Neither went past seventh grade, and my mother never held a serious job, but they were able to live in a middle-class neighborhood and send eight kids to parochial school. My next-oldest sibling and I were the only ones who got to college, mostly because we'd come along at the end, but all of us prospered one way or the other, with mostly just a high school education and for a few, a year of technical school or college.

The dollar was worth a lot more in terms of purchasing power then. When John started working for the State in 1970, his salary was $12,000, the equivalent of $59,000 in 2020. We easily managed rent on a three-bedroom apartment with built-in oak bookcases and hardwood floors, and a few years later, when I added a part-time salary, we bought a lovely, big house.

The thought of owning a house never crossed our minds until our lease was running out and we learned from neighbors that a house up the hill, kitty-corner from the large lot that housed the Chancellor of the University, was for sale for $37,000. We had no savings for the 10% down payment, but we managed it with an FHA loan for $1,000, co-signed by John's boss, plus several loans from family.

The house we bought on Forest Street in 1973 for $37,000 would sell for $100,000 when we sold it ten years later. In 2020, it would sell for $620,000.

In later years, I wondered when and why everything got so expensive, especially the big things like houses, rent, cars, and medicine. And college education. When I started my freshman year in 1956 at the state college in Eau Claire, tuition and books for one semester cost around $150.00. Because all my siblings were now gone, I was able to live at home free, and I managed to pay all four years of expenses myself by working summer and part-time jobs.

The more prosperous the nation became, the more expensive the cost of living became for most people.

I LOVED OUR HOUSE on Forest Street. It was stucco, with the 'battered' sloping walls of the prairie school. It had three full bedrooms, a den off the living room with one whole wall of bookshelves, and a south-facing porch with a tile floor and gracefully arched screens. The yard in spring was a wonder, with crocus, trillium, wild ginger, bleeding hearts, and Virginia bluebells planted by a previous owner sprouting up to surprise me every other day.

Our house on Forest Street

We'd never had such luxurious space, with rooms for each boy and a spacious master bedroom. There were large crank-out windows in every room; in summer the breezes wafted throughout the house, stirring the edges of the generous mass of fairy tale ivy covering the southeast side of the roof and attic windows.

The boys were nine and seven, still young enough to be good friends and playmates. They now abandoned the cardboard brick blocks that had served as forts for years of play for the lure of Legos, which would absorb them both for many years. It was the era before soccer moms, and outside of scouting, the boys had no organized activities or sports, nor did their friends. They rarely complained of boredom.

John, Peter, Johnny

Afternoons, with the house cleaned, the shopping done, the evening meal planned, I'd grab a novel and head for the couch, hungry for more stimulating worlds. Then one day, I put down Pride and Prejudice, which I was reading for at least the third time. It was time to find a job.

Thirteen years after college, the only experience on my resume was my Peace Corps tour and my fair gigs. I had tried one last time to get teaching credentials by applying to the University of Wisconsin for the semester of practice teaching I needed to teach high school English. My timing was bad, as there were more teachers now than teaching jobs.

Desperate, I hit on the idea of writing a guidebook to Madison and began researching the city's history and resources. John liked the idea, and with skills he'd learned working for our college paper, became my publishing partner. After the year it took me to write, I typed it out on a Selectric Typewriter, which produced professional typeface. John then cut and pasted the copy into a rectangular format, adding his own line drawings. We called the book *Getting the Most Out of Madison*.

When a mock-up was ready, John showed a boldness and self-confidence I lacked by approaching a local bank, suggesting they buy advance copies to give out to new accounts. To my surprise, they bought a thousand. The presale covered all of the printing costs for two thousand copies, leaving us half to sell at full profit.

The weeks before the book was reviewed, I regularly went limp with the certainty that no one would like it. To forestall taking my first glass of wine too early, I put on my Sears Keds every afternoon at 4:00 and ran two miles at the West High track. I was enormously relieved (and promptly quit running) when the book was well received. It would completely sell out in three years.

John and I had partnered well on the project. His drive and self-confidence made all the difference in getting the piece printed. Publishing a book in the pre-digital age was a big deal, and I would be continually surprised at how it impressed people more accomplished than I.

The guidebook got me an interview for a job developing the shop at the Elvehjem Museum of Art (pronounced *LVM*) on the UW campus. The director seemed relieved that I knew something about running a store and hired me.

Mother Earth had taught me the rudiments of store operations. At the Elvehjem, I learned I had a knack for buying, and in the years I was there, I began to learn the fine art of merchandising. I traveled to trade shows to find products that were related to the museum's collection, and when my work produced new, much needed cash for a museum whose funding mostly had strings attached, a new director gave me a raise. Customers liked the products I picked, and sales continued to climb.

Still, I never saw it as a retail job. It was more artsy than that, even academic, given that the Elvehjem was a teaching museum. I certainly never considered it a path to a permanent profession. Running a store seemed a poor second to the satisfaction of teaching, of waking young minds to great ideas and literature. But I liked not being confined to a desk for hours at a time, liked the freedom I had to move in and out of the store at will.

AFTER I WENT TO WORK, things looked tidy in my domestic world, but soon enough things changed in our family dynamic. Up to now, John had been our sole breadwinner. He'd been pleased when I got my job, and with my salary added to the pot, I thought he would relax. Instead, he became increasingly discontented. Every night after dinner he went to his desk and worked on inventing board games. His plan was to sell one to a national toy company, making his fortune and freeing him from his bureaucratic position. That never materialized, but he didn't give up, moving from project to project.

John was an attractive, interesting man, and people enjoyed him. He read widely, especially in history and current politics, and was a good conversationalist. But he didn't need many people. He only wanted to see people he worked with or people he liked. I grew tired of making excuses to people who invited us over, mostly my friends. Whenever I complained, his general response was a refusal to engage, leaving me with the options of screaming to get his attention or walking away. I hated fighting. There'd been too much of that in my family during my childhood. So, I disengaged.

Increasingly, I looked to my work to fill the inevitable void when my kids would leave home. Two co-workers at the Elvehjem, Anne Boyle and Doreen Holmgren, would become close friends for life. With them I gradually relaxed my boundaries with drinking, which were tight at home. Almost everyone in my family drank to excess, and I'd always watched myself closely. In those child-raising years, I occasionally lost control and drank to a danger point. One Thanksgiving, I drove a car full of John's visiting relatives up a one-way street after a celebration at a local tavern. Then, on a girlfriends' weekend away with my two new friends, I got so drunk one night I was barely able to function the next day. I saw my friends' reaction, and, appalled at what I'd done, became even more careful. I promised myself it would never happen again.

This episode disturbed me enough that I decided to see a therapist. When she asked me how much I drank every day, I cut the amount neatly in half, either ashamed to say how much or reluctant to give it up. Assuming the drinking had been situational, the therapist soon steered the sessions to my marriage, and before long suggested John and I do couples counseling. He agreed, and I was relieved when in the sessions he listened to me and acknowledged our marriage needed work.

This began the happiest period in our family life. John and I took our first vacation together since we'd had the children, flying to South Carolina to stay in a cabin on stilts on the Atlantic shore. That winter we bought cross-country skis for all of us and explored the trails in the city and nearby state parks. At home we bought a heated waterbed, just for fun, to put in the small room next to our bedroom, originally used as a nursery. It was for all of us, whoever claimed it first, a snug spot to read on a cold winter's day.

With two jobs and extra money, we started spending some of it on ourselves. We were having fun for a change. We had dinner parties at home with several neighbors who had become friends. It was fun to entertain in our wonderful house, and I remember well one dinner with two couples who lived on our block who we especially enjoyed. It was an evening of good food and drink and excellent conversation.

Years later, I would remember that night with pleasure and then pull up short when I realized that just five years after it took place, all three couples would be divorced.

FIVE

In a corner restaurant near our hotel in the French Quarter one day in 1977, I sat watching with a smile as Johnny, thirteen now, polished off the last of three large deep-fried shrimp, crunching to the very edge of each tail. We were on a rare family vacation in New Orleans. John and I had reservations that evening at a fancy restaurant in the Garden District and were feeding the kids before taking them back to the hotel. At ten, Peter was still in the hot dog stage and had dispatched the one the kitchen had found for him in about two minutes. Now he was pretending to nibble at a golden crab cake.

Johnny had loved seafood practically from infancy. When he was two and we lived in Boston, I'd park him in front of the lobster tank at the Star Market while I trotted up and down aisles grabbing cereal and toilet paper, returning to the cart periodically to unload. He watched the lobsters so intently, hardly moving, that I couldn't bring myself to pull him away a minute earlier than I had to. When he finally got to taste one, it was love for life.

When he spotted a seafood platter on the menu in New Orleans, he happily ordered it, waiting patiently in the small restaurant, the air fragrant with the smells of deep-fried cooking and Cajun spices. He'd already eaten a lobster tail, adeptly digging the tender white flesh out of the shell, dipping it into hot butter, smacking his lips in pleasure as he chewed. He carefully picked the meat from five steamed clams and put away a nice piece of salmon, saving a huge crab leg for last. I noticed a woman sitting at a table next to us eyeing him as he ate. Now as he gave his full attention to cracking the crab claw, she and her companion got up to leave. Stopping at our table, she broke into a smile, shook her head and said, "I've never seen a child eat like that!"

I was besotted by the French Quarter, by the sudden glimpses through narrow alleys of statues and purple bougainvillea, the charming, curlicued iron balconies on the two-story buildings in Jackson Square, the mellow strains of jazz drifting out of the painted pink storefronts. Oyster bars occupied almost every corner, with hundreds of the delectable shellfish wedged into mounds of ice. We'd stop at a bar, order a dozen on the half shell, and John and I and Johnny would squeeze on a little lemon juice and tip the oysters with their fresh, briny liquor into our mouths while Peter looked on in disgust.

New Orleans was a sensual delight unlike any place I'd ever been, and it was that sense of physical pleasure that fed into the creation of my first store. We'd wandered into Jackson Square one day, where the smell of sugar and roasted coffee beans drifted out from the open-air Café Du Monde. Heading in, we sat at a small table and ordered plates of the pillowy beignets lavishly sprinkled with powdered sugar. John and the boys ate a double order; I couldn't get enough of the café au lait, made with strong chicory coffee and steaming hot milk.

When we left, the boys wandered ahead of us into a square ringed with retail shops. Johnny had shot up a foot taller than his brother. He wore cut-off jeans and socks up to his knees, his unruly blond hair falling over his new glasses. Peter was dressed in khaki shorts and a striped polo shirt, hair neatly parted.

Suddenly I heard Peter call, "Mom, Dad, there's a toy store," as they ducked in the door. We followed them into a sunny room with 20-foot dragon kites draped along the ceiling. Shiny toys in bright blues, reds and yellows filled the shelves. Colorful cloth diamond kites spilled out of a tall wicker basket. I picked up a large wooden jigsaw puzzle of the world, each continent a different color.

"I've never seen a puzzle like this," I said to John, turning it over to read the label. It was from England.

He was holding a varnished wooden truck. "Look at the craft on these maple wheels. It's made in Vermont." I took the toy and ran my hand over its satiny finish.

The boys had already rushed to the back of the store, where Johnny was peering at instructions on a complex polyhedron building kit. Peter held up a wood dinosaur assembly kit. "These are cool! Can we get one?"

These toys were appealing and well-made, and I had never seen any of them in the toy stores in Madison. When I asked, the sales clerk told me the store was owned by a couple who had several other stores in the French Quarter. Curious, I visited one before we left. It was a tabletop store full of beautiful things I'd never seen before—plates and bowls in lush tropical colors, pitchers and platters covered with bold patterns of ferns and flowers, all so different from the pretty, traditional floral china sold in department stores. The stores themselves looked different, decorated more like a home than a retail space, with brightly painted walls, low tables for display, and polished hardwood floors.

I loved what I was seeing but would only understand later that these stores represented a new energy in storefront retail, a step-up in quality of design and product and a more sophisticated look. When I was growing up in Chippewa Falls, if you wanted to buy a gift you could either go to the hardware store where a shelf or two would hold bowl sets, mantle clocks, and decorative figurines, or the dime store, where I do remember happily walking out with a small bottle of lily-of-the-valley perfume for my mother.

As we walked the French Quarter that night, I found myself wondering how a toy store like the one we'd seen would do in Madison. I thought stores like these would do well in any kind of marketplace where lots of different people came together—places like city centers with pedestrian streets. A place like downtown Madison, maybe, although it was going through a transition now. It would be two years before I opened the Puzzlebox on State Street, but the germ of the idea came from this trip.

OUR GOLDEN TIME slid to an abrupt end when after almost three years at the Elvehjem, I quit my job. I'd started to worry some time ago that I'd grown too comfortable in a position with no future. I'd shared my doubts with John, told him I wanted more interesting work, but he was still surprised when I decided to leave to explore other possibilities. Despite my success with the store, John was not so confident that I could do better. But I felt sure I could and enrolled in a marketing course at the University to see if there was some other way to use the business talent that had unexpectedly emerged.

Unfortunately, reading case studies on milk distribution in Chile only depressed me. Before long, I found myself scrutinizing the want ads. Like most people who quit one job without another lined up, I started to feel sure I'd never work again.

Then John flabbergasted me by abruptly quitting his job to start his own consulting business. In retrospect, I should have seen it coming. I had naively assumed we were on the same page. I'd supported him for ten years while he moved from job to job, and now I expected the same of him. But he'd been working for nine years at a job he now found stultifying and had often made his unhappiness clear, still doing his duty to support the family. Then just when I had taken over some of the load, I quit my job. Now he quit his, and the message was clear: I'd better get back to work and fast.

Soon enough I got an interview for a well-paying job in the UW School of Nursing as assistant to the dean, with excellent benefits. I was surprised when, the day after my interview, the dean called to offer me the job. John was home, working in the basement, and I went downstairs to tell him.

"Great! When do you start?" he said, looking up from his bench saw.

"Wait! I haven't decided yet. It doesn't sound that great, except the salary. I'd set up meetings, take notes, take phone calls for the dean, kind of a glorified secretary, I think."

He was frowning. "It would be good experience, and the benefits are great. You're lucky to get an offer like this."

For me, the alarm bells were deafening.

"John, I had a good job I left because I knew I wouldn't be happy in it long term. This is only a step up in that it pays better."

"I don't know where in Madison you think you'll get a better job." Ouch! But he was right. There wasn't much here besides government jobs.

"I don't have to say yes right away," I said. "She gave me a week."

But the next day, knowing my resolve might weaken, I called the dean and turned down the job. When I told John, he barely concealed his frustration.

In truth, the quick offer had emboldened me to hold out for something better. The next three weeks got more and more uncomfortable, as John and I found little to say to each other. I acted normal on the outside, but inside I was scared. Our savings dwindled as few job prospects turned up.

It was a relief when I got an interview for an intriguing position as coordinator of the new State Street Mall and Capital Concourse, a makeover that took cars off State Street and the Capitol Square and incorporated newly widened sidewalks, new trees, benches, and bus shelters. I'd read the positive press on the new mall and the need for downtown rejuvenation. Over a hundred people had applied for what was seen as a prestigious post, even though it paid a low salary.

By the end of the seventies, the new regional malls that opened up all over the country had proved tough competition for free-standing stores in downtowns where there was no free, convenient parking. Madison still had a good number of stores on the Capitol Square, but newly empty storefronts were alarming, and on State Street, older stores were leaving without being replaced. Cities all over were struggling with dying downtowns.

In a few days, I sat down for my interview with Sue Springman, head of the Central Madison Council. She seemed very young to me, with long, wavy dark hair, friendly brown eyes, and an attractive air of crisp confidence. She questioned me closely about my experience and warned me that the city funding provided only a tiny promotional budget and no staff assistance.

I came home that afternoon discouraged about my chances. I just didn't think I was qualified for the job. John was eager to hear about it. When I described Sue, he stopped me. "How old do you think she is?"

"I don't know, maybe 25."

"Ha!" he snorted. "What are the chances she'd hire someone more than ten years older? No one wants to supervise a person with more life experience."

That seemed to settle the issue. But two days later, Sue called me in to a second interview, this time with a panel of city officials. It was brutal. The man who would be director of the new Civic Center grilled me on how I would "entice people back to a downtown they've deserted." I fumbled for an answer.

Two days later, Sue offered me the job. Apparently, she had the last word and had enough self-confidence not to let my age bother her. John was equally surprised, and I tried hard not to crow.

I was sure I'd made the right decision. It was my turn now.

SIX

Four months later, on a warm spring day, I sat on a bench on State Street listening to Chuck Bauer, co-owner of the Soap Opera on the 300 block, explaining his unlikely path to business. The store was a sliver of space always jammed with happy customers. He and his partner in both life and business, Chuck Beckwith, were both recent graduates of the University of Wisconsin with art degrees.

"Chuck and I both had parents who encouraged us to get liberal arts degrees. They trusted we'd find what we loved and follow that impulse. The truth is we stumbled into retail." He smiled. "We started selling handcrafts on the grass on Library Mall, like gypsies. But the city wanted something more permanent, so Chuck found a child's wagon at an antique shop and we sold leather hair barrettes out of that."

Eventually, they moved to a closet-sized space in a house on Lake Street and later to their current storefront. I was struck at how intuitively they had acted, making up their own business model as they went along.

"When we finally found a space, it was so small that it made sense to sell body care, mostly small items. Many of our wholesalers were young and innovative, and the products they sold were about the new environmental movement—biodegradability, herbal sources, and ecological packaging—that reflected our values, too. Our customers got it, liked it, bought it."

In fact, in only a few years, the Soap Opera would be what is known in the industry as a category killer: so well-patronized, so respected and loved by customers that no one could steal them away.

Bauer and Beckwith fit into the new era in another way. They had been life partners since college, and I can't remember a time when I didn't know that. But I wouldn't be surprised if I've forgotten, simply because at that time, few gay people were comfortable being out. Over their long tenure on the street, the two men would become respected icons of stability, in both the personal and business sense. In every way, they were a perfect fit for the newly emerging retail era.

TO PREPARE FOR my new job, I'd started paying attention to the business section in the daily paper. That was a novelty to me, but downtown merchants were affected by the economy, and I needed to know what was happening. Despite the turmoil of the last two decades, the economy had remained stable and strong. That year, 1978, U.S. manufacturing was at its height. The furnaces in our factories were burning non-stop. We were exporting goods to the world, with plenty left over for ourselves.

Politics had settled down as well. Jimmy Carter was a president made for the end of the seventies, a moral man whom people felt they could trust. Elected in 1977 after eight years of Republican rule, he was a Democrat but also an outsider, trusted to be above the deceit of Lyndon Johnson and the dirty tricks of Richard Nixon. A one-termer, he would take us into the eighties, when we would finally be able to put Vietnam in the rearview mirror.

A blockbuster anti-trust case against AT&T made lots of news that year, as the government moved forward to break the company into smaller units. I remembered the original Bell phone in my family home. It came only in black, had to be plugged into the wall, and was so heavy it hardly moved even when you pulled on the cord. But it was always there when you needed it. I loved that phone and understood the company's reluctance to change it. But years later, when I was able to work from home by calling into my office phone for messages, I appreciated the innovations that came out after AT&T was forced to reorganize, including voicemail, conference calling, and eventually cell phones.

But that would be the last big anti-trust case for many decades. Change was in the wind, as lawyers argued that even though monopolies killed off competition, they kept prices low for consumers. Even in 1979, companies had started to get bigger and the stock market stronger, and the eighties would bring multiple buy-outs and mergers. A general optimism had spread across the country. Smooth new roads were being built to get people in the shiny new suburbs to their spiffy new regional malls. Money abounded, and a corresponding cry went out to fix the abandoned downtowns. A new golden age of retail would follow that would be madly popular and make heroes of shopkeepers. And I was in a perfect place to be part of it.

THE BOYS WERE changing fast. Johnny had evolved into an introverted teen with messy personal habits, a total disregard for how he looked, and a sharp intellect. Peter was naturally neat, outgoing and popular, but missed the companionship of his increasingly solitary big brother. Peter and I were the extroverts in the family, while Johnny was more like his father, retreating to his room most of the time. That summer I'd taken tennis lessons at a near-by court, Peter happily walking with me to bang balls against the backboard while I practiced serving. He was cheerful when we walked home together in the warm summer night, swinging our rackets as we sang silly songs, laughing. He'd always enjoyed sitting side-by-side to watch TV. Then one night when I sat down close to him, nudging his shoulder with mine like I always did, he pulled away, letting me know he was getting too big for that, and I felt a rush of fear of the empty nest in my future.

Less than a year after counseling, John and I were once again on different pages. The old habits in our marriage resurfaced, including my distaste for conflict, and I simply stopped pushing for anything different. In a way, it worked well for me, allowing me to fall completely into my new work.

And it wasn't long until my job became the equivalent of a religion. There was a connection between my disaffection with national politics and my enthusiasm for my new mission. I was one of many in that post-Vietnam era who struck out in new work directions. In Madison, our 28-year-old mayor, Paul Soglin, had been arrested for demonstrating against the war while studying to be a lawyer. Now he advocated a liberal social agenda even as he paid close attention to the city's economy.

As I settled into my job, I met more shop owners on the street. Mary Lang, one of the first women owners there, had opened the Peacock, a woman's clothing boutique on the 400 block in 1968. A small-town Wisconsin girl, she'd come to Madison to enroll in the nursing school at St. Mary's Hospital.

"I stuttered when I was young," she told me one day over coffee. "I had a male professor who made fun of me. It was awful, humiliating. I took a night sewing class just to get some relief. I really loved it, and when the course ended, the teacher told me I had a flair for design and should consider fashion school."

She smoothed her hair, thinking. "Janice, when I first got to Madison, I loved seeing the hippies on State Street. A lot of them didn't even wear shoes. They sat on the curbs playing guitars. It felt so free, it was thrilling."

Mary dropped out of school and worked as a salesperson at Hilldale Mall. She laughed as she told me her story. "Would you believe that on a semester break, I hitchhiked to the east coast with my boyfriend?"

That did surprise me, this elegantly dressed woman, but I just smiled as she kept talking. "When I got to New York, I snagged interviews with boutique owners on Madison Avenue, came home and wrote a term paper on opening a clothing store called the Peacock. After that, I spent a year in Chicago as assistant buyer for a department store before I moved back to open the store. I'd saved a thousand dollars but didn't have collateral for a loan. My dad got a loan in his name and gave me the cash in exchange for monthly payments with interest."

While Mary was gone, her boyfriend found her a perfect space on the upper floor at 420 State. But after the store opened, only a handful of the hundreds of people streaming down State Street sidewalks made it up the stairs.

"I remember looking out our two tall windows, at the long line of cars at the stop light below," she said, "wondering if I'd survive. Desperate, I hit on the idea of hiring live models to pose in the windows at night. They showed up spectacularly well, with the light behind them."

The stalled motorists soon noticed, and word of mouth spread, brought publicity and new customers. By the second year, she'd tripled inventory, increased sales, paid off the loan to her father, and bought a house. Soon she moved to a ground floor location where The Peacock became a fixture on the street for over forty years.

I would remember this conversation years later, when I, too, faced with limitations, fell into a creative solution. I would find over time many new businesspeople had a similar story.

MY NEW JOB made me curious about cities in history. I read up on the agora, the famous centers of ancient Greek city-states, which were situated in large squares surrounded on all four sides by buildings. The agora was the focal point of community life. The open area served as a market but also a meeting place for political assemblies. The square was bordered by civic buildings, courts of law, religious temples, libraries, lecture halls for philosophers, including Socrates. I never heard anyone articulate it concretely, but I felt that Madison's downtown, with all the physical elements of the agora, was very close to the Greek ideal.

For more than a hundred years, downtown Madison had been the city's busy central marketplace. The big regional malls that opened in the sixties were stiff competition, though, and eventually the large stores on the Square that sold clothing, hardware, and housewares would close. But enough were still there when I started my job in 1978, and the pedestrian traffic was impressive. The Square and its side streets were home to five banks, two state office buildings, three department stores, two Rennebohm drugstores, two churches, half a dozen clothing stores, the local newspaper office, two hotels, two dime stores. Madison's excellent main public library was just one block off the Square and so was City Hall. Downtown was always much more than a place to shop. When voters got angry enough to organize, they marched up State Street to the Square to make themselves heard. But mostly they came for business, history, shopping, and pleasure.

In New Orleans, I'd seen a successful retail area made up of one-of-a-kind independent stores. We already had that on State Street, and I thought we could make it even better. The spaces there were small, with correspondingly modest rents. That allowed older stores to survive, stores like Patti Music, where you could buy sheet music, violin cases, and violins themselves. Close to campus, Paul's Books had recycled a wealth of academic and general books since 1954. Any empty storefronts that did appear were beginning to be quickly snatched up by some local startup, which the street would become famous for. It helped that the small spaces didn't work for chains, which needed more space to do well. And then there was the built-in market of downtown workers, students, and tourists.

Because of the malls' growing popularity, though, many people in the late seventies thought of downtown Madison as a declining retail district, when it was actually in an exhilarating stage of reinvention. Day after day, as I saw the bits and pieces of the culture that operated on all levels of the central city, I fell irrevocably in love with downtown, especially State Street. I never tired of walking the street, full of a remarkable range of people: students and their parents, state legislators in suits, tourists in shorts, mothers with toddlers, teenagers hanging out, fans in Badger shirts, state workers in pressed pants and shirt sleeves, remnant hippies wearing ragged jeans and sandals. The window shopping was world-class: greatcoats and parachutes at the Army-Navy store, Marimekko pillows at Tellus Mater, Tarot cards at The Medium, tall red boots at Goldi, hair brushes and lotion at the Soap Opera, oil paintings at the Garver Gallery, tiny kittens at Fir, Fin and Feather, skis at Fontana, bikes at Yellow Jersey, and a profusion of bell-bottomed trousers, chopsticks and bowls, incense and Buddhas, posters, typewriters, sheet music, lingerie, travel bags, perfume, new books, used books, long-playing records.

The street had a lightning kind of energy which transferred to me. I was completely at home there.

Working with only a tiny budget and no staff, I'd managed to program the new mall nicely in its first year, inaugurating weekly concerts and supporting new events like the Fantastic Flying Machine Contest, with kids bringing homemade mini-floats to parade around the Square. My best coup was wooing the Wisconsin dairy industry's annual event to the Capitol Square, with decadent cream puffs and real cows for kids to milk. I solicited my friends for names, and Anne Boyle, my steadfast Elvehjem colleague, came up with a name that has stuck for more than forty years: Cows on the Concourse.

I also mediated squabbles among food vendors for prime cart spaces and dealt with sluggish city committees to get activities approved, my least favorite part of the job.

Through most of that year as Mall Coordinator, I exuded self-confidence and energy. But as the summer trickled to an end, I started to wear down. To top off the first season, I'd planned a huge free dance on the eight-block Square, with a different band at each of the four corners. Short of energy and with only a few dollars left in my tiny budget, I'd failed to publicize the event adequately. It was an enormous space, and the hundreds of people who came didn't begin to fill it. The four bands I'd hired did not appreciate playing to what amounted to sparse crowds. It was my first failure, but it was a big one, and it hurt badly.

I'd spent the evening walking back and forth on the extensive dance floor, hoping that each hour would bring more people, finally slinking away as the bands packed up. John and the boys had gone north to a relative's cabin for the weekend, so I was alone with my failure. I came home bone-tired and depressed, and drank a bottle of wine to numb the pain of failure.

Sitting with the empty bottle, I recognized that I'd hit my limit. The job had stopped being a pleasure months ago, when it became impossible to do well with so few resources. I was sick of working without an assistant or a decent budget. I couldn't imagine another year like that. But what else could I do? The window had long closed on my early dream to teach. In Madison, most jobs were either at the University or with government, and I'd had my share this year of sitting in meetings waiting for approval for projects.

Somehow, I had to get out. But this time, I'd need to have a job before I quit.

SEVEN

A month after the band debacle on the Capitol Square, I got a call at work from Fanny Garver. "Janice, Sandra Hall told me she's willing to drop the sale price. Are you still interested in her business?"

My head cleared immediately.

Hall sold baskets from Africa and molas from Panama in her folk-art gallery in the Garver's lovely, old brick building on the 200 block. After our trip to New Orleans, John and I had talked idly about opening a toy store in Madison. I'd never taken it seriously. But John's goal was to be his own boss, so when Hall put her business up for sale a year before, he'd initiated a sit-down with her to discuss it. I'd agreed, mostly out of curiosity. The business was failing and basically worthless, but the space she occupied was prime. Under our day-dreamers scenario, if we bought it, I'd have to sell off her product, close, and open as a toy store. But her price was too high, and I had been just about to start the Mall job, so I hadn't really been interested.

Nonetheless, I kept thinking of how a stuffed giraffe I'd seen at a toy store in New Orleans had triggered a memory of a Christmas morning when I was seven. We were living on the farm in Tilden where I was born, money so tight that each of the kids in my family got just one gift from Santa. The year before, mine had been a disappointing wood-burning set, which I never quite got the hang of, and this year, I was hoping for a paint box like the one my friend Sally had. To my astonishment, when I ran to the tree Christmas morning I saw a standing easel blackboard, supported on each side by magnificent brown-and-white cut-out-wood giraffes. Printed in huge chalk letters on the board was a message: *Merry Christmas, Janice*! It took me awhile to understand this beautiful object was mine, and then I was filled with joy.

The happy memory of that Christmas morning had popped into my mind in the toy store in New Orleans. How fun it must be, I thought, to sell lovely toys that made children happy.

And the timing was perfect. With upper State Street shaping up so nicely and my choices narrowing, I quickly grew open to the idea of opening a store there. Sassafrass, a stylish clothing store for women, had moved to the 300 block from lower State; Goldi, a successful women's shoe store from Milwaukee, had opened a new store across the street next to the Soap Opera. On the corner of State and West Johnson, the Bakers Rooms and the Ovens of Brittany had begun to revolutionize restaurant culture in the city. And around the corner on West Johnson, in response to a movement that convinced publishers that women were a major new market, four women had gotten together to create a feminist bookstore called A Room of One's Own.

The 200 block was ripe for change. The new Civic Center was sure to increase traffic on the block. Some older stores—Singer Sewing Machine, Madison Pen and Card, the Christian Science Reading Room—were in last stages of life and would soon free up space for new stores. I'd seen in New Orleans how small stores located in a cluster could function like larger traditional gift stores, which offered a little bit of everything. Only now, you went to different stores, where you got a better selection in the category you wanted. I loved the idea that if I opened a store in Garver's building, I'd be part of the cluster of new, unusual shops.

Starting a store sounded like fun, sort of like putting on a play. I'd get to write the script, design the production, be the lead actor, hire people I liked, and direct the whole thing! After a year of answering to rules, regulations, and bureaucrats, it would be wonderful to be the boss of everything. But what about afterwards? What if the show wasn't a hit? What if I couldn't pull out a salary? And what if it got boring after the first run? I was at that point with this job. The active season was over, and I faced a long, dull winter of planning and sitting on committees.

"We need a good tenant, Janice," Fanny said, interrupting my fleeting thoughts. "I wish you'd consider it."

IT SOUNDED CRAZY even to me that I would open a store just to get out of my job. But that's what I did. Fanny's call was just the nudge I needed. I was nervous about telling Sue Springman I'd be leaving, but she surprised me by completely understanding. More than anyone else, she knew how frustrating my job had been with a tiny budget and no staff.

In retrospect, my eclectic series of jobs had inadvertently prepared me for business. I'd learned how to run a store at the Minnesota State Fair. That got me the job developing the museum shop, where I discovered I was a very good buyer. My job overseeing the new mall taught me the specifics of the downtown market as well as national retail trends. Maybe this sequence of jobs wasn't as accidental as I had assumed. I'd been drawn in this direction, and each job decision had been made consciously.

But the flow seemed perverse because it was a universe away from my early dream of being a great teacher. It was hard to see how running a store would be a serious profession. I had no idea then that in less than five years, I would become aware that a business career had become socially acceptable among highly educated people.

And everyone now, even the *New York Times*, was calling downtown the soul of the city. I could be part of something important, something bigger than just business, something with real moral authority.

I would not be stuck in a bullpen office with a dull metal desk, shuffling piles of reports and going to endless, boring meetings that produced even more paper no one would read.

When I thought of what my store might look like, I remembered the ones in New Orleans, with bursts of robin-egg blues and cherry reds, orderly piles of bright, shellacked toys, and sinuous dragon kites with long tails hanging from the ceiling. My store would be filled with clever wind-ups and dazzling kaleidoscopes and would fit into the retail renaissance I saw unfolding.

There was a creative surge in the nation's retail sector then, as some unusual groups of people opened stores. Many were activists who'd never taken a business course. Maybe, like the partners at the Soap Opera and Mary Lang at the Peacock, they didn't want to answer to a boss. And maybe, like me, they looked to owning a small business as a way to express personal values. Nor was making a lot of money the primary driving force for many of them. That never even occurred to me.

I wanted a store that reflected my values, like Dick Hayne, an ex-Vista Volunteer I'd read about, who with his wife Judy opened a store called Free People, a clothing store for the under-thirty set in Philadelphia. Later, Dick and a partner, Scott Belair, built the store into Urban Outfitters. In 1972, two ex-Peace Corps volunteers opened a flagship store in Berkeley called The Nature Company, which sold maps, fossils, gems, and other things that honored the earth.

The early innovators in retail were ahead of a national trend. Not long afterward, the Rouse Company, a Baltimore real estate developer, would build Harborplace in their hometown, their first of a line of successful festival marketplaces. Rouse brought an alluring array of shopping, food, music, and performing arts to their centers, which were designed with small spaces for just the kind of stores the new crop of businesspeople were opening. Rouse was the first developer to use specialty stores as anchors for malls, instead of the usual department store. Despite its location in a blighted downtown with little parking, foot traffic at Harborplace the first year equaled that of Disneyland.

In Madison at the end of the seventies, there was a remarkable confluence—the national retail trend, the right local players, and a unique physical space. State Street was an intact seven blocks of mostly small retail spaces that lent themselves to local stores and start-ups. Downtown already had all the physical and social attributes of a festival mall. It was naturally constructed to function perfectly in the new era.

It was a time when downtowns everywhere were filling up again after being emptied by the new malls. The nation needed to regroup, to heal its national soul, and downtown was the place to do it. It was where the artists were, as well as learning, and new politicians and the Wisconsin idea of extending the University's boundaries to the state.

State Street now hosted a regular slate of street musicians and performers—jugglers, mimes, musicians, pavement painters. In 1978, the Pail and Shovel Party won election to the student senate with a promise to bring the Statue of Liberty to Madison. One February morning in 1979, when I was poring through catalogs to find toys for my store's opening, the city woke up to see Liberty and the arm holding the torch emerging from the ice on Lake Mendota.

I felt a new era beginning, and I was thrilled to be part of it. My store would be in the middle of the action, right across from the Civic Center. I'd be two blocks from the Capitol in one direction and five blocks from the University in the other.

The last thing on my mind as I made my decision was where my small venture fit into the wider economy. In fact, as a sophomore in college, I had earned a D in a four-credit economics course, which my grade point average never quite recovered from. I'd found it boring, no match for the great ideas I was discovering in my lit and history classes.

I had no grasp of national economics, but I did have a sense in 1979 of something afoot. It turned out that a strong new business cycle was brewing, and yet few saw it coming. Richard Nixon had started it all with a surprise visit to China in 1972, most likely to drive a political wedge between China and Russia. Then, four months before I opened the Puzzlebox in 1979, Jimmy Carter would sign a bilateral trade agreement with China that in the short space of a decade would set off a tsunami of change in the U.S. economy.

Later in my career I would understand that luck and timing were both big factors in my success. It was my good luck to be starting a business at the peak of the second feminist wave, which emboldened me personally. More importantly, I would open my store on the cusp of a retail boom at the height of the American Century, although I had only a faint sense of that yet.

EIGHT

I woke in the dark, feeling sweat on my forehead. Then I remembered. Opening day. I kicked off the blankets, hot all over despite the cool morning air. Five o'clock. I grabbed a robe, tiptoed down the stairs, and opened the French doors to the screened porch. It was cold, and I wanted coffee, but if I started now I'd be jumpy by eight. Sitting on the wicker sofa in the dark, I pulled a wool throw over me and felt the fear. This wasn't just a new job. I was risking $10,000 of John's pension fund. And this wouldn't be as easy as the Elvehjem, where I had free rent, a volunteer staff, and a guaranteed salary.

A month earlier, I'd stopped at Shelley Rosenbaum's gallery on State Street, Exquisite Indian Crafts. When I'd told him I was going to open a toy store down the street, he looked at me in disbelief. "Toys? A toy store? But there aren't any kids downtown. In fact, there aren't any families living here at all. Janice, who will your customers be?"

I'd stumbled over my explanation and walked out in a panic. What if he was right? The toys I'd seen in New Orleans were for children, mostly European toys that had just started to be imported by American wholesalers. The bulk of my opening orders were those imports, along with a scattering of wooden toys made in the U.S. I began to think I should hedge my bets with some stuff for adults.

Most of the winter trade shows where I could see wholesale distributors had come and gone, but there was still one gift show in Chicago before the store opened. I'd been surprised when John said he wanted to come with me, since I'd traveled to trade shows alone when I ran the Elvehjem Museum shop. This was an alarming signal to me that he took the business as some kind of operational partnership rather than just a financial one. I assured him I was capable of doing the show alone, but he insisted. I knew then a conflict was inevitable.

John had consistently supported me in getting back into the work force. I probably wouldn't have published the guidebook without him. His technical skills and fearlessness in selling advance copies to Anchor Bank had been key. Maybe I wasn't being fair now.

Without John, I would have had a hard time starting the store. In fact, I couldn't even remember who had the idea first, but he had been the one to pursue the space on State Street. He'd drawn money from his retirement fund as equity for the bank loan. He'd negotiated the lease with the landlord and helped put the store together, painting and building shelving. He'd even come up with the name, inspired by a puzzle box he'd built in his workshop. Our collaboration on the guidebook had been similar, but there was a big difference. Once the book was published (and got me a job), we went our separate ways. I assumed this would be similar, but now it was feeling different. I knew he wanted independence above all else, and this business was looking like a route to that goal. But I wanted independence too, and his presence felt intrusive. I'd always assumed any profits would be jointly shared, but I saw the business as my work, just as his jobs were his.

When we got to the show, our different tastes and visions clashed. He stopped to admire a collection of wood toys that were well-made, but, to me, clunky and graceless. He engaged the vendor in conversation, then turned to me, eyebrows raised, as though I should place an order. I didn't, but it was awkward. Ignoring my cue, he asked the vendor to send a catalog. My stomach tightened. I had no intention of letting him step on my decisions and decided I'd better address it on the way home.

As always, he drove. Ever since we were married, he drove. Whenever I offered to take the wheel, he demurred, to a point where I realized he wasn't going to give it up without a fight. I hated fighting, so I just went along with it. After we made it out of the worst of city traffic, I turned to him, chin up, and said we needed to talk about his role in the business.

He must have known I was disturbed because he barely reacted. He had a way of going calm when I got intense. His eyes stayed on the road. "What do you mean?"

"You know you wouldn't have gone in on this venture if it hadn't been for the success I had at the museum shop. I'm a good buyer. I got promoted because sales went up, and you can't have profits without good sales."

"I know that," he said. "But I think I should have some say in the handmade toys, based on my woodworking experience."

That sounded so reasonable, but I saw the catch. My personal vision of the store had been growing and changing; John's was more conventional.

"I understand your fondness for those toys, but there's also taste involved, and our tastes are different. I appreciate your help in getting me started, but if you want me to be successful, I have to follow my own vision."

He said nothing, hands steady on the steering wheel, and we made the rest of the trip home in near silence.

It was crucial that I carry new, unusual toys. People went to the malls and department stores for their necessities. They came to State Street for entertainment, and they would want products that were fun and different. Besides that, I was hungry to express myself, and the selection of product was everything to me.

With a month to go before opening, I found a juried craft show in Rhinebeck, a small town in upstate New York. My sister Joan happened to be staying at a friend's apartment on the west side of Manhattan for a few weeks. I could bunk with her, making the trip affordable, take a train to the show the next morning, and return in the evening.

Unfortunately, after a heady evening drinking wine with my sister while admiring the evening view of Central Park, I overslept and missed my morning train. The only other one scheduled to Rhinebeck that day would get there just two hours before the show closed.

I felt sick with guilt. Had I blown the whole trip? It would be hard to explain to John when I came home with no orders, especially after I had insisted on going alone.

I waited a long four hours at Grand Central Station. When I finally got aboard, I was still a little hung-over, but it couldn't ruin the glorious train ride, winding along the Hudson River with steep, almost vertical cliffs rising hundreds of feet along each side of the river. It felt like everything would be all right. But when I arrived at the Rhinebeck stop, I found a deserted platform on a country road. I'd just missed the last shuttle. Around me was a scattering of houses, no taxis, and only an occasional car going by. Desperate, with one hand holding my handsome, new red leather briefcase, I put up my thumb to hitch a ride. Twenty minutes later, a kind woman picked me up, depositing me at the fairgrounds just an hour before the show would close.

I raced through the aisles, assessing products instantly. I saw beautiful art-level products, but few actually fit my category—I could hardly sell glass paperweights, sterling silver jewelry, or turned wooden bowls. But there's nothing like a deadline for focus. I made my decisions quickly, placing just six orders that day, but they were all excellent companies I would reorder from for years.

The items were almost all for adults: beveled glass kaleidoscopes that would grace a coffee table, a captivating series of hardboard Jumping Jack animal figures. One of them, a zebra with jointed arms and legs and a pink ruffle around its neck, would end up on my bedroom wall, where many years later my grandchildren would delight in pulling the ribbon that brought him alive. I ordered a variety of handsome, beautifully made hardwood game sets. My most important purchase would be a simple but clever baby rattle made out of a single piece of satiny maple. The rattle would sell steadily for the next ten years.

So much of what I did in the early days came purely from instinct and my personal taste. The home I'd been brought up in was conventional working class, with cork-tile floors in the living room, a very large blond-wood TV console, and Barcaloungers for my parents. Only a few inexpensive pictures of flowers hung on the walls. An art class in college piqued my interest in design, and my sophisticated sister Joan took me to museums and taught me about music, clothes, and food when I roomed with her while working a summer job in Minneapolis. Other than that, I'd felt my way, feeding my love of color and texture with needlework I'd done in my child-rearing years.

Many of my new buys at the Rhinebeck fair didn't fit the definition of a toy, but they were entertaining and well-designed, sometimes even beautiful. Their primary function was pleasure.

State Street 200 block

IT WAS ALMOST sunrise now on opening day. It was show time, and there was ache in the pit of my stomach; I was afraid people wouldn't like the store.

Two hours later, when I walked onto State Street, the Capitol building was brilliant in the morning light. It was an idyllic May day, refreshingly cool and sunny, the buds pushing out on the newly planted trees on the Mall. I'd planned a Saturday opening because it was the busiest day on the street, but the weather was a bonus.

I stopped to look at our front window, which we'd designed to tie in with the Farmers' Market on the Square. Anne Boyle, rapidly developing into a professional partner as well as a friend, had helped, filling the window with Vegimals, a clever line of stuffed velour toys. Six tiny peas snuggled inside a zippered green pod; an ear of corn with Velcro-tipped arms hugged itself.

I unlocked the door and stood a minute enjoying the quiet. Then I walked slowly toward the back, checking the long bank of wooden shelves filled with games, toys and stuffed animals. Light streamed in from the skylight above the fifteen-foot-high window facing State Street. I was the only one in the store, but I didn't feel alone.

I scanned the shelves, worried the store looked understocked. I had ordered ten thousand dollars' worth of inventory, but a quarter of it hadn't yet arrived. I'd put the most colorful products on shelves against the mirrored wall, the first things people would see as they walked in the door. If the window had brought them in, the Vegimals were right there where the customer could put their hands on them. On the shelf below, where children could reach, were a series of funny baseball hats with stuffed silver wings and short red horns attached.

The hats and the Vegimals were designed by Beverly Red, who owned a small, innovative company in Vermont called Freemountain Toys. They were new to Madison, and they were first-rate—good design, good materials, affordable prices.

The other prime shelves in the front of the store I'd filled with handmade toys, mostly regional. A Madison artist, Patti Davene Davis, had carved the quirky set of pick-up sticks in the forms of French fries and tacos. Next to them was a stuffed mother loon, a lake bird beloved by Midwesterners. It had a black and white polka dotted body, with two baby loons clinging to the Velcro on its back. The Minnesota company I bought it from, Lady Slipper Designs, also made the witty stuffed moose head trophy that hung on the wall.

After customers looked at the showy stuff, they could move to the imported toys on the rest of the shelves—Brio train sets from Sweden, wooden sailboats from England, Ambi hard plastic toys from the Netherlands, rattles and pull toys in bright, clean primary colors.

Most of the toys on the shelves that day were from small U.S. companies or imported from Europe. Later, when China got into the game, things would change, but for now, everything on the shelves was something special.

SOON JOHN AND the kids arrived, in time to open the store with me. I loved having the boys there, trying out toys, just hanging out, providing body heat. Peter at twelve was still a little boy who liked spending time with his parents. He'd happily helped set up the store. Johnny was fifteen, preoccupied with his gaming and friends, but curious about the new business. A few hours later, they'd had enough and took the bus home, leaving John and me behind the counter.

Standing there, we must have looked like a typical Madison couple at the end of the seventies. I had just turned forty, John was three years older. His brown hair was still full, on the long side, but he wore

John & I setting up Puzzlebox

horn-rimmed glasses now, and favored corduroy pants and cotton sport shirts. He hadn't changed in appearance much at all since our marriage.

As for me, the radical chic look I'd adopted with hip glasses, long hair, and short skirts had been replaced by what a close friend would later call my "mousy" look. I wore a lot of neutral colors—tan and camel mostly. My clothes were neat, but without personal style, eminently practical. I wore little make-up, and my straight hair, dark blonde now, was cut short. I'd loved the style of the new feminists, and I still admired the clothes I saw in the windows of Sassafrass down the street, but it was my growing career that held my attention.

Soon, five or six people who'd been to the Farmers' Market came in. They looked but didn't buy anything. I stood there woodenly, with nothing to do but smile. Then a man came up to the counter with a twelve-dollar cribbage board. My first sale. That was a relief, but then nobody bought anything for half an hour. John and I looked at each other doubtfully, and I had a sudden flash of an empty till at the end of the day. Was this all a stupid mistake?

Then more people came, and a few more. They stayed, and finally they bought. There were families with little kids, couples, groups of friends. I felt the energy of the crowd grow, with everyone touching the toys, playing with them, laughing, having fun.

My shoulders relaxed. Maybe we wouldn't make a lot of money, but there was no doubt people were having a good time. A group of three women in their thirties wound their way around the store, looking at everything, laughing together, and then brought armfuls of toys to the counter. I smiled at them happily.

"Where do you find these things?" a woman with a blonde ponytail asked as she set a wooden marble run on the counter. The toy had three ramps and a spinning wheel at the top that sent the marbles racing down the ramps.

"Cedar Rapids, Iowa," I said. I didn't mention that the old man who made the runs wouldn't ship them and would only take cash, so John and I and the boys had driven the four hours to Iowa to hand him the cash, pack up the runs, and bring them home in our station wagon. But I'd agreed with John that these were the best marble runs I'd ever seen, and good-looking as well.

The woman's friend held a felt mask of a clown over her face. A sleek black cat was stitched to the top, as though the cat were sitting on the clown's head. "What do you think?" she asked her friend, who smiled her approval.

"A New Orleans artist makes those for Mardi Gras," I said, eager to share how special the masks were. They came in the form of butterflies, bats, rainbows, and Cleopatra. I'd bought one from Elizabeth Bourne on our vacation, and when I knew I'd open a store, I'd called her to order some. She didn't sell wholesale, but I loved the masks so much I bought a dozen from her at full price, marking them only a few dollars more than I paid for them. They were clever and charming, and I just wanted them in the store.

By mid-afternoon sales were at a respectable $400 dollars, and I finally relaxed. Clearly, people liked the store, would tell their friends about it and come back.

A half hour before closing time, a handsome man in his fifties walked in the door with an entourage of three chic, young women and started picking up toys on a shelf near the door. I nudged John.

"I think that's Leo Famolare," I whispered.

"Who's he?"

"I'm wearing a pair of his shoes," I said. He looked at my feet doubtfully.

I'd read in the paper the day before that Leo Famolare would be in town that day, representing the Italian shoe company with his family name. He would fly in on his purple jet for a special promotion at Yost's, a women's department store just up the block. I'd paid special attention because I loved his shoes, which were built for comfort, and had purchased two pair at Yost's.

The man had an elegant look. I knew little of men's suits, but his was light gray with a faint stripe running through it. It had a slim cut that looked pleasantly relaxed. His shirt and tie were the same soft blue color. The women with him wore suits as well, the skirts well below the knee, the waists nipped tight with wide leather belts.

I stood in my khaki skirt wondering at these beautiful people walking through my store, curious about what they thought of it, but mostly enjoying their exotic aura. I watched as the man unzipped a peapod, took out the peas, fitted them back in, laughed, and tucked the toy under an arm. After ten minutes he brought the peas to the checkout counter, along with a baseball hat with silver wings and a wooden sailboat from England.

"It's wonderful to have you in our store, Mr. Famolare. I love your shoes," I said, holding up a foot to show him the sandal I was wearing. The group had been speaking Italian, so I wasn't sure how much he would understand. Enough, it seemed.

"Delighted," he said, smiling warmly.

After closing, we totaled our sales at over seven hundred dollars. It was well over my projection, and I was enormously relieved.

Later I would muse that it was only out of my fear that children's toys wouldn't sell well on State Street that I put so much effort into finding adult ones. And it was those toys that had been the biggest hit of the day. Happily and accidentally, I had landed on the successful and lasting concept of an all-age toy store, one that would do well where there were few children or families. It would take more time until I understood that when people bought toys at the Puzzlebox, they were taking the fun they'd had in the store home with them. And God knew we all needed fun.

But that day I wasn't thinking about that. I was thinking that if a rich man who dressed like a prince thought my toys were worth taking back to Italy, I must be on to something.

NINE

It was Monday, and I had bills to pay. I got the paperwork from the small office I'd carved out of a corner in the rear of the store and brought it to the front counter. I had an hour until opening, so I settled on a stool, lighting up a cigarette before the customers came. The kids had started to nag me to quit, but I just couldn't. Someday, when everything was under control, I'd do it.

Six months after opening, the excitement of the first day of business had faded into long, solitary days behind the counter, except for Saturdays when John helped out. People loved the store, but there weren't enough bodies on the street weekdays to make the kind of sales that would cover the cost of a staff. The new mall would eventually help everybody, but for now, it had taken the cars off the street, which made it feel way too quiet. I was starting to seriously wonder if I was going to make it.

Grabbing a calculator, I totaled the bills due this week. Then I checked my cash log and saw there was just enough money to pay them. I was counting on strong sales on the weekend to cover the bigger bills due next week.

The unpredictability of traffic made me crazy. If the weather was good, we did great on Saturdays. If the weather was bad, sales were bad. I was still a long way from covering expenses easily, and I didn't want to draw down our savings any more than necessary.

Someone was banging on the outside back door. I walked back and found Nick, the UPS guy, standing next to a stack of very large boxes. Maybe someone was moving into the office above the store. Then he added even more to the pile. He saw me coming and smiled. "Business must be good, Janice. These are all for you."

"What? That's impossible!"

"They've all got your name on the labels."

I found a box that had a packing slip taped on it, tore it open, and in a column that contained half a dozen other items I had ordered, I saw a notation for two B.B. Bears.

"It's a mistake, Nick. I've got to send them back." But I knew I'd have to wait for return labels from the company. I leaned against the door that led down to our stockroom. "If I put all these boxes into the basement, there won't be room for anything else."

Nick was sympathetic, but company rules forbade drivers to do anything but take boxes off the truck, and he packed up his dolly and left.

Annoyed at the mistake, I returned to the store, checked out a customer, and then found my original purchase order. Now I discovered my error. B.B. Bear was packed in dozens. I'd inadvertently ordered twenty-four. The company might take them back, but only if I paid freight and a restocking fee.

Groaning, I leaned on the counter with my head in my hands. The mistake I'd made was a small one, but at this stage of my business, it felt big and shook my self-confidence. I'd spent hundreds of dollars on two dozen bears that might not sell in a year, that would tie up cash and clog my stockroom. It was a novice's mistake. And I'd have to haul the dozen boxes downstairs myself. And later bring them back up for return.

Stuffed bears would become a major craze a few years later, but in 1979, they were kind of fuddy-duddy, with scrawny arms and legs. One day a month earlier, I'd been ordering from a catalog when I saw a picture of a large bear, twenty-four inches tall, with a round torso, short chubby legs and arms, and a friendly face. B.B. Bear, short for basic brown bear, cost sixteen dollars, which meant he'd sell for thirty-two. Madison's median income in 1979 was seventeen thousand dollars. It was a high-taste market with middle-class income, and thirty-two dollars was definitely high-end. I added two to my order anyway, for what my brother-in-law, Ed, who I'd worked for at the state fair, called flash-products that might never sell but provided color and excitement.

I only occasionally sold one of the colorful felt masks I had bought in New Orleans, which I made no money on, but people loved looking at them. In fact, just about anything I carried that cost over a hundred dollars, like a hand-carved chess set, had to wait for a tourist from Chicago who could afford it. Still, it was essential to have special things for people to see, even if they didn't sell easily.

I went home that night and kept my mistake to myself, brooding quietly in the kitchen, my thoughts interrupted frequently by laughter from the little den off the living room, where John and the boys were watching Happy Days.

In order to get the location on State Street, we'd paid too much money for a dubious thing called customer goodwill. But the previous customers were long gone, and our investment in the future wasn't yet paying off. I needed to deliver results soon.

Putting away dishes, I suddenly remembered the neighbor who'd told me that four out of five small businesses fail.

THE NEXT DAY I called Anne Boyle at her office. She'd been doing our window displays ever since the opening. She listened kindly while I berated myself for the stupid mistake, only asking: "Hmm, how much money are we talking about?"

I paused. "Almost four hundred dollars."

That didn't faze her. "Are you sure the bears will be that hard to sell?"

"They're cute enough, but they're just too expensive."

"What do they look like?"

"He's not like the old fashioned teddy bears with those skinny limbs. His fur and body is very soft, huggable. He's got this enormous rump, flat on the bottom, so he sits well. And his short arms just kinda hang. He has a very ... benign face. Sweet, but definitely masculine. His only problem is he costs too much."

"I need to see him! I'll stop by tomorrow, but I'll start thinking on it now."

She showed up the next morning dressed all in black, like the working artist she was, a flash of shiny silver earring peeking out from her long, straight brown hair. I took her into the stockroom where the boxes were piled up to the ceiling. She held a bear high, examined it carefully, sat it down on a box, and looked at it.

"They would look great massed in the window. Much better than just one or two. Let's put a dozen or so in the window for the opening of the Civic Center. When is it again?"

"In February," I said, thinking it was a long four months away. But a week of opening shows were already being publicized.

"We can do an opening show window," Anne was saying. "I'll build a stage and put a few of the bears in costume, performing somehow. The other bears can be the audience."

Basic Brown Bear

I felt a frisson of excitement as I pictured the bears en masse. I decided to keep the whole shipment.

DECEMBER THAT YEAR brought record snowfalls, followed by a cold snap that froze sales as well. I was learning that having a freestanding store in Wisconsin had a lot in common with farming:

Anne Boyle

Bad weather could sink a year's profits. I'd put a row of six B.B. Bears on the top shelf, but we only sold a few that Christmas.

While I was sure the window would amuse, I still worried about actually selling the bears, so I put together a print ad that offered B.B. Bear for a special price of twenty-five dollars on opening weekend. The expenses mounted as Anne bought materials for the components. On top of the four hundred for the bears, I'd now spent another hundred and fifty dollars. It was worrisome, but by now I was thoroughly hooked on the project and had no choice but to bury my doubts.

Two days before the opening, I climbed to the top rungs of a twelve-foot ladder and hung three bears with fish line until their toes touched the stage, as though they were dancing. The bear in the middle wore a pink tutu, with two male dancers in tights supporting her on either side. Five large yellow stars hung in an arc above the scene. We waited until opening day to arrange fifteen bear spectators on four benches facing the stage.

At six o'clock that evening, Anne and I stationed ourselves inside the store, waiting for the audience to arrive for the eight o'clock curtain. People came at first in a trickle, and as they approached our window, we saw them stop at the sight of fifteen caramel-colored bear backs topped with furry round heads with fuzzy ears. We watched in delight as hundreds of people stopped and looked, smiling and laughing out loud. The window was a smash. It was clear now that I was selling entertainment as well as toys. And I loved that. It felt very good to make people laugh, and I wanted to do more of it.

Opening Night, 1980

In the following week, the bears were so popular that sales began to decimate the window, and I had to reorder. I started with another dozen, and after that two dozen. And then two dozen again.

Sometime later I started getting press as a marketing whiz, all because of this window. Thanks to my ordering mistake and Anne's creative thinking, we attracted many new customers, which resulted in a general spike in sales. Just about everybody in the city came downtown to our block for the opening that month, and just about everybody came into the store after they saw the bears in the window. After that, my business grew steadily.

And I had learned a key marketing truth: Sometimes the most creative solutions come from responses to limitations.

I never tabulated how many B.B. Bears we sold over the years, but the twenty-four turned into thousands, and they never went on sale again. More importantly, the bears set up a wonderful marketing formula. With Anne's help, they appeared with regularity in increasingly complex costumes, poses, and situations. In time, they became a destination in themselves.

Mermaid Bear

In July that first year, heady with the success of the first window, we overreached a little, hanging more than a dozen bears dressed in shorts, sandals, and sun hats strolling by a line of Art Fair booths peopled by bear artists. The concept was good, but the window didn't read easily. Sometimes simple was better.

In winter, we reprised the opening window when Carmen played across the street at the Civic Center, with a bear diva in a glamorous black wig, a slinky red dress, and fishnet stockings.

Over salads at Gino's on lower State, Anne and I would laugh and laugh as we dreamed up ideas based on familiar human roles, foibles, and rituals. In fall, we did a back-to-school window, with small BBs wearing backpacks, sitting at tiny desks. A teacher pointed at a five-foot blackboard listing homework: juggling, kite flying, poker, Frisbee, magic. For a performance across the street based on *Cabaret*, Anne built small round tables where the bears sat watching the show, dressed in black tie, gowns, jewelry and furs, sipping champagne. No idea was too ambitious for my artist friend, and her sets were crucial to the window's charms.

Cabaret Bear

I used to say that B.B. Bear was like rice—he took on the flavor of anything we put on him, be it male, female, elegant, or silly. We dressed him as a nurse in a new baby unit, a football player in a UW jersey, a cheerleader with pom-poms, a detective in a fedora, a chanteuse in a silver sheath. One of the most popular windows ever was a tug of war between five B.B. Bears dressed in muscle shirts and five Paddington Bears in their traditional garb. We asked customers to bet on the winner, and one morning five Paddingtons lay on the ground, with BB victorious. That window provoked an anonymous pen-and-ink letter on fine laid paper that came in the mail protesting unfair treatment of English bears, signed neatly with the claw prints of Paddington Bear.

TEN

In the early eighties, State Street was seven, short, compressed blocks of retail stores of variety, color, ingenuity, and vitality, and I never saw that done better anywhere else in the country. The great thing about State Street then was that no matter how much the nature of the stores changed with the times, the small spaces and low rents made the street a natural business incubator. If one business didn't make it, another start-up would quickly take its place, and no one lost a lot of money. It was a lot easier to take a risk then.

With computers still in the future, finances were simpler. My first lease with the Garvers was one page, and no lawyer ever set eyes on it. I did my own bookkeeping, hiring an accountant only because government requirements were too complex for me to decipher. Few customers used credit cards much, so many stores worked with a simple cash box. We had no payments to the bank for credit card fees, which in the future would amount to 2% or more of sales. We used an inexpensive cash register that lasted for over a decade, renting another for the Christmas season. It computed sales tax and allowed us to ring up sales by categories. Our banking fees were close to nil. We kept on top of inventory by counting it manually in slow times. It was not difficult, and was a good way for staff to learn the stock.

Business-to-business ethics on State Street then were high. With my experience at the Elvehjem, it would have been more logical for me to sell gifts rather than toys, but a nice woman had opened a gift shop on the Square, just three blocks away. It never occurred to me to compete with her (she went out of business after a few years). Territory was respected. Stores earned their right to exclusivity, and no one infringed on their products. The result was dozens of stores with wares unique to each.

THE LOOK OF the new mall—the pebbled sidewalks, the friendly benches, the copious plantings—was copied from other cities, but the imaginative new stores, the street entertainers, the ex-activists now engaging in business and bringing their pasts with them were the crucial elements that gave State Street its famous flavor.

The anti-war movement had spawned a culture of do-goodism among young people. At least in the circles I'd traveled in, a business career wasn't really respectable. It was considered a crass occupation, all about money. But owning a store would turn out to be a way for many in the new generation to stay clear of the establishment they'd opposed. It allowed them to make a living while putting their values into practice by treating all classes and races equally, by selling high-quality products, pricing them fairly, and giving excellent customer service.

Some well-known figures from the protest movement operated food carts on the new mall. A prankster named Eddie Elson, who once sold $10 tickets to the Comet Kohoutek by promising to magically shrink people and store them in bushel baskets until it was time to beam up, brought in hot dog vending stands modeled on the ones in his native Chicago.

After serving seven years in prison, Karleton Armstrong, one of the gang that bombed Sterling Hall, opened a cart on Library Mall called Loose Juice. Later still, he would open a popular sandwich shop called Radical Rye on the 200 block opposite the Puzzlebox, in the spot formerly occupied by a pornographic bookstore.

The porn store had been an embarrassment after the new mall opened. Several people had tried to buy the building to get rid of the store, but it was so profitable the owner could command big city rent, giving him little incentive to sell. Years later, he'd finally get an offer he couldn't refuse from a handful of citizens who paid far more than the building was worth just to get pornography off the street.

As more new specialty stores opened on the street, I came to understand why they were successful. Surprisingly, some of it was due to the limitations of space. Like me, the owners had to choose carefully what they put on the shelves of their small stores if they wanted to survive. And many stores seemed to have an underpinning of values and energy that drove their success and created a common culture on the street.

A new store on the 300 block, The Jewelers' Workshop, intrigued me. A year before I'd opened, Richard Armstrong moved his jewelry shop from a 400-square-foot space on Gorham Street to a 2000-square-foot space near the Soap Opera.

Richard was one of the real hippies, a guy who listened to Abbie Hoffman *(Tune in, turn on, drop out)* speak at the March on the Pentagon in 1967, dropped out of graduate school, moved to the country, and started making jewelry. Raised in New York, he'd come to the UW to do graduate work in biochemistry. When he was called up for the draft in 1967, he traveled back to New Jersey to register, greatly relieved when he was excused for a dislocated arm. Back in Madison, he took art classes for relaxation, and like the Soap Opera founders, sold jewelry on Library Mall, on a concrete ledge where people could lay out their handicrafts. Both men and women had long hair then, so he started making hair barrettes for both sexes, in the shape of big silver butterflies. Eventually, he teamed up with a partner in a small store on Gorham Street, where they sold six pairs of Australian opal earrings a day at $60 a pair.

Richard liked to describe himself as a bad boy from New York, comfortable with all sorts of people and the era's drug culture. He distrusted authority and certainly didn't admire businesspeople, yet ended up a successful entrepreneur.

Like many others on State Street, he had no business plan. But one thing led to another, and when he was offered a large space on the 300 block, he followed the momentum. He borrowed money from friends, gutted the place, remodeled the front into sales, and built work benches for eight jewelers in the back. In the beginning when business was slow, he had them make stock, until the wall-to-wall cases were flush with handmade jewelry.

So, he did have a plan, born of his observation that hardly anyone in Madison was selling custom jewelry. Richard was an intuitive, voluble guy who loved to talk about jewelry. "Janice," he said to me one day, "buying custom jewelry is about showing a personal interest in someone. In fact, a man giving a woman custom jewelry is a high-end pass. You know, we're all selling products, but it's always something else."

Richard was right. I was selling toys, but my store was about fun and entertainment. And he was selling jewelry but also romance and pleasure. Before I'd opened the Puzzlebox, my business-savvy brother-in-law Ed protested the name: "Janice, the store's name should tell you what it sells." But I hung with the name, which suggested mystery and discovery, and never regretted it.

Many of the new stores had names totally unrelated to product. Down the street from us, Sassafrass, owned by Karen and Dan Fix, sold women's clothing. The windows were filled with slim mannequins in Ray Ban sunglasses wearing roomy sweaters with the slightly padded shoulders that were just starting to be popular. The name of the store was appealing to me, conjuring up an independent, fun-loving woman. Dan and Karen had opened the store on lower State Street in the '60s, but moved to the 300 block in the late '70s, sensing upper State was in their future. The clothes were high-quality, fashionable but often classic, with mid to high price tags.

On the same block, Jazzman reigned as the coolest men's clothing store in Madison. With Craig Butenhoff and Paul Strong at the helm, the store would become a favorite on the street. Like many of the new business owners on the street, both men were liberal arts graduates. Their sense of fashion felt cosmopolitan, appealing and fresh, never overtly trendy, even through decades of change. Jazzman's windows showcased classic button-down shirts in soft plaids and small prints and neat piles of good-looking jeans. Whether it was the fabric or the cut, their clothes were more sophisticated than those in most local stores. The faces of the men in my life always lit up when they unwrapped a box with a Jazzman label.

Both Sassafrass and Jazzman had two characteristics of excellent stores: expert buying and a high level of customer service. Just as I carefully screened products for the Puzzlebox from the thousands of items available in trade fair booths, these stores winnowed clothing brand choices to the best, based on their own taste and knowledge of their customers. The owners were frequently in the store to wait on customers, and when they weren't, they had well-trained salespeople on hand.

The sourced-food movement that would fill Madison in the next century with scores of high-quality, innovative restaurants had precedent in the post-Vietnam era on State Street. In 1972, a pair of country-style French restaurants, the Ovens of Brittany and the Bakers Rooms, revolutionized the city's traditional restaurant scene. The founder was a Chicago native, JoAnna Guthrie, who headed up a post-sixties coterie dedicated to improving the culture by paying attention to how food was cooked and served. Guthrie bought a big Victorian house in University Heights, where she housed her idealistic group of young workers. As one of its founding tenets, the restaurant served food grown on their own farm in southeastern Wisconsin.

Ovens was located on the corner of the 300 block; over time, it would expand to half-a-dozen beloved restaurants in the city. Just as important, it would generate many original restaurants started by ex-employees, most notably Odessa Piper, who developed a line of baked good for the Ovens, including the wildly popular morning bun, a delectable pastry of rolled strips of croissant dough baked with brown sugar and cinnamon. In 1976, Piper opened what would become an award-winning restaurant called L'Etoile in a second-story building on the Capitol Square. She cultivated a network of local farms as suppliers and was often seen wheeling a child's wagon around the farmer's market on the Square, loading it with fresh produce for that evening's menu.

For me, there was a kind of sweetness about the early eighties on State Street. I loved having a store to develop, loved being part of a new creative movement, loved the feeling I was developing myself as well. And the street itself encouraged the best in me. People wanted to make a living, but beyond that there was no pressure to get rich. We wanted to do well, but we also wanted to do good, and the culture of the street encouraged both.

THINGS MIGHT HAVE been going well on my street, but nationwide, certain economic trends were simmering, promising to change the tone and tenor of entrepreneurship. Ronald Reagan was our new president, a free-market advocate who welcomed a movement called Neoliberalism, which promoted the idea that only unregulated markets could benefit people fairly. The idea had been around since economist Milton Friedman in 1970 had made the statement that "corporations have no social responsibility except the sacred responsibility to make money." Followers of this movement believed it was the profit motive that could bring good to all classes. Neoliberalism led to deregulation in every sector and an era of leveraged buy-outs, putting wealth in fewer hands, squeezing profits out of companies while cutting jobs and pensions.

It all happened so gradually and out of the public view, though, that it would be many years until anyone suggested that the Sherman Anti-Trust Act of 1892 had in effect been subverted. In the moment, I was paying no attention to this. When things are going well, it's human nature to think it will go on forever. Reagan's term ushered in a new attitude toward money and business, and the effect on the culture was not foreseen by anyone I knew or anything I read. Life was sweet in Madison, and my business was doing well, so all was right in my world.

On Saturdays now, the Puzzlebox was so packed that people would walk in the door, look at the crowd, and leave. Fanny and John Garver noted this and soon offered a solution. The space behind our back wall, leased to an antique dealer who'd been arrested for bilking his elderly clients, was now available. The Garvers knocked out the wall, giving us another 300 square feet and a second large display window facing Johnson Street. The store was now sizable enough to increase the inventory and make better sales. It had always been an interesting space with its high ceilings and mirrored wall, but now it was beautiful.

JUST AS THE STREET was coming into its own as a festival marketplace, I, too, was undergoing a sea change. The jobs I'd held in the seventies had slowly built up my self-confidence, and all around me I felt the support of the swelling feminist movement. The surge in my business that followed the success of the bear windows felt empowering, and the shifts in my family life accelerated the change.

Despite the counseling John and I had done, we had both reverted to old behaviors. Not unlike most men of his generation, John took being in charge for granted. We still tended to see movies he wanted to see, spend time with people he liked. To keep the peace, I let him set the agenda way too much. Still, the differences between us should have been negotiable. My avoidance of conflict was a problem, but perhaps the real one was the absence of the deep connection that allows couples to survive their inevitable conflicts.

And changes in the boys compounded our issues. When we'd moved back to Madison in 1969, they'd been solid playmates. Now, adolescence had landed on Johnny fast and fierce. He quit growing, got pudgy, started wearing thick-lensed glasses, and became physically awkward. He was indifferent to grades, ignoring coursework that bored him. His low marks bothered both John and me, given the crucial part education had played in moving us into the middle class.

Johnny and Peter, 1981

Puberty was kinder to Peter, who stayed slender as he grew. He was physically graceful and good at sports, didn't need glasses, and was a popular, extroverted kid. He got average grades, but he was always more of a doer than a dreamer. His teachers liked him, as most everybody did. His class photos were always good because he smiled so genuinely. He loved being a boy scout, loving racing his skateboard around the block, had lots of friends. The only clues to the edge of anxiety he'd shown since childhood were his close-bitten fingernails. He still loved and admired his older brother, but their differences created a wedge between them.

As Peter got more social, Johnny went more inward, retreating to his messy room to read. Things got better for him when he joined a group of Dungeons and Dragons gamers and started making like-minded friends. Then he scored a spot on the high school paper, which showcased his writing skill and love of film. The movie reviews he turned in were fresh and insightful. One of his best pieces, a critique of the first *Star Trek* movie, began with a single word: *Plop!* I loved seeing my introverted, socially awkward son bask in his peers' approval.

John still worked in the store many Saturdays, but he deferred to the staff that worked with us now, more knowledgeable than he about customers and products. And he had respected the boundaries I'd set. When it came to the business, it was understood between us that the final decisions were mine.

My marriage might not have been what I wanted it to be, but my business success compensated. As long as I was able to operate independently, making my own choices there, I was willing to settle for less at home.

ELEVEN

Early one morning a year later, in the spring of 1981, I sat in my basement office paying bills and thinking about the future. By now the store was clearly a success, and yet my early doubts about a career in retail nagged me. I'd loved opening the store, loved creating the product mix, enjoyed making people happy. In fact, the marketing part of the business was fun and challenging, but the everyday management could be downright boring. It was kind of like all the meals I'd made for my family over the years that disappeared almost immediately, and the next day I had to do it all over again. I still couldn't see myself doing this forever, but I had no plan for an alternative.

Upstairs, my first full-time employee, Mary Ann Wilson, was covering the sales floor. She'd come to me as a senior at the University, smiling and self-assured. Her main reference, from the owner of a retail store in her hometown in Michigan, had given her a 9 out of 10 rating. From that time on, I didn't hire anyone who scored lower than an eight.

MaryAnn worked part-time that first year, proving quickly she was not only smart and competent but extremely personable. She'd told me when I hired her that she wanted to go to California when she graduated in the spring. But she didn't feel she had marketable skills yet, and when May came along, I happily lured her into becoming my first full-time employee.

Putting my papers aside, I went upstairs and found her standing near the stuffed animal shelf with two customers. As I watched, she slipped her hand inside the soft, green back of a stuffed turtle. Her hidden fingers pinched the turtle's head and pulled it quickly into his shell. The two women made happy clucking sounds, one picking up a squirrel and rubbing its paws together.

Mary Ann Wilson

Mary Ann stood beaming. She liked people, loved our toys, and sold a lot of Folkmanis puppets. The company founder had designed the first ones for her own children and grew the company in the seventies with cottage industry in Emeryville, California, which meant women made the toys at sewing machines in their homes.

I walked to the front of the store to take over the counter during Mary Ann's lunch break, looking for the stranger I'd noticed when I came up from the stockroom. He wasn't local, too well-dressed for a downtown Tuesday in Madison where the only people wearing suits were either lawyers or state legislators. He was young, maybe thirty, blond and good looking, six feet tall at least, with a solid but slender frame under his light gray suit.

I waited on a customer who bought a kite, and when I was finished, the man walked up to me. "Is this your store?" he asked, smiling.

When I said yes, he reached his hand across the counter, and I looked into a pair of earnest, blue eyes. "I'm Mark Brocato, with the Rouse Company. I wonder if you'd have a few minutes to talk."

My interest was piqued immediately. I'd followed the Rouse Company with interest since it opened Harborplace in Baltimore. Rouse was the Rolls Royce of retail development, so yes, I had a few minutes to talk to him. When Mary Ann came back from lunch, I took him downstairs to my basement office.

"I really like your store," he said as I led him through the aisles of shelves filled with toys to my small desk tucked into a corner. "Have you heard about our Grand Avenue project?"

"I have. It sounds very interesting." I'd read that they were partnering with the city of Milwaukee to take over a whole city block downtown. The project was even more remarkable because there was a recession going on. Of course, that downturn was hardly felt in Madison with its stable government economy.

"Let me show you some of the sketches our people have worked up," he said, opening the attaché case he was carrying. I watched as he unfolded several large pieces of drafting paper.

"Frankly," he said, "I'd like to talk to you about coming into our project. Do you have any other stores?"

The question surprised me. I shook my head. "No, this is the only one." I paused, then added, "Honestly, I'd love to see your drawings, but I'm not interested in expanding, certainly not in another city." I couldn't imagine the tedium of driving the hour and a half to Milwaukee regularly.

Mark just listened, nodding, and didn't press me. "Well, I'd like to show you the drawings anyway."

I spent a pleasant half an hour looking at his plans, which included a restoration of the Plankington Mall, a two-story historic downtown shopping arcade that had been partitioned mercilessly and mutilated visually over time. It looked like a great urban renewal project, especially attractive because the Plankington was so beautiful. But I knew what I didn't want, and we shook hands and he left. In the next few months, Mark Brocato stopped by the store once a week, always warm and friendly. I liked getting updates on the leasing—who and when they had signed—mostly Milwaukee stores, no one from Madison yet. He seemed genuinely interested in my business, questioning me about my customers and my products. He admired our merchandise mix, and despite his national leasing experience said he'd never seen many of the toys we sold. I always liked seeing him; it was a pleasure talking to someone so knowledgeable.

In fact, Mark didn't seem like a salesman at all, more like a professional friend. He never pressed me, but I always knew he hadn't given up. Then one day he asked to meet with me again. When we sat down, he told me that Rouse had authorized him to offer me a generous construction allowance that would take the risk out of the venture for me.

Flattered to be considered valuable to a company with such high standards, I started rethinking my refusal.

I went home that night imagining a Puzzlebox in that lovely project. I remembered a day driving to work a year after the store opened. Things were going well, sales growing nicely. And suddenly I had thought: Is this all there is?

Idly, I decided to do some research on the company and found a profile of its leader, James Rouse. The company had made a lot of money building regional malls in the fifties and sixties. It was only a year ago that they'd built their first festival marketplace in downtown Baltimore. Harborplace was built just a few blocks from declining Black neighborhoods with the hope of generating a revival of the city center. I read that Rouse was sometimes described as a "capitalist/idealist." Wow. Sounded like me, a little bit, and some of my friends on State Street. A businessperson who wanted a higher purpose than just making money.

In fact, the move to the suburbs in the fifties and sixties and the resulting growth of regional malls had changed the landscape of the U.S. Now, with the war finally over, there was a yearning to come together, to celebrate our country, both locally and nationally. This would manifest in a national movement to revive city centers, and Rouse was one of the companies making it happen.

I loved the idea of a new challenge, especially one that would get me out of daily management. I knew I could learn a lot from working with the Rouse Company. They did things so well, built beautiful buildings, hired good people, even had a higher purpose.

Mark had thrown out the bait, so subtly, with such patience, that he'd made me forget my reasons not to do it. In fact, he had sharpened the appetite for adventure that was dormant in me, bringing it to full consciousness.

TWELVE

When I was eight and we were living on our farm, Sunday night supper during strawberry season consisted of a very large strawberry shortcake. I would help pick the berries myself, eating my way through the patch, always cramming particularly toothsome berries in my mouth as I stooped over the thick, leafy bushes with their hidden treasure of succulent fruit, catching the juicy liquid running down my chin with a finger and licking it happily.

My mother made the flat, oval-shaped shortcake using an entire box of Bisquick. When it came out of the oven all brown and smelling of sugar, she sliced off the top, spread strawberries mashed with sugar on the still-hot bottom layer, put the top back on, and slathered that with more berries. She topped the whole thing with sweetened whipped cream and served it on an enormous oval platter with sides high enough to contain the runaway juices, presenting it to us like a birthday cake.

It was the memory of those nutritionally incorrect meals that led me to institute Friday night pancake dinners when my kids were little. Johnny was seventeen now, with an increasingly sophisticated palate. On the rare evenings we ate out, he quickly scanned the menu for the most exotic item, maybe a buffalo burger or shark-skin soup. But he still loved my buttermilk pancakes, made with a barely stirred batter that produced light, fluffy, moist cakes, enhanced with real maple syrup. Peter was still into hot dogs, which made him easy to feed and please, but he loved pancakes above all else and could eat two stacks before I turned around.

On a Friday night some weeks after Mark Brocato's offer of a construction allowance, my family assembled at the dinner table for our ritual meal. We ate together less often these days. Either one of the boys was likely to be at a friend's house as at home, and sometimes it was just John and me. It was going too fast, I thought, then pushed the thought away. Watching the pancakes disappear from the platter, I speared two for myself, added soft butter and syrup, and let a forkful of the doughy sweet confection melt in my mouth.

"Mark Brocato stopped by again today," I said to John between mouthfuls.

He paused, fork in mid-air, and looked at me. "What did he want?" His interest had heightened ever since Rouse had offered the construction allowance.

"Who's Mark Brocato?" Peter asked, looking up from a pile of pancakes liberally sprinkled with chocolate chips.

"He's the guy who wants Mom to open a Puzzlebox in Milwaukee, dummy," Johnny said. He snatched a piece of sharp cheddar from the plate of cheese.

"I liked Milwaukee," said Peter, licking chocolate off his mouth. "Remember when we went through it on our way to the car ferry?" He'd loved the trip to Michigan on the ferry.

"So what did he want," my husband asked again.

"A Rouse Company bigwig will be in Milwaukee next week. They'd like me to come look at the project."

Johnny looked up. "That's really cool, Mom."

"Thanks!" I said, warming at his approval. "It's nice to be wanted by such a good company."

John had stopped eating, head cocked to the side as he looked into the distance. "I should go to the Grand Avenue with you for that meeting," he said. "You could use someone else to hear what they offer."

"If you like," I said automatically, even as I was thinking I'd rather go alone. But I knew I could use another set of ears in that meeting. Then I quickly said: "I'm still not taking it seriously. I just think it would be fun to see the project."

FIVE DAYS LATER, John and I met Mark Brocato at the Plankington

Arcade on Wisconsin Avenue. Built in 1915 with two stories of shops looking out on a long skylit corridor, its striking feature was a central rotunda with an elaborate domed skylight. We were touring the site before the restoration construction began.

Even though the framework of the elegant skylight was still intact, the glass had been replaced with plywood. The second-story open arcade had been floored in to create rentable office space, and only part of it had been removed. The plaster on the pillars that lined the graceful walkways was crumbling. In the moment, I loved the idea of associating with a company that saw the value of restoring such a beautiful space, but I said nothing.

Mark led us to the bottom level, and as we threaded our way through the remains of old drywall, a man dressed in shabby clothes walked toward us, unshaven, unsteady—obviously a street person who had wandered in. He immediately engaged us in conversation, exclaiming over the mess, and Mark, always polite, introduced himself, explaining that his was the company doing the work. The man frowned: "Those rich people on the north shore will never shop here. Too many niggers downtown."

John and I looked at each other, shocked. Mark Brocato looked appalled, but the incident was a turning point for me. By opening a store here, I saw I could be part of an important moral imperative, a venture that would help renew the downtown in this deeply segregated city.

We moved up to the second story, where the vice-president of leasing for the project, a forty-something man named Robert Harris, soon joined us. He was attractive, tall and fit, with an open smile, a firm handshake, and an aura of energy. His handsome gray suit, light blue shirt, and yellow tie made me conscious of our casual Madison look—John in navy slacks and sport shirt, me in my simple jeans skirt and blouse.

Robert led us along the walkway where retail space would be created, speaking mainly to me as we walked, questioning me about my history and the products we carried. I was flattered by his interest and intrigued by his self-confident, sophisticated bearing. He looked good in his clothes, and I got the sense he was comfortable in them. In Madison, I sat on a Board with men who wore suits like assigned uniforms.

Robert stopped in the middle of the walkway to point at an empty space. "This would be a good location for your store."

John, who'd been following behind with Mark, spoke up. "What about one of the corner spaces looking out on the rotunda?" he asked.

Robert turned to him, startled. "That's prime space. The rent is expensive."

I wouldn't have had the nerve to ask for prime space, assuming Rouse would want more prestigious tenants for the corner spaces. I was glad John had asked. I jumped in immediately.

"It would be perfect for us, though," I said. "The corner would showcase our bear windows, and people love them."

Robert said nothing. I wondered what he was thinking.

In an office nearby, the two men rolled out blueprints of the reconstruction. In a project like this, you rented an empty space with steel supports and no walls. It was the tenant's space to build, and it was expensive, but that's why they'd offered me a construction allowance.

When we studied the plans, I thought the space he'd suggested for me looked awfully small, and I said so.

"The economics of a costly center like this one dictate small spaces," Robert said. "But the project will create a huge customer base, which means higher sales."

"I understand that," I said. "Still, I'm thinking that after putting in a bathroom and a small office, there'll be even less."

"You don't need a bathroom," Robert said quickly. "Mall space is too expensive to use for that. Employees can use the common area bathrooms."

"That's not acceptable to me," I said just as quickly, sitting straighter in my seat. "It's demeaning for staff to have to walk fifty yards to use a bathroom. Besides, it's inefficient to have an employee leave the store when it's busy."

Robert raised an eyebrow.

I was sure about this issue. It was a deal-breaker for me.

We also discussed the rent structure. It was clear the base rate was negotiable. What wasn't negotiable was the percentage rent assessed on sales over a number set by the mall. According to what I'd read, this was where the landlord made a profit. There were also common area fees, which would go up according to labor costs. But I didn't know that then, and they had every reason not to tell me.

On the drive back to Madison, John was excited, acting as though the store was a done deal. I was more cautious. "The base rent is higher than Madison, and I wonder just how that percentage rent will play out," I said.

"But their sales projections are so high the rent won't matter," John said.

"Look, John, it's a beautiful project, but I'm not sure I really want to expand. It would be fun to get the store ready, but then I'd have to run it. With two stores I'd be hauling product, managing another staff, and doing twice as much paperwork."

"Well, you wouldn't have to run it forever," he said. "We've got something successful here. My idea is to build it up to three stores and sell them off. This is an opportunity you can't turn down."

"What?" I turned to look at him as he drove. "Since when has money been a number one object in our lives? Certainly not when you ran for office or when you changed jobs in Boston and we had to move to Maine. It was all about good work that was important to you. Now it's my turn to find that."

He looked surprised but said nothing, and we drove home both in our own thoughts. I knew John wanted to own a business. He didn't like working for other people and had left jobs for that reason. We were both in our forties now, and it must have seemed time was running out for him.

And time was running out for me. His plan for multiple stores might have worked if our skill sets were more complementary, our goals the same, and our marriage solid. We'd been going along fine, but this expansion would change things. Consciously or not, I didn't see myself married to John forever. Another store would complicate things, precipitate an irresolvable conflict. I was grateful for the help he'd given me in the business, but the truth was I didn't need him to expand, and I didn't want to run a business with him. I wanted it to be my own, wanted to make my own mistakes and learn from them, and above all, I wanted work I loved, not just a paycheck.

When we got home that afternoon, Johnny had already eaten and gone off to a gaming session, and Peter was at his friend Dan's for dinner. So, it was just the two of us. I'd made a batch of Greek Avgolemono soup the day before, planning to serve it cold with another dish for the boys as well. Now I made a simple salad and set the table on the screened porch facing Chamberlain Avenue. I loved the porch, with its gracefully arched screens and private view of the neighborhood. We sipped the tart, creamy soup, looking out on our street through the bridal wreath shrubbery brushing the screens.

John looked up from his soup and said: "Just think, we can have a lot of meals like this now."

I got up abruptly, saying I wanted water, and walked to the kitchen. My chest felt tight. I put both my hands on the countertop and braced against it. In front of me was an open bottle of salad dressing, a few drops spilled on the counter. I reached for a cloth to clean it up.

My fears in the car had just played out, and so quickly. After John had spoken, I'd had a paralyzing vision of endless dinners with the kids' chairs empty now for good, just the two of us sitting at the small table.

THIRTEEN

Johnny stood in the middle of the living room, slightly slouched, chin forward, hands in his pockets, shuffling his feet. John was in the chair across from me with the daily paper in front of his face, but he looked up as Johnny spoke.

"Mom, Dad, there's something I need to tell you," he said, giving his father that quick wince that indicated he was nervous.

"What's up?" I said. "Is everything OK?"

"Oh sure," he said quickly. But he didn't look happy. Then he straightened his shoulders, looked first at me and then John as he blurted it out quickly. "I joined the Wisconsin Army Reserves."

We were both struck dumb.

He continued. "I'm signed up to go to basic training at Fort Knox, Kentucky, right after graduation."

He might as well have told his liberal, anti-war parents that he was joining a cult. I was dismayed at first, but after hearing him out, I accepted the news. My son had an unusual, perceptive mind, and he had trouble finding a place where he fit. He'd clashed with his father since adolescence over his indifference to his own grades. In a classic oldest son/father dynamic, John had chided him regularly for not living up to his potential. The basic training stint wouldn't delay his college entrance, as he was already signed on to the University of Wisconsin for the fall semester. But his decision was a clear rebellion.

Ironically, the Army, with its strict regulations, would be a good fit for my unconventional son. It would accept him as he was, appreciate his intelligence, and see him as officer material. In the Army, he would develop a gift for leadership he didn't know he had.

SIX MONTHS LATER, when Johnny was in training, I decided to leave my marriage. It was not what I'd planned, not while the kids were still at home. I'd always known they needed the security of a family, with parents united for their good. Because of that, I had worked hard not to let the problems between John and me become obvious to the boys.

I'd never been in a financial position to leave, anyway, and so I'd concentrated on making a pleasant home. Now the prospect of an empty nest, plus John's intrusion into my business, had renewed my discontent. The Grand Avenue offer could be a complication I didn't want—or an out I hadn't had. For the first time, I saw that I could make enough money to support myself and the kids for as long as they needed it.

When I told John I was finished with our marriage, he didn't take it seriously. To me, our relationship had turned so cool and matter-of-fact, so lacking in any demonstrated affection, that I couldn't believe he hadn't seen it coming. But when I moved into Johnny's vacant room, he finally believed me. It was a relief to crawl into bed alone at night, with slices of apple and cheese for comfort, escaping with a novel until I fell asleep.

A few months earlier, I'd started seeing a therapist, full of guilt at the thought of breaking up our family. But the therapist I saw seemed determined to bring me into the morality of the eighties. I remember two sessions clearly, one when I went on at length about the harmful effect of divorce on children. She suggested that children could also be harmed by parents who were unhappy together.

Another day when I described the depressions I would fall into and how I resented John's lack of sympathy, she brought me up short with a simple statement: "Depressed people aren't very attractive." That was hard to hear, but it was then that I started taking responsibility for my own feelings. John knew I'd been seeing a therapist and asked for a joint meeting. I agreed, but several sessions only reinforced my decision. Mostly, I listened as the therapist plumbed John's thoughts and feelings. It was clear we had been living in two different realities.

This shifting attitude toward divorce would only accelerate in the new era. Women like me, brought up to consider our roles as women paramount to everything, now were getting permission to break the rules and think of ourselves first. Only much later would I understand the adage, *Don't throw out the baby with the bath water*, as I and many others like me came to terms with the effect on children of broken marriages and single parent families.

My experience as a child of warring parents would play a big part in my children's difficulty in accepting the news. All of my siblings hated our parents' fights, which were never physical, just loud and full of vitriol, often resulting in some outrageous action, as when my dad tore the thermostat out of the wall because he liked it hot and she'd turned it down.

I vowed to myself that when I married, I would never, ever put my children through that, and I kept that vow. When John and I disagreed, I'd push back but never raise my voice. Somehow, that worked to his advantage, and I found myself giving way more than I should. It would be many years later, when my mother was near death and my dad able to openly express his affection, that I understood that in part their fights were a perverse manifestation of the passion that held their marriage together. I came to believe that because of their limited education, culture and resources, my parents never learned to resolve their differences with civility.

Sadly, my decision to spare my children seeing their parents fight had unexpected consequences. Both boys were stunned when John and I separated. And why not? They'd never seen us fight, so they had no reason to think we were unhappy. Peter, in particular, just going on 15 the year we split, was blindsided. I could never explain to him why it was happening. I didn't really understand it all myself until much later. I had been repressing my deepest feelings to the point of resentment, always a poisonous substance, and at the end I just wanted out. I saw Peter's pain, but at the moment had only enough energy to follow through on my decision. I'd make things right later.

John found an apartment downtown, overlooking Lake Mendota.

Johnny was living on campus, so Peter and I were alone in the house. I hadn't let myself think of how lonely it would feel until it happened. Because both my husband and oldest son were introverts, I didn't think their absence would make such a difference. Peter's focus was turning toward his friends, but he still had need for a family home, and I was feeling inadequate.

I'd told myself that when John moved out, I'd fill the house with friends, food, and laughter. Instead, my circle of friends shrank when one moved to Minneapolis and another to Philadelphia. And I badly missed the company of Anne Boyle, who had taken a job in graphic design at the Lincoln Park Zoo in Chicago. Much of the time, I came home at night to an empty house, a sad adolescent, and a blank social agenda.

ANNE MANAGED TO come back every three or four weeks to change our windows, building the props in her small apartment on California Avenue and driving them up in her car. Our creative partnership was a boon to my business and palliative to my soul.

She and I shared a respect for intuition, and our aesthetic tastes were similar. We both liked orderliness and symmetry, keys to sorting out our multitude of toys. And thus, the aesthetic of the Puzzlebox window displays formed, utilizing minimalism, color, and whimsy.

Anne brought art to her window designs, with basic principles of balance and white space. She taught me that odd numbers usually made for better balance—three bears in a row rather than four. She found ingenious ways to give a variety of form to the window space but always arranged things so people could see past the display into the store. Simple was often better, but not always. That's where intuition mattered. Sometimes a lot of bears were good!

Being able to follow my own taste and judgment in buying and merchandising was one of the rewards of ownership. I heard a common question from customers: "Where do you find this stuff?" In fact, I bought what I liked, mostly at trade shows, sometimes just from catalogs, and then let customers tell me what they liked by what they bought and what they didn't. Sometimes I deliberately bought stuff that probably wouldn't sell because it was too expensive or too arty. I bought it for flash.

There were also underlying principles I didn't talk about that determined what I bought. We didn't rely on bathroom humor for laughs. You could buy farting cushions at the mall but not at Puzzlebox. Our stuff made people laugh but in a kinder, wittier way. *Toys for the kid in everyone* became one of my tag lines in ads.

In general, taste was not discussed much in business, perhaps because it was so often considered the province of women. I observed that most men deferred to their wives' taste at home unless too much money was involved. When I had wanted to replace our old couch with a nicer new one, John nixed it, saying it was frivolous. But when he bought an expensive camping tent, somehow that was different.

Over time, I would find myself admired by men for my business success, but I don't think they linked it to a developed skill or a talent for buying so much as some clever gift for making sales. The men in my own family were surprised by my success. One brother accounted for my success by suggesting, wrongly, that I priced products exorbitantly. To me, success was not about money but the affirmation of my values and taste, and I loved the opportunity the business gave me to express them.

And, of course, the majority of my customers were women. By and large, men had less interest in toys, tabletop, and gifts, and consequently underestimated their importance to the economy.

Years later, Steve Jobs would talk about taste, about the importance of design and original ideas, about bringing culture to products. In designing his sleek, lovely-to-touch phones and devices, he made taste sexy. I had a good eye, but I wasn't really good at design, couldn't even draw well. So I thought it must have been what I saw in the products, even when they were simply toys—the swooping line of the chassis on a toy car, the fine cotton cloth sail on a boat, the quirky turned-up eyebrow on the face of a bear. I thought my picks were related to some element of art or design I'd seen, maybe even something I'd read. Taste was a mystery and one I found intriguing.

I STILL HAD RESERVATIONS about Grand Avenue, so one day I put in a call to Alan Filley, a highly respected professor in the business school, whose specialty was organizational structure. When we met a few days later in his office on campus, I was frank.

"I got my fill of bureaucracy working for the city and opened a store to escape a government job. But I'd never meant to make a career of it," I said. "People have received the store so well it's confusing. I'm gratified by the attention, and now this offer from Rouse is exciting. Part of me would love the challenge of a project with them. Maybe it's what I need to be happier in this work."

He paced as he answered me. "It's important to know what kind of business type you are. Some people are really good at starting things. We call them promotional types. Other people prefer to run things, to be administrators. You have to decide which model fits you."

I immediately knew that I preferred starting things, but then my strict childhood work ethic kicked in, and I thought, "Well, of course I prefer to start things, everybody does, but if you start something you need to finish it." I didn't want to be a frivolous person who only chased novelty.

But I didn't say that out loud that day. And he did not suggest we meet again. I knew that Filley worked with large companies and earned high fees, and I suspected he didn't want to charge me anything. Instead, he gave me some study materials and counseled me to give what he'd said some thought.

I DIDN'T KNOW MYSELF well enough in those days to trust the voice inside that said I wasn't meant to run a large business. A year into my marriage, the same inner voice had told me something was wrong, but I ignored it and went on. Now a voice assured me that I loved developing things, and maybe the price of that was running them as well. It didn't occur to me then that I might not be so great at the second part of the equation.

Rouse eventually offered the choice corner spot facing the rotunda, the final nudge I needed to sign a lease. The store would open in October, just five months away. I started adding up costs, knowing that even with the construction allowance, I'd need money for fixtures and inventory. So, I set up a meeting with the loan officer at First Wisconsin Bank who had authorized the start-up money for the first store.

Three years earlier, John had gone in with me to get the loan, but I had done the work of assembling a five-year cash flow projection based on a model from a small business book. When I'd shown it to the banker, a man I'll call Bill, he'd looked it over carefully, clearly surprised, and commented that he wished more loan applicants would be as prepared. With $10,000 of our own cash for equity, we'd easily gotten a $12,000 loan.

Three years later, I was going in with a track record, so I thought it would be easy. I had cash from the store as equity, plus my inventory as collateral, so drawing up the projected cash flow was a breeze. Rouse had given me an idea of what sales I could expect.

When I'd called Bill to make the appointment, I'd told him I'd be coming in alone and explained why. The business had always been in my name, as sole proprietor, so nothing was fundamentally different.

But when I passed my new sales and cash projection across the desk to Bill, he studied it for some minutes, his pale face serious, his lips pursed. Then he began asking questions, mostly about what I'd based my projections on, all of which I answered easily. He fiddled with his glasses, took them off, and pinched his nose.

"It's going to be difficult handling your business alone now." His voice was stern.

I sat up straight, surprised by his words and his tone. "I've been handling it alone since the beginning. John just helped out a little, mostly because he wanted to."

"But now, with this new store, you'll have two operations to run, and you'll have to go to Milwaukee as well."

I shrugged. "Once a week, maybe more sometimes. I don't see a problem."

"Well, yes," he said. He lowered his chin, his eyes peering over the top of his wire-rimmed glasses, his eyebrows stretched into a severe line. "But you could have an accident driving over by yourself. Then who'll run the business?"

What? I could hardly credit what he was saying. That because I was a woman I might crash my car? My body went rigid. Then he went off on another track.

"This is a much riskier loan than your first. I can only approve it if you go through the SBA."

I was thinking furiously, getting quietly angry. I knew that Small Business Administration loans took all the risk out of it for the bank by guaranteeing most of the loan. It was a good tool for people with no money or experience who couldn't get a bank loan. But it was also a cumbersome, time-consuming paperwork process, and to ask me to go through it was insulting.

I got up, thanked him for his time and left. Walking back to the office, mad but calm, I decided to call Ann Kovich, a loan officer from M&I, a local downtown bank. She had stopped in the store and introduced herself a year ago, offering her services. I'd liked her but had no dissatisfaction with First Wisconsin at that point, and I told her so. Nonetheless, she continued to stop regularly, just to say hello.

I met with her the next day and had my loan approved within days, on excellent, no-fuss terms. I closed my checking and savings accounts at my old bank and transferred them over. A few weeks later, I called Sue Springman, my former boss at the Central Madison Council, and asked if she was still on the Board at First Wisconsin. She was, and when I told her about my experience, she promised to bring it to the attention of the Board. Bill didn't get fired, but Sue told me they would never let him near another woman client again.

FOURTEEN

After I'd signed the Grand Avenue lease, I sometimes felt like I'd jumped off a cliff. I was in it alone now; the risk was all mine. But, ironically, the incident with Bill the banker gave my self-confidence an enormous boost. From then on, I would love my new freedom. With no husband or boss to oversee me, I made decisions quickly, never looking back.

The personal adjustments would not be so easy. It helped that the boys and I stayed in our Forest Street house for a year. After that, adapting to a new single life would be far more difficult than I'd imagined.

The Grand Avenue, 1984

It turned out I didn't mind the hour-and-a-half drive to Milwaukee at all. Every Wednesday I got into my new blue cargo van, turned on the tape player, and headed out to the interstate. Springsteen's *Born to Run* thundered through my van during every trip for a year. In Milwaukee, I stepped out into the Grand Avenue parking lot and breathed in the delectable aroma of chocolate from the Ambrosia candy factory.

The beauty of the Plankington restoration still thrilled me every time I walked into the mall. Our store overlooked the ground-floor arcade, shaped like a cross, its two rectangular wings meeting at a central rotunda, blazingly elegant, all light and many shades of white. The sparkling-clear glass skylight above the rotunda stretched down both arms of the arcade, illuminating the ivory pillars, the creamy arched walkways that lined the second-floor balcony, and the gleaming eggshell tile floors.

Grand Avenue customers were better dressed than people on the street in Madison, where government jobs allowed relaxed dress codes. Milwaukee was a city of major business corporations, and the professional women I saw in the Plankington wore dark suits much like their male counterparts, only with silk bow ties. At lunch time the elevators emptied dozens of professional workers right next to our store from offices on the floors above the center. Men in suits outnumbered women three-to-one, but that seemed to be working in our favor. Every day the store filled up with men who spontaneously put down their briefcases to play.

It was my good luck that Laura Goldstein had arrived in my first group of interviews for store manager. As an art student in Madison she had worked at the Elvehjem shop for a short period just before I left. Since then, she'd been assistant shop manager both at the Art Institute in Chicago and a housewares store in Milwaukee. She was witty, quirky, smart and in both aesthetics and temperament, in tune with me. She was on the diminutive side yet carried herself with authority and confidence. Her dark, curly hair usually looked nicely wild, as though her energy had moved through her body and given it a jolt.

Both Laura and her assistant manager had a feeling for the Puzzlebox culture and had similar work ethics. Janis was an attractive brunette, with short, stylish hair, the first woman I knew who had a tattoo, a small lightning bolt on her right bicep she liked to show off with sleeveless shirts.

Laura Goldstein

The complications of a mall store appeared within the first weeks. With no storage at all in the Plankington building, most stores had merchandise shipped directly to the shop. Our store was too small and crowded for that, so we had everything shipped to Madison, stored in our large basement, and then loaded as needed into my van for my weekly trek. Laura was having trouble finding good part-time help for the long mall hours. Unlike Madison, there was no nearby university with an easy supply of college students.

Milwaukee had far more wealth than Madison, but sales there always lagged behind the State Street store. Expensive items sold much better at Grand Avenue, but the mall lacked State Street's steady tourist traffic. And Madison had a loyal base of local residents, whereas the rich Milwaukee suburbs never took to the Grand Avenue.

Every week, the two managers and I did a store walk-through, and Laura and Janis reported what was selling, what wasn't, and what customers said about the store. I'd already observed that the store had its share of what was known as the carriage trade, rich ladies with a lot of time on their hands and a need for attention, something we didn't see in Madison.

As I headed home from our meeting, driving in stop-and-go highway traffic, I had to tamp down my feelings about the negatives I'd come to associate with the Grand Avenue, no matter how well it was designed and managed. I needed to stay positive and never shared my doubts with staff, but as I gripped the steering wheel a little harder, I ran down the list. It would be inconvenient and expensive to go offsite for storage. Evening hours and Sundays were compulsory, whereas in Madison it was our choice, and it was easy to find students to cover those shifts. The percentage rent penalized you for high sales, and the monthly common area maintenance fees went up annually. And there were the difficult customers who tied up staff time and didn't appreciate our store. That may have hurt the most. I was used to getting compliments and even affection from customers.

AT THE END OF 1983, I was running two stores in two cities with little more than a telephone, a cargo van, and a pair of cash registers that were mostly change makers. We still wrote out purchase orders, mailing the originals and keeping carbon copies to check in the merchandise when it arrived. If we needed an order fast, we'd call it in.

I could never have guessed when I opened the second store that we were approaching the end of an era. In fact, we were on the cusp of a digital revolution that would overturn most conventions of selling goods. Point-of-sale registers that tracked sales and stock would become available a few years later, saving many hours of labor. Of course, they came at the cost of expensive equipment that needed frequent updating and replacement. For now, we continued to do the work by hand, using a simple one-page system Laura had brought with her from her last job. Often, part-timers would do the counts when business was slow.

But counting stock was not just a rote exercise. As Laura once expounded, "You don't just count the items, you end up cleaning the whole shelf, you play with the stuff. You get to know the feel of it. You never say to a customer, 'I haven't played with that toy.' You can answer any question a customer might have: 'Yes, and you should see what else it can do. The Freemountain shark puppet is not just a shark. When you turn it inside out, it turns into a swimmer."

The paperwork continued to increase—more invoices received, paid, and filed, more sales records kept, cash flow projected. I needed profit and loss statements for each store now as well as a consolidated one. Most of the time, I felt more like the coordinator of paperwork than owner. Surely it would ease over time.

I continued to work Saturdays on State Street with Mary Ann—I held on to that. But the rest of the week, I was mostly dealing with purchase orders, bills, and budgets.

My office space in the basement grew inadequate, so I rented a large space on the second floor of the building. It had very long, steep stairs, which might have contributed to the heart attack of the dentist who'd had his office there for years.

FOR A WHOLE YEAR after the new store opened, my schedule was so full I could ignore my lack of a social life, happy most nights just to go home tired. But home was soon disrupted.

John and I had agreed to use the same attorney for the divorce, a man recommended by trusted neighbors. We'd already reached a settlement that split the money from the sale of the house, our only major asset. He'd take the family car; I'd keep most of the furniture. We'd share custody, although it was understood the boys would live with me. I would keep the business but pay back John's initial investment with interest. Our entire attorney's fee was $150.

There was not yet a marital property law in Wisconsin. If there had been, the law that eventually passed, designed to protect unemployed housewives, would have automatically given John half of the business. Still, I thought our settlement was fair. John's support and the money we'd used from his pension fund had made the business possible, but it was I who did the work to make it successful. The cash settlement acknowledged his contribution. But only with sole ownership would I have true independence. It didn't cross my mind then, but it did later, that a married man in my position then would not likely have retained full ownership.

I would have liked to stay in the house until Peter was out of high school, but the property had appreciated $60,000 since we'd bought it eight years earlier, and I could hardly blame John for wanting his share. He would use the money from the sale to buy a triplex on the east side.

Our neighborhood was desirable, so selling the house was easy. What wasn't easy was finding a place to rent close to Peter's school and friends. I wanted a room for Johnny when he came home from school. I finally found a two-story, three-bedroom duplex three blocks away, with a screened porch on one side, which made losing our old one less painful.

Our new place was only six blocks from our old house, but once we moved in, it felt more like ten miles. I missed my neighbors, missed the quiet street, missed the tall oaks that shaded the house and the Jack-in-the-Pulpits and Virginia Bluebells that sprang up in the yard every spring like old friends.

During this period, I sometimes felt unsettled and alone in a way I never had before. The children were still there but not for much longer.

My mother and sisters were many miles away, my friends mostly moved by now. Years later, I would find a therapist to help sort things out, but for now it was all on me, and I felt a terrible failure, to my children, to myself.

I missed the comfort of church. I vividly remembered singing the Gregorian chant at daily mass at Holy Ghost when I was still in grade school. The 7:00 a.m. mass usually had only a handful of worshipers. A nun played the organ, and I and two other classmates sang, our girlish voices clear in the near-empty church. I came to love the Kyrie Eleison, the prayer for mercy. God have mercy on me, Christ have mercy on me. I remember walking the two blocks home afterwards happy and calm.

I had had no quarrel with religion, only with the strict dogma of the Catholic church. When John and I decided to marry, we had confessed to the parish priest that although we no longer believed in the creed, we wanted the ceremony. We quickly learned the church did not compromise. From that time on, our personal ethics were reflected in social action and politics, and our boys were raised accordingly.

So there I was, a liberated woman of the seventies and eighties, struggling to find an identity as a single parent and budding entrepreneur without the familiar comforts of conventional family and faith.

Many years later, in a new role as aspiring filmmaker, I visited my hometown fair and rode the Ferris wheel with Pinky Lee, a co-owner of the fair, whom I had interviewed for a documentary.

"Pinky," I said, enjoying the view of the Chippewa Valley in front of us, "I love the way people recognize my family name here. All I have to say is 'Rubenzer,' and they say, 'How's Joan doing?' or 'I saw Ron at the beer tent yesterday. He's still a card!' It feels so good, like I still belong here."

Sitting across from me, our bucket seat rocking at the top of the wheel, Pinky smiled. "Janice, they call those roots."

I thought about my difficulty in adjusting to becoming a single mother in the years after my divorce. The truth was that by making the decision to leave my hometown and live in Madison, I'd followed the modern American move from town to city, cutting myself off from family and old friends.

And now I had to sell our family home, which everybody loved. Peter hated leaving the most. He didn't like his smaller bedroom, missed our old block, our yard, his nearby friends. Once we moved he rarely complained, but I knew he wasn't happy, and I was feeling guilty. The divorce had yanked him out of a happy family home into a single-parent rental. I started thinking I'd better move us back to the neighborhood as soon as I could afford to buy another house.

Naively, I thought life would be better for all of us after the divorce. I'd believed my therapist when she'd minimized the lasting effects of the divorce. She had the boys in for an hour of reassurance, which did provide a temporary fix.

But the tension in the household had turned out to be mostly mine. Johnny was more aware of it and recovered in time. But Peter continued to be baffled by the split.

My easily affectionate son was smiling less, sometimes avoiding me when I tried to engage him. He'd always brought friends home, which I loved, but now mostly stayed at their houses after school. Desperate, I had a couple from our old block over, but it felt awkward with just the three of us. I was learning what it was like to be a single parent.

The business now had to be more than satisfying work. I had to watch the bottom line carefully, keep the store profitable so we could afford a good place to live. Despite the headaches the Milwaukee store caused, I needed it badly. Sometimes, I felt trapped by the obligation. Surprisingly, I realized how John must have felt, stuck in his well-paying bureaucratic job with the state.

As the parent who had left the marriage, I felt a powerful obligation to make the money we needed. It was up to me to compensate for my boys' losses.

I was the breadwinner now.

FIFTEEN

One morning on my way to work two years later, with the air filled with the smoky scent of early fall, I noticed that the trees on the four-year-old mall now reached above some storefronts. Even at 8:30 in the morning, people were walking on both sides of the street, some students with backpacks headed for campus, but the rest were regular people with few clues as to their destinations. I'd often wondered just who the people were who walked on State Street all hours of the day, every day. Didn't anybody work nine to five anymore? Whatever the reason, it was good for business.

In the four years I'd been on the street, almost two dozen new stores had opened, including the first coffee shops. I felt happy to be part of the new energy that infused downtown, and especially State Street. Urban renewal was underway all over the country. The Rouse Company had two new city projects in the works that would open soon—South Street Seaport in New York City and the Waterside in Norfolk, Virginia.

I was feeling fine. I had achieved a kind of equilibrium with the business. After two years, the Grand Avenue was operating smoothly with Laura and Janis at the helm, per sales meeting early projections. I'd learned to accept the shortcomings of doing business in a mall, and my weekly trips still gave me a nice break from Madison. And I still felt close to the State Street store, which continued to be highly popular and profitable.

At the Puzzlebox, I stopped at the window to look at the seven-foot-tall wood skeleton of a Tyrannosaurus Rex built for us by a local carpenter. It was an exact replica of the wood assembly kits we sold, and customers loved it. Mary Ann had filled the carpeted floor of the window with brightly colored plastic dinosaurs marching in regimented rows. Standing behind the sales counter inside, I'd seen people on the street stop to look at the T-Rex, walk in the door, and stop at the table where half a dozen assembled dinosaurs stood on neat stacks of the flat packages, along with glass bowls of plastic dinosaurs. The customer could put her hand on the product immediately. And the price was right: just $9.00 for the kits and $1.00 for the plastic toys. Some windows sold product better than others. This window was a terrific seller.

MY YOUNG MANAGER had exceeded my expectations. She kept the store well-stocked and well-run. She'd hired new part-time staff to work the new evening shifts, and she was learning to supervise them effectively. A few months earlier, I'd been shocked one morning to learn she'd fired a night employee who'd forgotten to lock the rear door. While I admired her courage at taking on the hardest task a manager can have, I assured her such human error was a forgivable offense. No dogmatist, she promptly hired him back.

Mary Ann had quickly learned the importance of product placement. The most accessible shelves—at waist, chest, or eye level—were for products that sold well. I'd been amazed to see how careful attention to this principle could increase sales, especially if you could reorder the product quickly. You just never let it run out.

The bear windows continued to wow the public. They'd achieved some local fame with a cartoon in the downtown weekly *Isthmus*. Over a drawing of the Garver building a headline read: *Madison is a great town for the fine arts.* On the right side was the Gallery window, filled with paintings. On the left, a couple stood in front of our window, which featured B.B. Bear in a loin cloth, hanging from a vine. The man's hand was around the woman's waist as she said: "Oh, honey—look at the cute bears."

THINGS WERE GOING WELL at work, but at home in my apartment one evening, I felt my new self-confidence fading. I wanted to celebrate but had no one to do it with. I poured a glass of wine and walked out on the screened porch. In our old house, the morning sun was filtered through hundred-year-old oak trees. Afternoons and evenings, the porch was shady and cool. This one faced west, with no trees to break the fierce afternoon sun. It didn't cool down until after dark.

The apartment now felt like a mistake. The living room walls throbbed when the neighbor in the apartment next to us played his hi-fi. The landlord was a sour-faced man who charged me $50 extra a month for my well-behaved cat. Six months were left on the lease, but I was ready to leave.

A narrow concrete porch in the back of the house did get shade, and it had become my smoking room. The kids hated my habit, and I wanted to quit but just couldn't yet. Wine in hand, I walked to the back, sat down on a lawn chair, and lit up. The smoke was acrid in the heat, the red wine sour on my lips.

I'd lost my cool porch and my beautiful house, my beloved sons were growing up and away from me, the rest of my family was hundreds of miles away. I had only one friend left in town to call for a movie or dinner, and she was gone for the weekend. I hadn't had a date since John had left and had no idea how to get one.

ONE DAY A FEW WEEKS LATER, Peter came home after spending the day with his dad. I smiled when he walked into the kitchen. At almost 17, he was close to my height. His face had lost its roundness, sharpened by high cheekbones, his straight hair cut short, one bang sweeping down his forehead. Everything fit—his straight nose, his quirky eyebrows, his neat ears tucked flat against his head. Peter had always been fun and funny, and this year he'd become downright witty, delivering lines that made me laugh and sometimes wince. He'd become master of the ironic quip, exhibiting a talent for zeroing in on human foibles. But tonight his usually happy face was troubled.

"Mom, I hate having to visit Dad in that little apartment. It eats up my whole Saturday. I still don't get why you two had to split."

My throat tightened. I just didn't know how to explain our divorce past lame platitudes like "Sometimes people grow apart." It especially hurt because Peter and I had been so close in the past. Once again, I wished I'd found a middle ground between noisy fights and quiet withdrawal.

The continuing, troubling problem with my new freedom was that it came at the cost of knowing where I fit, and the same could be said for my kids, who had had no say in my decision. I would move five times in the next ten years trying to find the right place.

I couldn't give Peter his intact nuclear family, but I could move us back into the old neighborhood. Soon I found an affordable house on Allen Street, just a block from our old one. It was smaller, plainer, with more street traffic, but it had three bedrooms and a screened porch that was shady most of the day.

I loved seeing Peter's cheerful face when he came home from school with a friend, loved it that our outdoor cat Spike was back in familiar territory, even if he was still naughty about coming home at night. It surprised me what a difference it made to be just a few blocks closer to our old house and all the familiars of the block.

Although Johnny, now mostly called John by Peter and me, was living on campus, he took possession of the finished basement, moving in for a semester before moving on eventually to live on his own. Old neighbors were near, and Peter's friends visited more often.

It wasn't perfect, but at last I felt I had restored some sense of home and place for my sons.

SIXTEEN

Much later, I came to think of the first five years of the Puzzlebox as a kind of magic hour. Through luck and timing, I'd landed in 1979 on what would become one of the best, most vital retail streets in the country at the beginning of a national shopping spree. I had no idea then that I'd stumbled into a remarkable period, but I'd smelled opportunity and ran with it.

Maybe my best work was in those first years, with modest beginnings and low expectations. My only financial goal was a good salary. The idea of selling toys for adults as well as children came from my fear of failure, but the belief that adults needed play as much as children came from my heart. And it was gratifying to have people respond with heart-felt enthusiasm. It would take years, but eventually this growing feeling of largesse would seep into my personal life, as I gave myself permission to buy a handsome sofa, embellish it with embroidered pillows, hang my walls with original art, and trade in my sensible khaki skirts for swingy, soft silk ones.

I loved Saturdays behind the counter in Madison, loved seeing the regulars, laughing with them as I showed them a new wind-up toy. A recent store survey had revealed that a high number of people came in as often as once a week. Madison customers had always been a joy, appreciative of the store and open to uncommon products. Marketing people called them early adopters. They gave me permission to buy cutting-edge stuff that might not sell easily. We had customers like that in Milwaukee too, but more of them in Madison.

State Street on weekends had an air of excitement that affected everyone, and that festival atmosphere was especially strong in spring. In good weather, I loved to play merchant, taking a long time sweeping the sidewalk. Then I'd go inside and choose the music for the first hour, often favorite opera arias. Later we'd move on to the Stevie Wonder mix tape a student employee had put together for us that had a way of making everybody move to the beat.

The store filled up early on Saturdays with shoppers out for pleasure, for the easy strolling up and down the tree-lined, pebble-concrete sidewalks, the unhurried browsing in the small, quirky stores, the long lunches at Gino's or the Baker's Rooms.

For years I had my own Saturday lunch break agenda: picking up a bottle of rain-scented hand lotion at the Soap Opera, or a new album at B-Side Records, a package of purple napkins at Leslie Watkins's Paperteria, just around the corner on Fairchild next to Fontana's Sporting Goods store. Or I'd just grab a burger at the Plaza and then stop at Tellus Mater for some street talk with Richard Crabs.

There was an infectious joy and creativity to those early years on State Street. My adrenalin flowed constantly. I felt I had permission to do anything as long as it was fun. We rang a bell at odd intervals on Saturdays and gave a prize to a customer, just for the fun of it. One Halloween, I dressed as a nurse in a white uniform and fright wig, stethoscope around my neck, and listened to customers' heartbeats. I hired a photographer to take B.B. Bear's picture with a white bow tied around his neck and gave autographed photos to members of the B.B. Bear fan club (no charge to join).

Halloween, 1984

The new culture was intoxicating, and it felt like there was value behind our stores in both Madison and Milwaukee, as opposed to the soulless suburbs. I was running a popular, successful business, sales were getting better and better, and I was doing it my way.

THE TRANSITION TO TWO STORES would have been difficult without Mary Ann, who was consistently quick, smart, and hard-working. She was also fun to be around. I'd observed with envy that Mary Ann had her hair cut differently every few months. When I hit on a hair style that flattered me, I stuck with it. Once she got rocker hair—a short, choppy bob. She quickly grew it out to her shoulders and then abruptly got a boy cut that showed her ears. Every time she changed the style, she bought a pair of earrings, always dangly. When I asked her about it, she just smiled and said it had become a ritual. Sometimes I felt like I was getting life lessons from her. I was twenty years older, but it had never occurred to me to have so much fun with my personal style.

The students I hired in the early eighties embraced social good and the search for a kinder world. They majored in political science, literature, or the social sciences, were conscientious and good with customers, needing only gentle training. Their work ethic was strong. By the third year we'd expanded our hours, and we hired students to staff Sundays and evenings. No one asked for time off their schedule unless it was an emergency.

In those early years, most of our student staff were smart, well-read, and non-materialistic. They liked to drink, and plenty smoked dope, although not at our parties. The Puzzlebox appealed to them because it was fun and had an ethical base—no war toys, no sexist dolls, no class differences. Our handbook decreed that all customers were equal, even the wealthy ones.

Helene Metzenberg, a silversmith who had become a mainstay employee at the store, was a slender, intense woman with silver-gray hair and a glint in her eye that didn't come from her glasses. She wore neat skirts, crisp blouses, was matter-of-fact efficient, loved tasks, and never just stood around. To my gratification, she took pleasure in running the vacuum cleaner tube under the counters before we opened.

This pleasant artist, wife of a professor, was cynical about human behavior and was always on the lookout for shoplifters. She wondered why I wasn't.

"Don't you think everyone can be tempted, Janice?" she asked one day when we were working together. She had a wry smile on her lips, which made me defensive. I didn't think I was terribly naïve about human nature.

"Well," I hedged, "I think people would prefer to be honest if they have a choice. I know we have some shoplifting, but I don't think it's serious. I don't want staff to look suspiciously at customers as they walk around the store. Besides, I've read that employee theft is a bigger problem than shoplifting. But I think you can prevent that by hiring well."

"Maybe," she said, looking doubtful. "I think some people just like to steal. And why put temptation in front of a young staff person who doesn't have a lot of pocket change?"

Helene convinced me that careless management invited stealing. We instituted checks to reduce temptation for employees, putting simple procedures in place for refunds and cash handling, things I would have preferred not to bother about. We tried to make sure the most tempting and easy-to-steal items were in clear sight of the checkout.

Helene's best contribution was the transformation of a Kleenex box into a safe. She showed us how to cut around three sides of the bottom to make a flap. We always kept $100 out of the day's sales in the register overnight to start business with the next day. Now when closing, we took the night cash from the register and put it there, under the tissues. On the shelf, it looked like a normal box of Kleenex. I was sure she was overly suspicious, but it worked almost immediately when robbers broke the glass in the rear door. They took a few toys but never found the cash in the Kleenex box. There was just change in the register, and the daily cash and checks were in a real safe in the locked basement. From then on, we gratefully used Helene's trick in all our stores.

Another remarkable student employee, Chip, often came to work in his pajama bottoms. When he arrived for his Saturday shift, he looked like he'd just rolled out of bed. He was over six feet tall, with a handsome face he tried to disguise with a three-day beard so he'd be taken more seriously. He came to the Puzzlebox in his freshman year from Minnesota, and he proudly called himself a radical—passionate about justice and social change. Everybody loved his pajama bottoms, which were always clean and attractive, and I'm sure he wore underwear. I think he just liked to be comfortable. He biked year-round, even in snow and ice, throwing a long coat over the pajamas. He was friendly and excellent with customers and a delight to have on staff.

The characteristics of employees were to change over the years, always reflecting cultural changes, but the first batch was definitely my favorite. Maybe they were just happy the war was over. They'd grown up with the ominous sound of helicopters descending into the jungles during the news hour. If the war had gone on a little longer, our male student staffers would have faced the wrenching choice of being drafted or moving to Canada. And then, affluence hadn't yet hit and spoiled any of us, as it would later in the eighties. Almost all students worked, even if their parents' incomes didn't require it.

In Madison at that time, most full-time jobs were secure and protected by a civil service system. The benefits were great, with both health insurance and a solid pension plan. It was easy to be politically liberal with all that security, and sometimes the city forgot that the rest of the state wasn't so fortunate. The governor then, Lee Dreyfus, famously referred to Madison in a speech as "thirty square miles surrounded by reality."

In that golden fall of 1984, as both my stores settled into a solid period of steady growth, I was too preoccupied with my own success to pay much attention to national economics. I knew that Ronald Reagan had successfully passed a tax cut of 27% for just about everyone, and I knew the stock market loved it. The bull market would last for years, helped along by low interest rates and Reagan's hands-off-business policy.

I'd read in the morning business section that in other cities jobs were starting to shift from manufacturing to service. Big-box stores were appearing everywhere, seducing consumers with their low, low prices, but that wasn't affecting us. People came to us for fun and unique products, a winning formula I intended to continue. It never occurred to me to worry about the future.

In fact, my business reality was sweet those days. If anything was bothering me, it was my personal life, which badly needed reinvention. And that was something my marketing skills couldn't help a whit.

SEVENTEEN

I looked into the salon mirror, aghast. Two-inch curls had sprouted up all over my head, like early ferns in spring. I swallowed hard, reached up and touched one. It sprang back when I pulled my hand away, like a Slinky. I didn't know what to think. Why had I let my hairdresser talk me into a perm?

Carol brushed the curls out, framing my face with a few tendrils. She stood behind me, hands on my shoulders, smiling widely. I thought I looked like some silent-era movie star with tight, plastered-to-the-head girlie curls. Still, it couldn't be that bad, or Carol wouldn't be so happy.

For years, she'd been giving my straight, dark blonde hair a simple cut, never more than a half-hour process. As she snipped away, she'd routinely shared details of her personal life, not excluding sex. I suspected she'd used her own confidences as bait to worm the details of my marriage and divorce from me. She knew I wanted to date but had taken no action. For half a year, she'd been suggesting I change my hair and even dye it a lighter color.

"Perming your hair would soften the lines of your face, give you a more feminine look," she'd cooed. "Everyone in business knows your professional success, Janice, but you hide your sex appeal under your straight hair and casual clothes."

Nobody else talked to me like this. I'd thought I looked good. I'd inherited my mother's smooth, clear skin and my dad's slender build. But feminine was not a word I'd applied to myself for years, perhaps a residue of my marriage of convenience. I'd buried my passion some years ago, sublimating it into my kids and now my work.

I think I'd assumed someone right would just show up, but no knight on a white horse had magically appeared. I didn't even feel confident enough to flirt. Carol said I had a wall around me. She may have been right. I was lonely and determined to change but felt frozen in place. In the eighties, the tools for dating were bars and newspaper ads. I was way too imbued with fifties morality to look for one-night stands. So perming my hair was a simple first step.

It was after six when I left the salon for home. I darted into my car, hoping I wouldn't see anyone I knew. Johnny was sharing an apartment off-campus now but had promised to come for dinner when I'd mentioned lasagna.

The boys were watching a rerun of *All in the Family*, feet up on the coffee table, laughing hard as I walked into the room. I waited nervously behind the sofa for a commercial before interrupting.

"Hey, guys!"

John looked up first. His face was blank as he registered the change. Peter turned, took in the perm, and squealed: "Mom, you look like Little Orphan Annie," and both boys laughed. Cowed, I went to the mirror on the hall door and looked at my image. It was hopeless, and I couldn't change it.

Curly

My new curls settled down after a month, and I gradually grew into the look. Fashions were changing, blouses and skirts getting longer and fuller. With new courage, I went to Sassafrass and bought a deceptively simple Norma Kamali white cotton-knit skirt that I loved as soon as I tried it on. It was cut on the bias so skillfully that the fabric moved almost caressingly around my legs when I walked. Pink was a color I'd avoided as overly girlie, but after the saleswoman pointed out that it went well with my complexion, I went home with a soft pink cotton sweater. Combined with my newly curled hair, the look was soft, feminine, and flattering. Now all I needed was a date.

"**WHAT ARE YOU DOING** tonight, Janice?" Mary Ann asked one Saturday at 5:00 as we were turning the store over to the night staff. "Mike and I are going to a big party."

"I'm just going home. I'm always ready to get off my feet on Saturdays."

She frowned. "I've been thinking you need to hear some good music. Let's go see a band next Friday. I'll check and see who's playing."

I couldn't imagine going out with her to a club. Her crowd was twenty years younger. Besides, it wasn't a good idea to socialize with staff. But it was nice of her to think of it.

Six days later I found myself in the back row of a pulsing crowd of people, most of them young men in jeans and T-shirts printed with images of rock bands. We were at O'Cayz Corral, a popular downtown venue. The air was heavy with smoke and sweat. Mary Ann had gone to the bar, and now she came back and handed me a Dos Equis. A Madison band called The Appliances was hammering away on a small stage at the end of the small room.

The deafening music now shifted to a song with a strong bass. Suddenly, the men around me were popping up and down like bobbins on a lake, straight up and down, arms pressed to their sides. I was fascinated, stimulated, and wildly entertained. Mary Ann started jumping too, and then a tall guy in a sleeveless T-shirt jumped up on the stage, flexed his biceps, bent his knees, and dove into the crowd. The cheering crowd easily caught him and began to pass his outstretched body.

This was my first exposure to the new music scene in Madison. Every couple of weeks, Mary Ann took me to see a different band. We never stayed overly long, ending up at a quiet bar to talk over the evening. She was a wonderful companion, and I found myself opening up about my marriage and divorce.

One night we went to a large venue called the Church Key. A band from Minneapolis called The Replacements, a pioneer of alternative rock, was the headliner. The guitarist had been too incapacitated to play standing up, so someone had brought him a chair. He sat for a while, playing, then suddenly stopped, sat still for some minutes, and then simply rolled off the chair onto the floor. The band played on as he lay there.

I couldn't take my eyes off him, or the band, or the large crowd around me massed in front of the stage, few of whom seemed to notice that he'd fallen. What I was seeing and hearing, musically, culturally, was radically different from my college nights drinking beer at the Pines in Eau Claire, where the band's repertoire was limited to slow dances and polkas. Mary Ann was the only woman I knew who loved rock and roll with a deep passion. She was knowledgeable about bands and music in general, and I was always interested in her interest. I felt real energy in the music, even if much of it was fueled by drugs and alcohol.

As part of the end-of-decade creative surge, all kinds of local bands had started up, a kind of parallel to all the new stores on State Street. Smart Studios opened on East Washington Avenue the same year I first saw body passing, and it became a recording mecca for punk and grunge rock bands. One of its founders, Butch Vig, had such a gift for bringing out the special sound a band possessed that the studio eventually attracted national groups, including the headliner Nirvana, who came to Madison to record in the plain two-story brick building a lot of people thought was a drug house.

Mary Ann was determined to bring me up to full cultural snuff, so one Friday, she took me to the weekly midnight showing of *The Rocky Horror Picture Show* at the Majestic Theater on King Street. I didn't know the plot but knew the audience often dressed like characters in the movie, which explained the woman next to us in line dressed as a maid in a short black skirt and a white apron and cap. The audience was raucous, screaming well-loved dialogue along with the actors, throwing rice at a wedding couple and pieces of toast for no reason I could discern.

My other favorite film outing came when the Majestic screened Jonathan Demme's *Stop Making Sense*. I couldn't get enough of the Talking Heads after that, singing along to *Psycho Killer* in the basement stockroom where I was marking Christmas ornaments with a student staffer.

Sometimes I worried about breaking rules by socializing too much with staff. But Mary Ann and I worked so well together, and she was such a responsible, self-starting, and valuable employee, it felt like we were equals, so I stopped worrying about it. I let myself relax into the sheer novelty of the evenings, of the close-up view of a new generation.

Throughout my life, I would be interested in tracking culture, almost in an academic way. I found the drug culture generally unattractive, but I accepted it as part of the times. It never occurred to me then that some people might put alcohol in the same category.

I never drank much at the clubs, not in public. But I always went home and had more than one nightcap, reviewing the evening, incorporating what I'd seen, lulling myself into a state of sleep. It got to be a habit, drinking alone late at night, but I wouldn't worry about it now. Alcohol was kind of like my best friend, helping me get through some uncertain times.

EIGHTEEN

In 1984, even as I was undergoing my own makeover, business suddenly got sexy.

Society's heroes in the sixties and seventies had been people who helped others—teachers, public defenders, political activists. In the 80s, Americans were tired of social struggle. People wanted to make money and enjoy life. The hero became a person who helped himself, and a successful store owner fit the new profile perfectly. Yuppies appeared—young urban professionals who lived to work and spend money. Students flocked to the business schools in record numbers. A local paper ran a photo of me hugging two bears to illustrate a story about my business success.

There was a tremendous turnover on State Street as the last vestiges of old retail either went out of business or moved to the suburbs. More new stores opened, most of which would stay on the street for decades. Ragstock, a used clothing store with an irresistible mix of vintage, grunge, and Army surplus, moved into a large space on the 300 block, previously occupied by a travel agency and a liquor store. For the Puzzlebox staff, Ragstock was an unending source of fun Halloween costumes—wedding gowns, cocktail dresses, fatigue jackets.

Just three spaces up our block, a women's accessory store called Que Sera replaced Madison Pen and Card. I shopped there regularly, buying cut-glass dangling earrings from Czechoslovakia, patterned socks, and a silver-studded leather belt.

A few blocks further down, Sacred Feather was thriving in one of the last houses on State Street, formerly a lingerie shop. The owner, Tony

Badame, had originally operated a push-cart on the street. The store sold hats for men and women and a line of local leather products. On the same block, a U.S. Army recruiting station closed, making room for B-Side Records, with an expert, eclectic collection of albums.

The Puzzlebox was nominated for the Best of Madison toy store that year, and when I wanted something special for the awards party, I went to Sassafrass for a two-piece turquoise cotton dress with an off-the-shoulder top and a long skirt with a sassy ruffle on the bottom.

After the Grand Avenue store opened, we'd felt a rush of sales in both cities. People streamed into the stores, eager to buy—little things like wind-up alligators, pig stickers, and Groucho glasses, or big things like train sets or fancy kaleidoscopes. Once, Mary Ann laughed and said we could put No. 2 pencils on the shelves and people would queue up to buy them. Suddenly, everyone loved shopping. It used to be functional, but now it became entertainment.

I observed these new trends, wondered at them, worried they were too hedonistic, but also profited from them. Sometimes I missed the idealism of the early era, but it passed quickly as sales skyrocketed.

KEEPING TRACK OF changing wants and needs was important in my business, and I thought I was pretty good at it. Futurist John Naisbitt had written a book called Megatrends in 1982, and among the top trends he forecast were the shift from an industrial to an information society, and the emergence of a world economy. But I got no sense in the book of the changes the digital revolution and globalization would bring, certainly no sense of how jobs would shift radically, creating a new class of loser as well as big winners, as corporations moved factories abroad for the cheap labor, killing blue-collar jobs here in the process.

None of these trends seemed earth-shaking to me, maybe because of Madison's stable, non-industrial economy. State Street was booming, the Grand Avenue store was doing well, and I couldn't see any reason for either to change.

My interest was piqued, however, by Naisbitt's prediction of a shift from traditional pyramid business structure to a flatter network. Intel, an innovative semi-conductor company founded in the late 60s, was getting attention in business circles for its horizontal structure, with the boss coming in at the same time as everybody else and vying for a parking space as well. I wanted to talk to my business adviser, Bill Pinkovitz, about that. I was feeling the burden of the increased administrative work, an unpleasant corollary to the good sales. I thought I'd be fine with sharing the power with my managers, but I wasn't as sure about showing up for work as early as they did, or staying as late. More and more, I found myself lingering over coffee and the paper at home until nine or even ten a.m., which was quite pleasant.

IN A BOON TIME, it's easy to see only what's happening in front of you. What I saw was that our sales were growing, and cash was accumulating in my bank account. I could afford good salaries for everyone, and for the first time, for myself.

The mid-eighties were years of success upon success, happiness flowing from our stores to customers. The bear windows continued to wow, Anne gamely trekking up from Chicago every month or two. We put the wooden sailboats in the window again, now with two B.B. mermaids lounging on rocks, dressed in shimmering gold, lame fish tails, gold lame bras, strings of pearls, and tropical flowers behind their ears. Times like those, we all felt like we were ten again.

Anne found someone to make a life-sized Raggedy Ann and Andy. In spring, the couple flew kites; in February they kissed for Valentine's Day. But the bear came back in fall. A dozen stuffed geese flew above the window, while B.B. Bear, dressed in camouflage with a stuffed rifle on his lap, slept beneath. There was nothing that bear couldn't do.

Rouse was so pleased with the performance of the Grand Avenue store that Mark Brocato called one day to ask if I was ready to open another store. A new project in St. Louis would open in summer of 1985.

I laughed. "I've just gotten used to making the weekly trek to Milwaukee, Mark. I don't see a third store fitting into my operation."

"You know how to do it now," he said. "You know you'll be successful. And this is a great project. You should come down and see it. They've just started renovating the terminal waiting room. It's going to make a spectacular restaurant and bar."

He'd sent me some pictures, and of course, it was impressive. But it didn't make sense for us. Too far away, too expensive.

NINETEEN

I woke abruptly one morning that summer of 1984 to a phone call from my sister Freddie, who lived across the alley from my parents in Chippewa Falls. My mother had had a stroke the night before and had been taken to St. Joseph's hospital. I was too shocked to absorb the news. Mom was 82, but that was young for our family tree. She had been so strong, such a rock for all of us, that she seemed invincible. I couldn't imagine life without her.

When she was released from the hospital two days after her stroke, I drove home to spend the weekend with her and my dad in our brick house on South Main Street. When he'd opened the door to let me in, his face had been strained, and as he hugged me, I felt his thinning body tremble as he whispered, "Jannie, I'm so glad you're here."

When I walked into the small bedroom just off the living room, Mom was a little fuzzy-headed. She greeted me by name, but that was to be the last time she was knew who I was.

My mother's life had been a hard, physical one, raising eight children and even running our farm for years when my dad was working at the rubber plant during the war. Our modest house in town had only one full bath on the second floor, shared by everyone. So when Mom's brother Fritz died and left her a little money, she'd used it to have a second, more elaborate bath built off the first-floor bedroom. In her old age she loved indulging herself with what small luxuries she could—a deep tub, a pretty vanity, soft Turkish towels.

Before I'd left Madison I'd stopped at the Perfume Shop to buy something special for her. The store's owner knew his products well, and when I explained what I wanted and described my mother, he brought out a jar of J'ai Ose by Guy Laroche. He explained that it was classified as an oriental perfume—soft, spicy, and long lasting. When I held it to my nose, I saw desert pavilions and swaying palm trees.

Now I handed her the wrapped box. "It's French, Mom."

She loved gifts and opened it eagerly, unscrewing the gleaming gold lid of the small frosted glass jar. She held it to her nose and smiled. "I love it. Would you rub some on my back?"

My dad quickly spoke up. "Let me do it." He'd had been hovering nearby, obviously distraught.

My mother had taken the bus to Madison a month earlier to see a specialist for mysterious symptoms her doctor couldn't identify. The specialist had found nothing wrong. I'd gone with Mom and was relieved when the doctor told her she had no need to worry. That night in my apartment, my mother had told me how well my father had been treating her since she'd been sick. Through much of my adult life, she'd complained that she'd wanted to divorce him but didn't have the resources. So, I was surprised when she wanted to cut her visit short to get back home. She seemed more concerned about him than herself.

Now Pop gently pulled her gown over her head. I helped her into a comfortable position as he began to massage the cream into her naked back with a gentleness I had rarely seen in him.

She moaned with pleasure. The scent of citrus wafted up, or maybe peach, and sandalwood. After a while, my dad gave me a turn, and as I rubbed the cream into her dry skin, I thought of how her body had changed in the last few years. Mom had done floor exercises for twenty minutes almost every morning of her life. She'd been proud of her trim body. Now she had rolls of flesh around her belly and back.

My mother was old and sick now, her back broad, hair thinned out, veins pushing out on her arms and hands. And yet, I marveled at how little it mattered to me. I felt her essence as never before, the spirit that transcended her body. My father and I were together that day in understanding how much we would miss that essence—tart, bossy, loving, vulnerable. I felt an ache in my heart at the strength of her spirit and the fact that I might lose it.

I'd brought another gift with me that day, a gray stuffed baby puma from the store. It was oddly elegant, so soft it snugged easily into her body when she held it.

MY MOTHER SLIPPED AWAY over the next four months. I visited her frequently at the rest home she'd gone to soon after another stroke took most of her memory. At home in Madison, I often retreated to the new screened porch after dark and drank until I was tired enough to sleep. Through my own volition, I'd lost my family unit, and now my mother was dying. I felt my mortality, felt my age, felt a failure.

By ten in the evening, the traffic was light, almost soothing. The darkened porch provided a cloak of invisibility. I'd sip my wine and let myself sink into the feelings I'd repressed all day. The porch was my refuge, the wine the narcotic I needed to numb the pain.

Too many times in those months before Mom died, Peter caught me there on the porch, drinking. One night I heard him come down from his room and stand in the doorway behind me. I turned as he spoke. "Are you OK, Mom?" He stood braced against the door jamb in the dark, his face barely visible, his arms crossed against his chest. His voice was worried but a little distant, as if he was hoping he was just imagining I was acting weird. I put a fist to my chin to try to hide my face, keenly aware of the half-empty bottle of wine in front of me. I smiled as best I could and reassured him. "I'm OK, sweetheart, don't worry. I'm just thinking about Grandma. I'll go to bed in a minute."

He didn't move, didn't speak. Finally, he nodded, turned and left, with a quiet "Goodnight, Mom."

THE DAY I GOT THE PHONE CALL that my mother died, I felt only relief. I was just glad it was over. My own response shocked me. Later I realized I'd done my grieving in advance. The next time I was in Chippewa, I brought home the puma I'd given Mom. The French body cream had been all used up, but the puma was infused with its scent—heady, soft, spicy, and long lasting. In the weeks after, I woke each morning with a headache and a deep feeling of dread. Then I remembered drinking myself to sleep the night before because I didn't want to face my loss, didn't want to think about how much I'd miss Mom, didn't want to think about how there was no buffer now between me and death.

But the drinking wasn't working. It just postponed the reality of the loss. And it was affecting my work. I needed to give my business my full attention now. My survival instinct kicked in. I couldn't stop drinking, but I could moderate my intake, and I did.

I started thinking about the future. I couldn't see myself as the owner of these two stores forever. But I had no idea what else I could do. And who was I kidding, anyway. I needed money, a real income, and I couldn't think of another way to make it.

Then Mark Brocato called with a surprising offer from Rouse. They would pay for the entire cost of construction, including fixtures, if I opened a store in St. Louis next year. They wanted to take the risk out of the venture for me. All I'd have to do was bring in the inventory.

Rouse still valued me. They wouldn't take this kind of chance if they didn't have full confidence in me.

I felt the knot in my muscles ease. Suddenly, the negatives I'd seen before—the distance, the price tag, the exponential growth—didn't look so bad. With that kind of subsidy, I could afford to make the changes necessary to manage the growth. Maybe this was the challenge that would push me in a new direction. The hole I'd been in since Mom died was suddenly diminished by the bright light of a new project.

Another good reason to go ahead was the growth opportunity for my managers. I was keenly aware of my standing in the community as a feminist model. I valued Mary Ann and Laura, wanted them to stay with me, wanted them to grow along with me. And to be honest, I needed them to make that growth happen.

This could be a huge professional boost for us all. I was about to take the business to a new level. A week ago, I'd felt unmoored, sorry for myself. Now I was feeling like a forerunner and a winner.

A WEEK AFTER MARK'S CALL, Mary Ann and Laura sat silent in my office above the store, looking at me expectantly. I'd told them both about the offer ahead of time to give them a chance to think about it.

"If we do this, your jobs will change," I said. "I'll need help setting up the new store, and then we'll have a whole new structure. You'll have to turn more of your work over to your assistant managers."

"Cathy is ready to take over here," said Mary Ann. "She can do everything I do. She just needs experience doing it."

"Janis, too," Laura said. "She loves working for the Puzzlebox and will take on whatever I give her."

They were both sitting up straight, eager, faces animated. I tried to slow it down.

"Look, I don't know where this will take us. I feel I'm going in a little blind—three stores in three cities. It's a risk." But even as I said it, I felt a thrill.

Mary Ann frowned. "If it's a Rouse project, how risky can it be? They don't fail, do they?"

"Not that I know of. But some of their stores must fail."

"I love working with the Rouse management at Grand Avenue," Laura said. "But I know some of the stores with less desirable locations don't do as well."

"Then Janice will have to negotiate a good space," Mary Ann said, looking at me.

"I'm thinking of the distance," I said. "It's an eight-hour drive, so we'd have to fly there, stay overnight. It'll be expensive. The store will have to be totally self-sufficient in terms of getting product."

Laura frowned. "That's a real problem. I don't see how you could do it without a decent-sized stockroom on site. Would they give you that?"

I didn't know. "Maybe if we had a bigger space, we could have stock shipped to the store. It might be worth the extra rent."

We were all silent, thinking. I needed to voice a caveat.

"No one in St. Louis knows who we are, knows how good our product is, knows our culture. Even if we can attract a good manager, how will we keep it from being just another mall store?"

Mary Ann got up and started pacing. Laura looked at me, eyebrows raised. Then Mary Ann spoke. "So, let's find a good manager and bring her here for a couple of weeks. She can stay with me, work in the store every day, visit Grand Avenue to see how Laura runs a Rouse mall store."

Laura let out a cackle. "We'll feed her propaganda! We'll brainwash her!"

We all laughed. Then I said, "So what do you think, guys?"

"Let's do it," Laura said decisively.

"You only live once," Mary Ann said. They both looked at me happily, expectantly, as if to say, let's get on with this new adventure.

My mother had had to wait until she was old to get a few luxuries into her life. She was smart and had more energy than anyone else I ever met, but she never held a serious paying job. The travel she and my dad did in retirement was mostly to visit one of their kids in a different state.

What possible reason was there for me, her single, forty-six-year-old daughter, to say no to this generous offer from the Rouse Company? I'd seen photos of the train station in St. Louis, a magnificent limestone building that looked like a castle. Rouse would build a gorgeous, exciting center in it, and the Puzzlebox would be part of it. I'd be part of it, traveling to supervise construction in that stimulating environment, in a new city, meeting new people. To hell with caution.

It was high time I found out just what I had in me.

TWENTY

The trip from my arrival gate to the taxi stand at the St. Louis airport was starting to feel almost as long as the short flight. Getting up in the dark to make the 6:00 a.m. plane had been bad enough.

Outside the terminal, the February air was mild but damp, actually clammy. The sky was blanketed with dark gray clouds. I looked toward the first cab in line, and the driver popped out of his door. He was wearing a brown leather jacket and what could only be a vintage Yellow Cab cap, with Taxi in black script above the shiny black brim. Seeing I had only a briefcase, he moved quickly to open the passenger door.

I was meeting Mark Brocato in half an hour at Union Station, which the driver told me was twenty minutes away. Two years ago, I'd resisted opening the Milwaukee store because of the hour-and-a-half drive. This commute was much longer and a lot more expensive. I felt a moment of panic. What had I been thinking?

We sped past bare brown fields dotted with pancake restaurants, low office buildings, and billboards advertising personal injury lawyers. Then the fields disappeared into acres of one-story tract housing.

"It seems pretty flat here," I said, "and a lot warmer than when I boarded in Wisconsin."

"It's flat all right," the driver said, laughing. "The elevation's only 400 feet. St. Louis is hot and humid in summer, just plain humid in winter. The tropical heat from the Gulf floats right up the river and gets trapped here. The airport gets fogged in regularly, both summer and winter."

But he was so good-humored I started to cheer up.

"How long have you lived here?" I asked.

"Born and raised in St. Louis," he said. "My grandparents came from Mississippi a long time ago." He smiled in the rearview mirror. His skin was smooth and brown.

"How big is the city now?" I asked.

"About 400,000," he said. "It used to be a lot bigger."

"What happened?"

He met my eyes in the rearview mirror and shrugged. "The suburbs, I guess."

Hmm. I'd have to find out more about that.

"I'm thinking about opening a store in the Union Station project," I said. "Do you know anything about it?"

"Oh yeah! Everybody here is excited about it. This was the biggest railroad station in the country once. The waiting room was fancier than Grand Central in New York. When I was in the Army, I used train stations all over Europe and never saw one more beautiful than this one." I was struck by the driver's easy self-confidence and store of information. He seemed to take a perverse pride in the odd weather. Maybe the city would reveal higher attributes, I thought, even as the scenery changed to taller office buildings, parking ramps jammed with cars, and Budweiser billboards.

The driver lifted his hand from the steering wheel and pointed ahead. "Keep your eyes on that spot. We're coming up on downtown."

Now I saw the tip of something very high and shiny: the arch. We turned south toward the city and the graceful, curved lines of the stainless-steel sculpture seemed to emerge inch by inch. A ray of sunlight broke through, sending slivers of light bouncing off the beams. It was sheer genius, I thought, to place this unexpected beauty in such an otherwise featureless place.

"When the fog recedes, the arch seems to be rising right out of it," my driver said.

A few blocks down Market Street, we pulled up to Union Station, a horizontal stone building four stories high, with a steep, red-tiled roof and a tall clock tower on one side.

Thanking the cabbie for the wealth of information, I paid the fare and stepped inside the terminal. I looked up at a vast barrel-vaulted ceiling that explained the steep roof. Except for a dozen workmen and a row of ladders, the enormous room was empty. A faint sound of hammering came from a distance. Around me were elaborate stained-glass windows and ornate plasterwork on the walls and ceiling. Above an arched mezzanine on one end of the room was a frieze of three female figures holding torches in both hands above their heads.

A man on a very tall ladder worked at one wall, and as I moved toward him, a shower of small bits of shiny paper drifted in front of me. I caught one in my hand. It lay gleaming in my palm, golden and delicate as tissue.

"Janice," someone called.

Mark Brocato was coming through a door opposite me, dressed in khaki pants and a polo shirt. "Can you imagine how much gold leaf this ceiling is going to take?" he asked as he walked up to me. I looked up and realized the workmen were applying sheets of gold leaf to the elaborate friezes on the wall. The bits floating down were discards. I resisted the impulse to scoop up a handful and slip them in my purse.

"This room will be the restaurant and bar for the hotel," he said. Omni, a hotelier with a reputation for good taste, was building a six-story hotel under the train shed, right next to this room.

We walked out the door and stood at the top of a staircase that in the past must have led to the boarding platform. Someone was hammering steel, a buzz saw whined in the distance, and I caught a scent of warm shaved wood. In the enormous area below, workers were putting up one- and two-story frameworks, presumably for stores and restaurants. I looked up at the arched steel-frame ceiling that covered the train shed. It was huge, most of it covered with wood.

"The original shed covered eleven acres," Mark said. "All the plywood will be replaced with glass when we're finished." He pointed straight across the empty area below. "That's your space right there."

I sucked in my breath. It was prime. I could see only a shell now, waiting to be built out, but it was front and center. The large plaza in front of it, John told me, would hold a large ornamental fountain. No one who came into the place would miss our store.

A sense of lightness came over me for the first time since my mother's death. Maybe there was a bright future, with this project in it. As my eyes roamed over the scene below, I saw that the center would be magnificent, a shopping mecca of delights under a brilliant steel and glass ceiling that would shield shoppers from the humid air. And it would be anchored by a snazzy modern hotel where I could stay when I made site visits. Add to that the breathtaking terminal restaurant and bar, open to anyone. I felt a tingle of pleasure at the thought of creating a beautiful store in this beautiful place.

I flew back to Madison excited about the project, but far from the glitter of the golden terminal, the lingering effects of my mother's death and the uncertainty of my future anchored my spirits.

Peter was now a senior at West High, more independent each day, with a steady girlfriend and a gang of good friends. I'd learned not to make dinner unless he promised in advance to be home. John was living off-campus with friends. Next year Peter would be a freshman at the University. He'd live at home the first year, but after that he'd likely start rooming with friends as well. The house would feel empty then, no slamming door when he came into the house asking what was for dinner, no companionable nights watching TV with the cat sneaking from my lap to Peter's.

For my social needs, I still relied heavily on my relationships at work—an occasional musical outing with Mary Ann, staff parties every few months. That summer we initiated an annual softball game—Madison vs. Milwaukee. It was a happy time, with both my sons there with my full staff. In the Puzzlebox family, we all fit.

After Mom died, I often drove to Chippewa for an overnight with my dad, who was glad for the company. I liked his company too, but the trip also saved me from my lonely Saturday nights after work. My sister Freddie would join us for dinner at a local supper club, and afterwards, back at the house, Pop would hand me the TV remote while he fetched frozen Snicker bars from the kitchen. I knew I needed to widen my circle, but I didn't have the energy now to try. Later, I'd think about that.

I signed the lease for St. Louis a few weeks after my trip. I didn't see it as a financial risk in any way. My banker, Ann Kovich, liked to say that I was a cautious risk-taker. The store was already paid for, and the mall looked like a winner. This project felt fool proof.

TWENTY-ONE

Two weeks before the projected opening of the St. Louis store, a glaziers' strike brought construction to a halt. We couldn't even set the glass shelves on the brackets already installed on the wall in our store. I felt frustrated and scared. Expenses for the new store had somehow run over my construction allowance, which had seemed more than generous. I'd let the architect do a few extras, including a framework of brightly colored construction tubes around the front window. The store needed to look special, and this would showcase our bear windows.

St. Louis store window

If the strike didn't end soon, I would have to pay labor, rent, and utility costs without sales to cover them. The 13% mortgage payment on our new house on Allen Street left me cash poor. My six-year-old business was flourishing, so the high rate hadn't concerned me. But now I worried I'd run out of cash for everything.

The Union Station store had proved more complicated than my first two. I'd needed a St. Louis bank to handle deposits and deliver a line of credit for Christmas. The bank had been tough, negotiating a third position on my house. It felt like everybody had a piece of me now.

To my relief, the strike ended just days before the opening. We had to scramble, but we managed to get everything in order in time for a grand preopening party the night before.

When I walked down from the hotel dressed in the short black cocktail dress I'd brought for the party, I was too tired to fully enjoy the glittering crowd of wealthy St. Louis citizens who'd paid hundreds of dollars to attend this hotly anticipated opening. Despite the men in tuxedos and women in satin gowns sipping champagne in the courtyard right next to our store, I was just glad to be going home the next day. I now had another beautiful store in another prestigious project, with a good staff ready to take over. I was very lucky. Still, the strike, the budget overages, the financial strain were all weighing on me.

Mark Brocato, spiffy in black tie, approached me where I stood inside the store looking out and asked me if I was ready for another project. Rouse would be renovating a beautiful old train station in Washington D.C.

"Mark, this store has not come easily. Right now, all I want to do is go home, get rested, and get my energy back."

He wasn't put off by my lack of enthusiasm, just nodded. "We've learned that each retailer has different limits. Some want to push as far as they can; some find a sweet spot and stay there. Maybe three stores is the right number for you."

Perversely, that bothered me. I didn't like to feel I had limits.

THREE MONTHS LATER, the sales at the new store were way, way over projection. At Christmas, the store's total sales came close to beating each of our Wisconsin stores. It seemed we'd skipped the usual slow build. I was still too stung by the early difficulties to assume sales would continue at that height, but it was gratifying, nonetheless.

Our St. Louis manager, Rose Ellery, was a pretty brunette with a shy, warm smile, quiet by nature, a serious woman in her early twenties. Her references were excellent and borne out by her performance in the first months. I'd liked it that she wasn't afraid to get her hands dirty unpacking boxes and cleaning shelves. But even after two weeks of immersion training in Madison and Milwaukee, it was obvious we were still a bit of a mystery to her. She had a distinctive southern style, more deliberate and paced than the three of us. The delay had caused her more stress than anyone except me.

I'd raised Mary Ann and Laura's salaries to match their new responsibilities. Laura's job was to tend to the look of the Milwaukee and St. Louis stores, flying down to change the windows as needed. Mary Ann would oversee sales, analyze inventory counts from the store, and put together reorders until our new manager learned to do them.

I loved my stays at the Omni on my biweekly trips to St. Louis. In the morning, I'd slide out of the crisp sheets of my excellent bed, put in a call to room service, and step into the black-and-white tiled shower. I'd scarcely have dried myself when my breakfast arrived, a pot of strong, hot coffee and a toasted bagel with cream cheese. Despite these pleasant trappings, I'd yet to venture out from the glass-domed station to see much of the city, and my trips were beginning to feel a little claustrophobic. With the notable exception of the arch and a famous Louis Sullivan office building, there wasn't a lot to see downtown. St. Louis was built on the majestic Mississippi, but when I'd gone to get a close-up look, I'd been disappointed to find it quite narrow, a sluggish muddy brown. I was used to the clear, rushing water of the upper Mississippi, miles wide in some parts.

Before opening, I'd had dinner with Mark Brocato in the Central West End, a pretty, near-west neighborhood that was home to the hot restaurant scene. Our youngish fellow diners looked affluent, the women in stylish dresses and the men in handsome suits. But I hadn't ventured farther west. St. Louis had prestigious universities, plenty of parks, and a vibrant art scene, but things were not concentrated in one area as they were in Madison. Rose told me that people in St. Louis centered their social life in their neighborhoods. In order to explore them, I would have to rent a car, and by the time I finished my work at the store, I was more than ready to go home.

But any disappointments in the city faded fast with the spectacular sales at our store, way ahead of Madison and Milwaukee week for week. I was initially cautious—maybe it was just an opening bump—but as the months went on and it continued strong, I relaxed.

I liked the diversity of the St. Louis part-time staff—men, women, White, Black. Few black workers had ever applied to work in Milwaukee, where almost 25% of the population was Black. The few people of color on staff Laura had recruited by word-of-mouth. In St. Louis, the population was about 12.5% yet many Black workers applied to work with us. The difference was difficult to understand at first. Later I would learn that many people of color were second- or third-generation St. Louisianians. During the years when manufacturing provided well-paying jobs, a Black middle class grew, and its neighborhoods prospered.

It was different in Milwaukee, where many Blacks had migrated in the 1950s for manufacturing jobs that soon began to disappear, leaving a large population with few resources to support it. As a result, the city was segregated and tenuous for many Black residents.

Our customers at Union Station were to be a mix of downtown workers, locals, and tourists. It was odd to be behind the counter where people who came in the store had never heard of us. In Milwaukee, many people knew Madison and our store there. Still, in St. Louis we did hear the familiar question: "Where do you find this stuff?"

And yet, I found myself wondering if this store, or any store outside of Madison or Milwaukee, could ever have the same feeling as the original one. The risk was less about sales or profits than the hard-to-define store culture that had made our stores beloved in Wisconsin. But St. Louis was showing that we didn't need that culture to succeed. The city was showering money on us, and I loved it. It gave me a sense of real power. There was evidence now that the Puzzlebox concept could work anywhere.

As Anne Boyle's presence receded with distance, a new artist appeared who would have a similar major impact on the Puzzlebox. John Ribble was a talented illustrator who taught graphic arts at Madison Technical College. His true love was illustration, and he started a Puzzlebox tradition when he designed an original and gorgeous poster-sized calendar full of bears, kids and a few dozen choice toys. Starting that year, we gave away the calendar at Christmas.

John had keen observational skills, and I loved talking to him about the culture and the changing country, often over lunch at Gino's as we planned the next ad campaign.

"Sometimes I'm amazed at how much has changed since I opened the store six years ago," I said one day.

He raised an eyebrow, pausing over a fork of lasagna. I went on.

"I was a snob about business, didn't consider it anything a person with a brain and a social conscience would go into. Now a business career is considered glamorous. What happened?"

He smiled. "The eighties. People like making money now. It's the thing to do once you hit 25, anyway. But Janice, everyone loves the Puzzlebox and respects you. Your business is different."

I sat back, gratified by his praise, but still a little dissatisfied. He laughed. "Relax and enjoy it. You're very good at what you do. And I love doing work for your company."

There was really no reason for me to have these recurring doubts. Maybe I really was that good. Listening to my instincts had worked for me in business.

Later, I would come to understand I was the unsuspecting beneficiary of a national trend toward acquisition. It was happening everywhere: big corporations swallowing up small companies, big boxes like Target and Walmart beating out chain stores in malls, and people lining up to buy consumer goods in all forms, including toys. Acquisition was peaking, and it would soon become socially acceptable to buy from big stores with cheaper prices even if it meant the death of small local stores and main streets. Listening to my instincts had worked for me in business, but they only went so far.

That day in 1986, I did not see these trends yet. In St. Louis I'd thrown my hat into the ring with a first-class retail developer. It was true that I'd read a quote from someone in the Rouse Company that just before Union Station opened, they thought they'd made a big mistake, that maybe the St. Louis market wasn't big enough or urban enough to pull in the kind of crowds Rouse usually got. Well, that just showed everyone had doubts.

BY WINTER OF 1986, I was fairly confident I could have my cake and eat it too. I felt a little like the godfather, sitting in my office with Laura, Mary Ann, and Marty King, our bookkeeper, now elevated to a full-time position as Chief Financial Officer. With St. Louis so successful, we'd started thinking seriously about growing, wherever the moon might take us. It was heady to think about how much cash was coming in. It felt like we were sitting on a gold mine.

Marty was a petite, thirty-five-year-old brunette who had been an accountant at a bank in North Carolina. She was introverted, as numbers people often are, but personable. When she'd come on as part-time bookkeeper, she'd brought a maturity and experience to my team that would prove valuable. For today's meeting, I'd asked her to prepare projections for various expansion scenarios.

I'd still be in charge of development and marketing, but my staff would take over operations. With Mary Ann and Laura now full-time administrative managers, there would be a general bump-up of employees on the store level, with current assistants promoted to managers. I decided to give Laura and Mary Ann a small percentage of Puzzlebox stock so they would feel real ownership. Everyone would get raises and benefits, and I'd asked Marty to see what income we would need to cover the new expenses.

Her projections showed we would need five stores to make the cash flow work. The economy was very strong, the stock market still booming, people still shopping like crazy.

Soon after this meeting, I sat with my managers over drinks at Victor's Coffee at the corner of State and Gorham. I remembered Victor Allen telling me a few years earlier that coffee was just at the beginning of its marketing curve.

New stores kept opening on State Street: an Art Mart two doors away where we could buy supplies for the windows, and Pegasus Games for a new generation of gamers a few blocks toward campus. Even though we had every reason to feel confident about Puzzlebox, we were wary of some changes on the street and in the culture.

"State Street is changing again," Laura said.

"We've got competition for the first time," Mary Ann said, her eyes narrowing. We'd just come from a store that had recently moved onto the street from another location. They carried half a dozen of our product lines.

"No one would have done that five years ago," I said.

"Do you think that's really changing?" Laura asked.

"I think it fits with the new attitudes toward business," I said. "It's OK to move into your competitor's market, even smart. Why not carry a product someone else had first? It's a proven seller. It feels different than when I started. Remember, I opened a toy store because a woman already had a gift store on the square."

"Customers have changed too," Mary Ann said. "Most of our regulars are great, but sometimes on weekends the store feels full of strangers. They make a mess and don't put things back."

"Shoplifting has definitely picked up in the Grand Avenue," Laura said. "I wonder what that's about."

We all sat thinking. Maybe it was the Reagan years. The economy continued to grow, the stock market climbed. Our sales went up solidly every year. Did people think businesses had so much money it was OK to steal from them?

Kvetch as we did, we were still full of self-confidence. Our stores were unique, successful, highly popular. St. Louis had put us into another category. Mark Brocato had called again about their new project in Washington D.C., but I was smart enough now to know that a store that far away would be foolhardy. Instead, we were eyeing Bayshore Mall in a suburb in north Milwaukee. I was also looking for another location in Madison. It was time to concentrate our stores in the same cities so they were more economical to run.

Not many women were doing the kind of business I was, and that was heady. I liked being a forerunner, and I liked empowering my staff. It was exciting and massaged my ego. But I did recognize I had shortcomings as a CEO, mainly around finances.

Anyone coming into our store on a day when it was jammed with customers must have assumed I was making a million. Maybe I could have gotten rich if I'd just put the extra cash into the bank or investments. But that wasn't what I did, and not what I wanted to do. I put any extra money back into the business, to make store improvements and maintain good wages and benefits. And expansion cost money and added debt, before any profits kicked in.

Technology had not affected my business much yet. Even with three stores, the tools had not changed appreciably. But the trend to use credit instead of cash was accelerating, as the swift transfer of money became possible. Since 2% of every sale would be paid to the bank or a credit card company, it was only a matter of time until profits would erode. But that had not happened yet.

I needed to be careful with money for many reasons. I'd used up my portion of the cash from the sale of our family house on the down-payment for our new one. I'd just turned 47 and had no retirement plan in place. My life was all about growing the business now, and I needed to make it profitable soon. Thankfully, Marty would help with that.

Despite this hard-headed calculus about my finances, I now decided it was time to delegate more responsibility to my talented young staffers. They were eager for opportunity, eager to take on more. Their young energy could take the Puzzlebox to a new level. I would act as Chief Operating Officer and leave the details of running the business to them. The unexpected success of St. Louis was providing money now to buy my freedom from the routine work.

In the fall, I'd signed up for a class in American Foreign Policy at the University. The few hours a week I spent there were highly stimulating. I was in the second semester now and was loving it. I'd be doing a primary research paper this spring on the U.S.'s loss of China to Russia after World War II. I couldn't wait to get out of the office and into the stacks at the State Historical Society library.

The crazy thought occasionally flitted through my head now that it might not be too late to get a PhD in history.

TWENTY-TWO

The elegant, three-story reading room in the State Historical Society Library was one of my favorite study spots on campus. But I preferred the small, dark room in the stacks of the building that held the U.S. State Department documents. To get there I had to go through a plain, linoleum-floored hallway, down a narrow stairwell with flaking paint and worn rubber stair treads. But then I turned a corner, and my eyes fell happily on the improbable glass floor below. The room was modest, almost ascetic, with low ceilings, antiquated steam pipes lining the walls, and long rows of bookshelves separated by narrow aisles. So, the thick, translucent green-glass floor seemed a mysterious extravagance. Although the windows in the room were heavily shaded to protect the old books, enough light sneaked in the edges to illuminate the enchanting sea-green glass. Sometimes, I'd sit cross-legged on the floor in one of the narrow aisles, perusing a book, just to feel the cool, roughened glass through my jeans.

There was a faintly metallic smell from the hundreds of feet of sturdy iron bookshelves, an odor that had become strangely pleasant to me. Otherwise, the air smelled clean and fresh, despite the antiquity of the documents. More than once, I drew a finger over the tops of books, sure I'd find dust, but I never did.

The room was scrupulously ordered, with thousands of books lined up precisely on the shelves, like troops waiting for inspection. When I walked in the door, my muscles relaxed, and my mind cleared, even as my adrenaline rose at the thought of possible discoveries. Wellbeing flooded my body. I was happy just being there.

Today I needed to find specific material for my spring paper. In 1949, the Chinese Communists, led by young rebels Mao Tse-tung and Zhou Enlai, were engaged in a bloody war with Chiang Kai-shek, the corrupt nationalist leader who was backed by the U.S. The rebels defeated Chiang's army, which likely influenced the U.S. decision later to hold the line against communism in Vietnam. It was a huge turn in history, and its origins were muddy.

I walked down the aisle of darkened stacks, switched on a fluorescent light, and pulled a dark red book labeled *Foreign Affairs of the United State, China, 1944* off a shelf. I sat at one of the old wooden desks that lined one wall, the heavy wooden chair screeching as it scraped the glass floor. I was the only one there today. The room had a perfect white noise, a faint, underlying buzz. Occasionally, people came and went. Rarely, the old elevator wheezed its way past the floor.

I was soon lost in the text, mostly telegrams from the diplomats in China to the State Department in Washington, telegrams from President Roosevelt to his ambassador, and later to a personal envoy. I was now convinced from these documents that if anyone was responsible for losing China, it was FDR himself. He had ignored the advice from his career diplomats to align with the communists. In fact, the rebels had told the diplomats they'd rather go with the U.S. than Russia. But FDR disregarded the advice, heeding instead his personal envoy, a civilian named Hurley, who was more comfortable with Chiang as a more stable force.

My sessions at this desk had a timeless quality. Mao Tse-tung and Zhou Enlai were not the remote figures of our time but were young, vigorous, and idealistic, camped out in caves for much of the war. How different history might have been if we had held out a hand then. China could have been an ally against Russia in the Cold War period. The Vietnam War might never have happened.

The hours I spent in this room nourished me, satisfied my need for intellectual engagement, and gave me a challenging new project. My mind drifted back four years to the question Professor Filly asked me when I consulted him about opening a second store: "Are you the kind of person who likes to start things or run them?"

I'd chosen to start things, all right, and now I had to run them. Even with Laura and Mary Ann taking over supervision of store managers, I still spent a solid three days a week checking inventory levels, monitoring sales, reviewing bills, signing checks, keeping my own cash log, and supervising Mary Ann and Laura. We'd started a regular Tuesday morning weekly meeting, crucial for communications. I'd never liked meetings, was already tired of this one, but I couldn't afford to skip it.

But I was OK with the new level of administrative work, mostly because of this class. With the enrichment it brought me, I found it easier to accept the growing piles of paper on my desk.

I STILL ENJOYED MY SATURDAYS with customers on the sales floor in Madison, a great antidote to the solitude of my office. One afternoon in March of 1986, I was working with Mary Ann at the counter when I suddenly realized the feeling in the store had changed. Fewer people made friendly eye contact when they entered. A group of seven chattering teens, some wearing letter jackets from a school in a nearby town, went straight to the counter with the wind-up toys, trying out every model on the shelf. They stood bunched in a group, backs facing outward, making it hard for anyone to get past them. Several families moved around them to leave, pulling their small children with them. When the group left without buying anything, many of the wind-ups had migrated to other shelves and perhaps into a few jacket pockets.

"Those kids really trashed the store," I said, feeling my own frown.

"I know," Mary Ann said. "The regulars still come in on Saturdays but mostly in the mornings. After that it's kids from the suburbs and out-of-towners."

I should have known. But I'd been too busy setting up the new store in St. Louis. I needed to spend time behind the counter more, not just in Madison, but in the other stores, too. It was way too easy to lose track of customers.

But then my mind went somewhere else.

Just a few feet away, a tall display of clear plastic bins held little inexpensive toys—plastic dinosaurs, soft pig noses, fake foam bricks, kazoos, rubber cockroaches, yo-yos, and bottles of soap bubbles.

"Compared to St. Louis, this store looks a jumble," I said. "The bins are stacked so high you can barely see over them."

Mary Ann stopped and looked around, her forehead wrinkling. "Well, it's smaller than St. Louis. We've got a lot of inventory now, and we've got to put it somewhere." She shrugged. "And customers seem to love it. More stuff to look at, more stuff to buy."

When the store had opened seven years earlier, I'd been meticulous about displays, making sure categories of toys were well separated. I'd wanted customers to move easily from each well-defined display to another. Now toys were crammed together, fighting for space on the narrow shelves.

Just then, the marketing director of Downtown Madison, Susanne Voeltz, walked in. She wore a long, deep-pink tunic over a pair of narrow trousers, with a striped red scarf casually hooked over one shoulder, an outfit that accentuated her slender frame. If she hadn't been so nice, I would have felt outclassed in my working jeans and simple sweater. I was a Board member of the downtown group she led and liked the new promotions she was doing. She and her husband had driven to St. Louis for the Union Station opening, and after that we had become friends,

"How's the St. Louis store going, Janice?" As always, I wondered how she kept the scarf from simply falling off her shoulder.

Susi was married to James McFadden, an architect who shared her keen sense of visual style. At Union Station, the three of us had enjoyed a drink together in plush-velvet armchairs in the Grand Terminal bar.

"The sales in St. Louis are good, much better than projected."

"That's wonderful. It's a beautiful project, and your store is the best one there." She flashed a winning smile.

This was unabashed flattery, but I enjoyed it anyway. Maybe I believed it.

"I was just telling Mary Ann that this store looks a little shabby compared to St. Louis. I like the shelves full, but too much is crammed in here."

"Why not give it a makeover?" she said, "You should talk to James about it. He could give you some ideas."

I listened, but I was cautious. My experience with the architects who designed my two mall stores had been disappointing. In Milwaukee, the architect had spoken of a playful mirrored ceiling, but in the end my budget had only paid for painted drywall, wood shelves against the wall, a standard check-out, and a tiny bathroom. In St. Louis, I'd been thrilled by the architect's description of a Palladium-style design with columns and arches. But the end product, while attractive, looked like a conventional toy store for kids.

So I was wary. This time I had no construction allowance. But cash flow was good, and I could afford a simple renovation. I decided to meet with James.

JAMES MCFADDEN WAS the third influential artist with whom I established an enriching, creative partnership. Anne Boyle had created our wildly popular window displays. John Ribble gave us stylish ads and brilliant watercolor illustrations for the annual calendar. Now James would transform the physical space of the store itself, in a way that I would never have imagined.

He came to our meeting dressed in pleated gray trousers and a handsome checked jacket. When he sat listening, he was all attention. His sharp sense of humor was often expressed in a pealing laugh.

We toured the store while I explained how everything functioned. He nodded and listened. A few days later, we sat down with his simply drawn plan. James proposed modernizing the long-mirrored wall with new hardwood columns that would conceal badly needed lights for the shelves. The columns would be stained with dark red paint instead of varnish. The other long wall would be covered with new hardwood shelves, stained a soft green.

"Staining wood is kind of unusual, isn't it?" I asked.

"You're right, it's not done much." He stood up and smiled. "Let's go to the store for a minute. I want to show you something."

At the back of the Puzzlebox, James picked up a toy tri-plane, made of stained hardwood. The plane had three red wings, a green tail, and a light-yellow body.

"See how nicely the grain shows through? You see the wood but get the color, unlike paint or varnish."

Holding the little plane, I ran one hand over the smooth wings. I liked the soft effect of the color, and I loved it that James had used one of our toys for inspiration.

We stood looking through the long narrow space as he revealed his organizing motif. "It will be a Wisconsin spring dawn," he said, explaining that the 20-foot ceiling would be painted blue-black and the high walls a light, airy blue. Much of the other woodwork and shelves would be stained spring green with touches of red, like shooting rays of sun. All the carpentry, including several new fixtures, could be started immediately, and most of it stained in the shop. The rest of the displays could be reconfigured out of the stainless steel and glass elements we owned.

And then he told me he wanted to hang clouds from the ceiling. I was baffled. He'd put clouds in that lovely space? For the first time, I faltered. I asked him why.

"The clouds will be very close to the dark ceiling and painted pink. The space is narrow and long, allowing us to create a natural path through the store with the clouds, drawing you deeper into it." He was vague as to what the clouds would be made of and said he was still working on it.

I was nervous about being closed too long. "It would be best if we didn't lose our weekend sales," I said tentatively.

"With so much of the work done out of the store," he said with confidence, "I think we can be done in four days. The construction company I'm using will have no problem with working nights."

Only later I would realize what a phenomenally short construction period that would be for the elaborate remodel James had designed, far shorter than the simpler build-outs in our mall stores, which had taken many weeks to complete.

I gave James the go-ahead that day. I wanted something special for this store, and I knew that to get it, I had to trust him to express his vision. It was unusual and somewhat hard to visualize, but from the start, my intuition told me James's design would work well for the Puzzlebox.

We made plans to close the store on a Sunday late in April and open five days later, on a Saturday in May. As it happened, it would be the week of the store's seventh birthday.

TWENTY-THREE

The splendid space that emerged from James's simple drawing was a slow reveal. Jim Erickson and Sam Breidenbach, partners in a small, just-forming company called TDS Construction, were the first pleasant surprise. They were true craftsmen, hard-working perfectionists who did the work as James promised, in four days and four nights. We found them polite, well-spoken, and considerate. Jim was tall, dark-haired, with a slow smile, Sam compact, blond, and amiable. The Puzzlebox staff loved being around them. Compared to the lengthy construction schedules in our two mall stores, their efforts were herculean.

There had been a stunning surprise on the second day when the crew pulled up the old carpet to lay the new. Underneath was a beautiful, white ceramic tile floor abundantly sprinkled with black swastikas. It was shocking, even though I quickly computed that the floor had gone down sixty-some years before the Nazis had co opted the ancient symbol.

On the third day, I was there with James when the crew brought in the stained wood shelves. The forest green wood had a soft textured look and was satiny to the touch. I loved it.

The three wooden fixtures James had designed made it clear that nothing in his universe was allowed to be straight unless pure function demanded it. The green wood checkout counter was a graceful half-circle, maybe not so efficient as a straight one for storage, but well worth any inconvenience. The display for soft toys was an oval, freestanding, four-foot-tall island of green shelves.

"We're calling it Bear Island," James said, his laugh booming across the empty space.

On the evening of the third day, Jim and Sam hung the clouds, twelve lengths of architectural foam core painted a rosy pink, one end on each cloud curved down smartly. James had them hung diagonally, close to the blue/black ceiling.

I wasn't there when James stopped by after midnight to find the crew had hung them backwards. There was precedent for this, we were to learn, in Grand Central Station in New York, where the constellations of the Zodiac are reversed left to right on the ceiling of the terminal. As in our case, the workers had read the blueprints upside down. At Grand Central, it was impossible to fix without doing the whole thing over. In our case, James took to his couch that night and solved the problem.

Early in the morning on the fourth and final day, the crew took the clouds down, cut and pasted one end to the other, and hung them as James originally envisioned, with the curved edges gracefully leading customers through the store. With the clouds up, a total sense of beauty and fantasy emerged.

After the last of the shelves were hung that day, our staff came in to stock the store. Everything seemed to fit better in the new space. The beauty of the new store would become an incentive to keep things ordered.

Puzzlebox before remodeling

When we were done, I felt intensely happy. It was a different feeling than in the Rouse malls, where the pride came from being part of a larger project. This was very personal. It had been a pleasure to work with James, with Jim and Sam, the carpenters, the painters, and the company called Lost Finishes that stained the wood. It was and would be the most beautiful store we had and at the least expense. It was a continuation of the way things had always come together easily for me in Madison, with its special mix of talented people doing things they loved.

WEEKS BEFORE, Mary Ann had sold me on the idea of celebrating the new store design with a party for customers, city leaders, and friends. I decided to send a hand-written invitation to a nice guy named Jeff, a developer who'd come to my office a month ago to discuss a project. I'd turned down his project but liked him and felt it was mutual. Finally, I felt I was ready for a date.

Then, on the Saturday before we had closed for the remodel, a customer had walked into the Puzzlebox who had caught my eye once or twice before with his good looks. He was tall, with a big frame and curly brown hair. He looked faintly academic in a corduroy jacket with leather patches on the elbows. I watched him as he explored the shelves, clearly pleased with what he found. He came to the bins by the checkout, and as he leaned over to examine a fake brick, I noticed the line of his jockey shorts under his pants. It startled me that I'd been looking that closely. Foam brick in hand, he walked to the back of the store, and I turned to Mary Ann.

"Have you seen that guy in the store before?"

"I have. He's usually in on Saturdays. Why?"

"I just think he's attractive. I wonder who he is."

"I'll invite him to the opening party," she said, and before I could stop her, she walked back to where he stood looking at a book. She talked to him for a minute, he smiled and nodded, and she returned. I was feeling warm all over, sure he'd figured out we had been talking about him.

"So?" I said.

"He said he'd try to make it. He doesn't live here."

I felt relief and disappointment all at once. He was making his way to the checkout, and I felt self-conscious, avoiding his eyes until he walked right in front of me. He set the fake brick and a rubber rat on the counter.

"Are you ready to check out?" I asked, meeting his eyes, brown, warm.

"I am. These will be great to use with my patients." He was smiling.

It got busy then, with people lined up to pay, so I didn't pursue the conversation. He wrote his check while I packaged his toys, and after he left I looked at the name printed on the check. Dr. Michael Keown, PhD, with an address in Tomah, a small town a few hours north.

Hmm. A doctor. I didn't think PhDs used Doctor in front of their names—it struck me as odd, and I wondered what he did for a living. Tomah had little industry, only a big VA Hospital.

We were counting out the cash registers just after closing when he rapped on the glass door. I wondered if he'd left something behind. Mary Ann went to the door, talked for a few seconds, and came back holding a bouquet of flowers she handed to me.

"For you," she smiled.

I was shocked and then ridiculously pleased. I couldn't remember the last time anyone had given me flowers. And these were roses.

TWO DAYS BEFORE THE PARTY, I went to Sassafrass for a new outfit, choosing a pair of slim, soft white trousers and a silky spring sweater in a shade of pink that reminded me of the roses. The sweater was extra roomy, a rapidly emerging style, but hung nicely on my frame. With it, I would wear long, sparkling, pink glass earrings. I'd never looked better.

As I got ready for the evening, I felt at the top of my form. I had a successful business, a staff I loved and respected, a beautiful store produced by an innovative architect. And now I had a new outfit and not one but two good prospects for romance.

Walking into the store an hour before the party, I stopped to take a long, fresh look. There was a clear line of vision from the front of the store all the way to the rear window, accentuated by the trail of pink clouds. I saw that James's vivid colors seemed to bring the toys more into focus. Someone had put an Ella Fitzgerald tape on, and I smiled as the lyrics of Blue Skies pealed through the store.

Sam Breidenbach was on a stepladder fixing one of the fan-like paper shades on the new light fixtures at the top of the stained red columns. "Everything looks great, Sam. You and Jim did an amazing job." He looked at me blearily and smiled. James told me later that Sam fell asleep at a celebratory dinner after the party, head falling silently into his bowl of pasta.

I usually disliked cocktail parties, with the obligatory move from one brief encounter to the next, but our party that night was joyful. As I made my way through the crowd I saw my developer friend, Jeff, leaning against a counter casually, hands in pockets. When I walked up to him, he thanked me for the invitation, smiling warmly, but I already suspected I would not take it further with him. The roses from the stranger had done their work.

Mike showed up soon and followed me around wherever I went, as though he were my date. I didn't know what to make of it, but in the end, I liked him being close, and his unveiled interest pleased me. When he looked at me, I felt beautiful. I found him easy to talk to, had no trouble engaging with him as I often did with other men.

In a quiet moment an hour into the party, he asked if we could get away from the crowd. Peering at him sideways, I looked into his eyes.

"We could take a walk."

He smiled, happy. I led him out the back door, avoiding questions from friends. On the sidewalk he moved quickly to the outside position on the sidewalk, a gentlemanly gesture that surprised and pleased me.

"I noticed you the first time I came in the store," he said. "You were doing this little dance of life behind the counter." He paused. "I just assumed you were a salesclerk. So you're an owner."

I was quiet. I liked the dance of life bit, but I wasn't sure how to handle the owner part. I didn't want to scare him off. A lot of men were uncomfortable with women who had power, especially in business. But then I thought: to hell with it. I hadn't come this far to go back to hiding who I was.

"I'm the only owner," I said, looking directly at him. "And I have two other stores too, in Milwaukee and St. Louis."

His eyebrows shot up, but his face didn't change. If anything, he looked pleased. So, he didn't have issues with strong women. Then without prompting he started telling me about himself, starting with the fact that he was divorced.

He was a Ph.D. psychologist who'd moved from Colorado to treat Vietnam veterans at the VA hospital. I was impressed, and then charmed when he told me he lived in an old schoolhouse outside Tomah.

As he spoke and we walked, I was free to examine him closely. His hair was so thick and curly it invited touch. He had a strong profile, nice ears, straight nose, smooth, tanned skin. I thought he was about six feet, well-filled out. He looked at me, and I didn't turn away. Instead, I bent my head to the side and smiled. I may even have tossed my hair a little.

I left my staff in charge of the party before it was over, and Mike and I walked across the street to the Ovens of Brittany for dinner. On the way, he put the palm of his hand on my back protectively as we crossed the street. The slight pressure felt startlingly intimate. On the way to our table we passed a group of acquaintances who greeted me, examining my companion closely. I liked the feeling that at long last, I had a date and with someone attractive.

Mike

During our meal, he told me about his work with veterans who had post-traumatic stress disorder, a new field then. When he described the specific nature of one of his patient's trauma, I was a little surprised at his candor, but I thought his work sounded meaningful and interesting. I suggested we go Dutch on the check, and he had no trouble with that at all.

He would be in town the next weekend and invited me to a picnic dinner, which he would bring. Of course, I said yes.

TWENTY-FOUR

Picnic Point is a long, idyllic finger of forested land that juts out into Lake Mendota. Mike picked me up from work the next Saturday, and we walked to a picnic spot near the end of the peninsula, a concrete bench with a sweeping view across the lake to the Capitol building. He looked handsome in khaki shorts and a blue plaid sport shirt. Tiny tufts of curly chest hair peeked out from the open neck. He spread a red and blue checked cloth on the bench for the sandwiches and wine he'd bought at the Upstairs Downstairs deli next to the Puzzlebox. He'd gone down the block to Tellus Mater for the colorful cloth and wine glasses. The price stickers were still on the glasses.

As we sat eating and talking, sailboats drifted past. A cardinal trilled, squirrels scuttled, a mallard made a smooth landing on a path near us. Mike sat boyishly cross-legged on the cement bench. I was keenly aware of his legs, attractively tanned, sturdy, and covered with more fine, curly hair. We stayed until sunset and then drove to my house, where we made love on my old iron bed. I was surprised and pleased at how quickly my defenses had fallen.

I'd had one moment of doubt early in the evening when I first saw Mike's car that night. It was an old, tan Chevy sedan, with rust edging the bottoms of the fenders. Not exactly a doctor's car, I thought, but determined to enjoy the evening, I stowed the detail for future reckoning.

Peter was still living at home, so the next weekend we ended the evening at Mike's motel on the west side of town. The weekend after that, I drove to his home in Tomah. I was having a fling, and I loved it.

It would end when the time was right.

In the course of a long life I would learn there were different components to sexual attraction, but at that time, I was inexperienced. I certainly had liked my husband John's good looks—his handsome face, wonderful head of hair, nicely modeled lips—but it was his brain and ambition that brought zing to the relationship. Later in life, I would meet a man whose powerful, vital, energy was a force I couldn't resist. But with Mike, the attraction was first and foremost physical.

I loved his body, loved the way he looked and felt. I'd never before felt attracted to hirsute men, but I loved the nest of hair on Mike's chest. I loved his strong legs, thighs like trunks of small trees. When he stood shaving at the bathroom sink, I loved standing behind him, melting my body into his.

Years later I had a cat I loved, a big gorgeous tabby named Jackson, not a particularly kind or affectionate cat, but one whose imperious stance and noble head made me see that sometimes beauty is its own justification. It was kind of like that with Mike.

Sometimes, I felt there was a string attached from one of Mike's ribs to one of mine. When we walked he automatically took my hand, the only man I was ever with who did. When he drove, his right hand wandered to my thigh and lay there, making the connection. I loved waking up in the morning with him next to me.

As the year went on, my favorite time with Mike was Sunday morning. I'd get the paper and bring coffee up to the second-floor bedroom, which looked out on the treetops. We'd settle in against the headboard, me with the papers and Mike with a book, often one about Carl Jung. He was generous in sharing what he read, and I remember best a book called *Art and Physics*, whose author made an impressive case that every major discovery in physics had been foreshadowed by some artist's work. I was crazy about ideas and loved being exposed to new ones. The combined attractions of Mike's body and brain were irresistible.

AS MY MANAGERS continued to take on a lot of my work, I relaxed my schedule, going in a little later in the morning, which allowed me the luxury of taking a long time to read the papers in bed with my coffee on days other than Sunday. Now that I was able to get the *New York Times* delivered to my door, I read it daily, and I'd started paying attention to the growing story of the AIDs epidemic. Day after day, the obituary section was full of photos of its victims, frequently successful young men in the professions of fashion, design, theater, law, and business. Through the eighties and into the nineties, the deaths would number over a hundred thousand. It felt like a terrible death watch.

The big business news in the early months of 1987 was the continued rise of the stock market. Everybody was profiting, whether as investors, brokers, business owners, or shoppers. The prevalent philosophy was growth through mergers. Junk bonds was a new catchphrase, used to describe bonds with a higher risk attached. Corporations got bigger and more profitable. Small companies succumbed to acquisition or died from overwhelming competition. Investors were convinced the market would keep growing. The mentality on Wall Street was that everybody was making money, so why shouldn't I?

But I never read in the Times the reason for the accelerated growth, nor was I all that curious then. But this would be the decade when trust-busting quit, when companies were allowed to skirt the Sherman Anti-Trust Act and grow into monopolies by keeping prices low. Thirty years later I would read that two Chicago school academics had put forth the new argument that the original intent of the Sherman Act was consumer welfare, rather than the suffocating effect on competition or even the community good, which had been the criteria used since the turn of the century. From that time on, unless someone made the case that a monopoly meant higher prices, the state courts that heard most anti-trust cases ruled on the simpler definition.

Other consequential things were gestating in that decade of great change, but a lot of us didn't see them. Technology would bring small miracles to our daily lives, but it would also enable a new globalism that would change the nature of the U.S. economy, decimating blue-collar factory jobs. Soon the world would open up to free trade, advocated by leaders in both political parties who preached the dream of an economic wave that would raise all ships.

In combination with the growth of monopolies, more money went to fewer corporations and a smaller percentage of people. There was a national preening in the pleasure of it all: the good jobs, the good living, the fine food, the spacious new houses, the sleek, powerful new cars.

Hardly anyone was noticing how the income gap was beginning to grow.

In 1987, the local papers took note of the new energy, covering Madison business with new vigor, and State Street got its due. Store spaces had always turned regularly there, as people tried out and discarded business ideas, but now many of the businesses that had opened since the mid-seventies were still there, and the street was filled end to end.

A scattering of older stores survived the decade changes—Patti Music, Ella's Deli, Stemp Typewriter, Oriental Specialties. Some were to last well past the millennium: the Chocolate House, Gino's Italian Restaurant, Paul's Books. Notably, the makeup of the street that summer was to remain largely intact for the next thirty years.

The Square did not fare so well. Manchester's, the oldest, most prestigious department store in the city, had now closed, as had the Emporium, the downtown Penneys, and the multi-storied Wolff-Kubly Hardware store. Other smaller stores moved to the malls—Woldenberg's dress shop, Carmen's coat store. Some would hang on a little longer: the Fanny Farmer candy store where I bought a box of chocolates every Christmas Eve, the Hub clothing store for men, two dime stores, and the Badger Candy Kitchen. The Perfume Shop where I bought Mom's special body cream would move to a west side location.

The national business news reported that all downtowns were in transition, not just ours. The recurring theme in Madison was the urgent need to get people back downtown. The empty buildings on the Square and the consequent lack of pedestrians frightened many members of the Central Madison Council Board, who assumed the whole downtown was dying. At Board meetings, I would point out that people of all ages were there in greater numbers than ever, shopping on State Street in a different way for different products, but no one seemed to credit that, as though the Puzzlebox was the exception. And then, many of the suits on the Board rarely ventured down State Street.

But I saw every day how many people were on the street, and good stores that gave them what they wanted were doing fine. The Square needed to reconfigure somehow, and would, but State Street was in a groove as a specialty shopping street. In fact, it seemed to me I wasn't just a shopkeeper anymore, on a small street in Wisconsin. I was part of an emerging and important retail movement, one that lent credence to my expansion plans. It never occurred to me that specialty stores might be vulnerable as well to the new forces. Rather, it felt like we were the future.

In those late years of the 80s, with the second feminist wave well underway, I felt I had found myself. It turned out I was an entrepreneur, a perfect heroine for the decade, when business was glamorous and paid well. Mike Nichols had nailed it in a new movie called *Working Girl*. His heroine, Melanie Griffith, played a high school grad from Brooklyn who beat out her educated, elitist woman boss, not only for a good job but for Harrison Ford as well. That was me, kind of. And then there was *Baby Boom*, where Diane Keaton lost her corporate job when she brought her baby to work. She moved to the country, invented a successful baby food company, and even got the guy, an improbably handsome veterinarian played by Sam Shepherd.

The new morality that had emerged in the seventies had convinced many of us that any behavior was OK as long as it didn't hurt anybody. So lots of people did exactly what they wanted—used drugs, had a lot of sex, got divorced, gained weight from all the good eating, indulged themselves on a regular basis. I didn't come near doing much of that, but it was a time when I moved away from my country, from politics, from involvement in anything much beyond my business, my classes, and my new lover, all of which took up all the space in my head.

And why not? The Puzzlebox couldn't have been doing better. Both Wisconsin stores were headed for double-digit increases for the year. St. Louis had a phenomenal summer, as tourists kept our cash registers ringing. Its sales were well above the other two stores, providing lavish cash flow.

There were a few critics who questioned the strength of the new economy, but they mostly aimed it at Wall Street corruption. I read part of a serial by Tom Wolfe in Rolling Stone called 'Bonfire of the Vanities,' which would be published as a novel the next year. The protagonist was a wealthy New York bond trader, a "master of the universe," who epitomized ambition, racism, social class snobbery, and greed in New York in the eighties.

But all that was a long way from Madison. I couldn't see any reason why my business wouldn't keep growing. In July, I sent Mary Ann to St. Louis in my place. The store's sales were so strong that keeping up with reorders was most important, and she could handle that better than I.

TWENTY-FIVE

Meeting Mike had given me hope for a happy future despite the loss of my nuclear family. Peter had finished his first year at the University and was home less and less, totally engrossed in his studies and new social life. He was ready to live independently and planned to move to a dorm in late August.

I'd been looking for a new place to live, one more suited to my newly single life. Luckily, I found an apartment downtown, just a seven-minute walk to the store. It was on the second floor of an old house, a pleasant, airy space that looked out on the treetops of Langdon Street. I was very good at moving, having done it thirteen times. In three days, I had everything unpacked and my pictures on the walls. I enrolled in another class, American Colonial history, and got ready for a new life.

MY AFFAIR WITH MIKE had done wonders for my self-image. I felt feminine, attractive, and strong. I'd loved the extravagant gifts he enjoyed giving me, but I'd come to see they often left him with cash shortages. I'd worked hard to create stability for my children and our home and wanted a partner who supported that. I didn't stop seeing him but understood that at some point I would tell him our relationship couldn't be exclusive. I needed space to find somebody else.

One night soon after I was in my new place, I decided it was time for that talk. I put it off until after dinner, when we were sitting over coffee in the living room. I fidgeted in my chair, telling myself he'd understand. I started talking, indirectly framing it around my feeling of transition now that the boys were out of the house. Finally, I spit it out.

"Mike, I like you so much, love the time we've spent together, but I think it would be better if we just took a bit of a break, still see each other, but not every single weekend."

His face was expressionless, then his brows knit, his eyes narrowed. "Are you telling me you want to see other people?"

"No, no," I quickly said. "That's not what I mean. But it's gone so fast. I think I need a little time to be alone now."

He sat looking at the floor for a full minute. I said nothing, waiting. Then he abruptly got up, picked up the bag he'd dropped by the door.

I jumped up. "Where are you going?" I said, feeling panic.

"Home," he said as he left.

Two days passed, and he didn't call. I was devastated, with a sense of abandonment I'd never felt before. I finally called him, and he came, and I took back what I'd said. With him, it was all or nothing, although we never discussed specifics. By this time, I realized I was in love with him. I didn't want to give up the affection, warmth, and companionship I'd had after my lonely years.

And Mike had some excellent character attributes. After I finally introduced him to my sons, he was very good with them, paying attention to their interests. He got on especially well with John, whom he gave the great gift of admiration. They were both brainy introverts, and Mike recognized qualities my shy son hid from all but the most perceptive.

Peter warmed less to Mike than John, although he was always polite. He was emerging as more worldly and practical than John, and I wondered if seeing Mike's beat-up car influenced his feelings. Peter had begun a life-long love affair with the automobile that would manifest in a new car for every phase of life. I thought he couldn't help but judge Mike by the car he drove. He was also highly intuitive, and he may have sensed there was something off about my new boyfriend.

Mike was something of a paradox. A prodigious reader, his IQ was near genius. He read primarily in his field and retained most of what he read. I was amazed at the facts he remembered from specific college courses. And yet, he seemed incapable of keeping a personal financial balance sheet. He had no interest in spectator sports and had few male buddies. He loved browsing and shopping, and had a surprising talent for food garnishment, fanning a dozen shrimp out on a plate, shaking out small cloth napkins to tuck into our water glasses. For a long time, he brought me a perfect single rose every Friday. I loved his pleasure in beautiful things, and the way he knew I loved them, too. So, I continued to enjoy losing myself in the pleasures of the moment.

I was taking a bit of a vacation from the business that fall and was a little alarmed when September sales in St. Louis ended sixteen percent down. But it was only the second year, and fluctuations were to be expected. I flew down to take a reading, but nothing seemed changed. In October they were up five percent, in November down five. Then in December they roared back, up thirteen percent over last year, and I breathed freely again. I'd have to get used to the St. Louis store's variable rhythm.

IT WAS CHRISTMAS EVE, the first in my new apartment. I always worked in the store that day for any staff who had family elsewhere. Mary Ann, Helene, and I closed the store at 4:00 and drank ritual champagne sitting on the floor, celebrating the end of a successful season.

John and Peter were coming for dinner, and I was delighted that Mary Ann, who'd be traveling the next day, would join us as well. Both boys knew and liked her, and would appreciate the addition of a pretty young woman to our party. Mike was en route from Tomah. I walked around my apartment, loving the piney scent of the fresh-cut tree mingling with the smell of the chicken roasting in the oven. I'd already set the table with my best linens and china. Nat King Cole was crooning about roasting chestnuts. The people I loved most in the world would be with me soon.

The apartment seemed to shimmer, the tiny colored lights of the Christmas tree reflected in the windows of the small living room. I was still in my pink phase, and the one wall of the living room I'd painted a soft rose glowed in the mellow light. I'd hung glittery bulbs, birds, and angels on the tree. Then I hung the dozen old ornaments the boys and I had made together when they were small, remembering our shared pleasure in the task.

When everyone was there, we gathered in the living room for a first course of fresh oysters and a country pate from Mary Ann. Mike did oyster duty, shucking the shells enthusiastically. I brought out tall, thin crystal glasses for champagne. We were all smiling and laughing, sliding the oysters into our mouths, savoring the fresh taste, chasing it with a drink of bubbly, then forking a piece of the pate, coarse and chewy, tasting of pork and garlic.

Late in the evening, when the others had left, Mike suggested I open a gift from under the tree. It was a large, six-sided hatbox covered with floral cloth. I removed the top and breathed in a fragrant, woody smell from a bouquet of fresh flowers nestled in the box. Tucked into the greenery was a small jewelry box. I opened it to see a shiny ring, with a large garnet gem set in silver and gold, studded with small, sparkling diamonds. I felt a rush of joy. It was lovely, and as I took it out of the box, I wondered which finger of which hand he had meant it for.

I looked at Mike happily, and with only a slight hesitation, put it on the ring finger of my right hand, where it fit perfectly. Without doubt, it was the most beautiful piece of jewelry I had ever owned.

Mike had been at his best tonight, and I relaxed into the happiness of the evening. My life felt infinitely better than a year ago. I had my family, a successful business, a new history class beginning in January, and most of all, I had romance and love.

TWENTY-SIX

God, I love this airline, I thought, as I buckled myself into the roomy, supple leather seat on the Midwest Express flight to New York. Formerly serving strictly corporate clients, the company had transformed itself into a one-class airline offering the same remarkable amenities and service to the general public.

Across the wide aisle, Mary Ann and Laura smiled at me. They were outfitted for the city, Laura in a black wool sheath with shoulder pads, Mary Ann in a short black skirt and a svelte black jacket. We'd be walking all day, so we all wore flats. Soon, the rich aroma of brewing coffee drifted into the cabin from the tiny galley kitchen. I thought happily of the breakfast that would be served after takeoff—an omelet perhaps, croissants for sure, warm enough to melt the creamy pats of hard butter served with it. And before the short trip was over, the comforting smell of chocolate, butter, and sugar melting together in the baked-on-board chocolate chip cookies.

Life was good and about to get better. We were on our way to Toy Fair.

TOY FAIR WAS AS MUCH FUN as it sounds. In the showrooms at the Toy Building at 200 Fifth Avenue, men in three-piece suits rolled hula hoops around their thick middles and cuddled baby dolls. Major toys were launched there—the Rubik's Cube, Nerf balls, Pictionary. One of the toys projected to be big this year, 1987, was Hasbro's Dolly Surprise, a doll whose hair grew when her arm was raised.

The first time I went to the show, I stayed at the Wyndham, a small hotel on 58th Street, near Fifth Avenue and Central Park. It was an old hotel, recommended by one of my sales reps for its charm and moderate rates. The owners had theatre connections, and the roomy suites were often used for extended stays by semi-retired movie stars. Once, when I was eating breakfast in the tiny dining room, my beaming waiter told me that he had just delivered a room service breakfast to "Miss Carol Burnett." Another time, I was thrilled to learn that Laurence Olivier was staying there while doing a benefit at the Hilton a few blocks away.

In the early years when I went alone, I took pleasure in walking the thirty blocks from the hotel to the Toy Building. I liked to walk fast, just like a New Yorker, savoring the changing landscape—Bergdorf Goodman and Tiffany on upper Fifth, where the women on the street wore furs and high heels, and the air smelled clean with a hint of hot salted pretzels. Beyond that, Rockefeller Center was full of tourists any time of day, and I'd often duck into St. Patrick's Cathedral across the street to get a quick whiff of the incense so familiar from my youth. At some point past the New York Public Library, people wore modest cloth coats and tennis shoes, and the elegant avenue evolved into blocks of gaudy stores with windows crammed with rugs, cameras, watches, and radios. Here, the meaty, sweet smell of roasting lamb from Greek restaurants sandwiched between stores competed with the spicy tomato and cheese aromas of the pizza-by-the-slice joints.

TWO HOURS AFTER we landed at LaGuardia, Laura, Mary Ann and I stepped out of the subway to see a gaggle of photographers in front of the Toy Building, snapping shots of Mr. Potato Head, Yogi Bear, and Barbie mixing with the crowd. Inside the glittering marble and brass lobby, we squeezed into a crowded elevator. We were not the usual Toy Fair shoppers. The big mass market companies—Tonka, Mattel, Parker Brothers—dominated the Toy Building. Their customers, mostly male, represented traditional toy stores, department stores, and increasingly big-box stores like Toys"R"Us and Walmart. But our two major importers of European toys had a showroom there as well, and after we wrote orders with them, we'd hunt for new companies in a temporary show attached to the fair.

That night we walked from our hotel on the west side of Central Park up Columbus Avenue to dinner. Ever since my first buying trip seven years ago, I'd stopped at a small toy store on Columbus with an outstanding collection of tin wind-ups, many of them new editions of old favorites—merry-go-rounds, clowns on bicycles, elephants dancing on rear legs.

Now, I was dismayed to see that the small store was gone, replaced by a national cosmetics chain store. The loss was inevitable, given the rapidly rising real estate prices in New York. I'd always felt Columbus Avenue akin to State Street, with its eclectic mix of small stores. I'd seen the shift on Fifth Avenue already, where Disney had taken over a large corner space near my hotel. Now the trend was spreading to the smaller streets.

After I'd made the decision to expand to five stores, I'd asked Laura to get some information on possible store locations in Chicago, in the Michigan Avenue district. The city was just a three-hour drive from Madison, and a downtown location would be perfect. But the realtor Laura consulted informed her that the area we liked was prohibitively expensive. That was the first time I heard the phrase *billboard rent*. Many of the small local stores that made browsing so much fun had been replaced by national and international chains that opened stores in high profile places strictly for advertising purposes. It didn't matter to them that the demand had driven the rents up so high that their stores couldn't make any money. The store was just another billboard for them.

Now Columbus Avenue was feeling the pressure, and it wouldn't be long until the small stores that had given the street its special charm would be gone. I wondered if I'd still love going to New York when everything started to look alike.

I felt a rush of gratitude for State Street, with most of the stores still local. Truth was, the spaces there were too small for chains, so we were safe from the kind of encroachment this street was suffering.

That evening, we dressed up for the industry banquet on the top floor of a Sixth Avenue skyscraper, where the Puzzlebox would receive a national award from *Playthings Magazine* for James' design of the store on State Street. It had been a thrill to see a full-color photo of the interior of our store on the cover of the magazine's current issue, stacked on tables all over the Toy Building. After I accepted the ornate plaque at

Playthings Award 1987

the banquet, the publisher announced that *Playthings* had arranged for news of our award to crawl across the electronic strip that announced breaking news in Times Square at midnight.

Excited, we hired a limousine to take us in style to the famed crossroads. And so, amid the glitz of Times Square, still gaudy and racy before the gentrification that would sweep it clean in the nineties, we stood on a sidewalk with hustlers selling sex shows and hookers in spandex, watching happily from our spot as the electronic feed rolled out the news of the winner of best store design: *The Puzzlebox, Madison, Wisconsin*.

I HAD RELUCTANTLY left the three store managers at home on this trip. Managers had the most contact with customers, so, ideally, they should attend shows. They were more likely to sell the toys if they helped pick them, and they knew best what their customers wanted.

But a party of six was cumbersome and expensive, and Mary Ann and Laura knew the stores well. We'd compensate by taking everyone to the more affordable Chicago Gift Show later. Still, I couldn't shake the feeling that something had been lost. The new managers were farther from me and the decision making than Laura and Mary Ann had been in their positions. It seemed that was just one of the costs of getting bigger.

The next six months ushered in an awkward transition period. Our second Milwaukee store would open in October. We'd not been able to find a freestanding location on a street with the good foot traffic we needed, so we'd settled for a space in Bay Shore Mall, a small regional center in a suburb north of the city. Laura would oversee it along with Grand Avenue, while Mary Ann was responsible for Madison and St. Louis.

In her eighth year with Puzzlebox, Mary Ann was invaluable; we'd worked as a team for years. I needed her to keep the Madison store first-rate and profitable, and I trusted her to transfer our operations and culture to St. Louis.

The expansion in Milwaukee would have been iffy without Laura. Her presence in the city guaranteed the Puzzlebox culture would be safe. Aesthetics were important to our success, and Laura's art training was a big asset. I trusted her completely with product choice, window design, and display. She would train and supervise both Milwaukee store managers and travel to St. Louis once a month to install windows and do general merchandising. The three of us would meet regularly in Madison to make sure we were all on the same page.

The St. Louis sales had been so much higher than we'd ever expected that I hadn't paid too much attention when they had gone down a little the year before. In August, I took a closer look and was startled to see that since January sales were down 15%. Grand Avenue had gone down a little, too, but usually rebounded the next month. We'd probably have to go a little longer until St. Louis sales settled into a norm.

When we'd had minor sales slumps in the past, I could usually get a quick reading from Mary Ann or Laura—bad weather, low traffic, holidays falling on odd days. But they were not on the floor regularly anymore, and the new managers were still too inexperienced to help much.

But Madison, our flagship store, held steady. In fact, it had been rare in our eight-year history to have any off-month there at all. With so many people employed in safe public jobs by city and state government, the University of Wisconsin, and a large medical community, the economy was constant and strong.

MY HONEYMOON PERIOD with Mike after that idyllic Christmas soon came to a pause. Too often lately he was short of cash, and to avoid embarrassment when we were out together, I hit on the idea of a joint money jar which we would fund equally with cash once a week. When we went out to dinner or a movie, we'd dip into the jar.

Mike agreed to the plan, and as it evolved, he would generally be in charge of the cash, paying the bills and buying the tickets. This made him happy, and I had to admit that I, as well, liked having him in that traditional role.

My boys had gone their own way that year, both living away from home. In May, John got his degree and started job hunting in Madison. He loved the city and was determined to stay, even though the job prospects were thin outside of government or academic jobs. He picked up more hours driving Union Cab, and started working part-time for a software support telemarketing company. It was arduous, brain-numbing, low-paying work helping customers non-stop on the phone, but it was a job. I could only hope my talented, brainy son would find his place eventually.

Peter

Then Peter came to dinner one night, wanting to talk. I could tell something was up when he walked into the kitchen where I was chopping vegetables. His face was uncharacteristically serious. My youngest son was growing to adulthood so quickly. He'd shot up again, nearly 6-feet now, still slender, his blond hair still light. His voice was strong and confident.

"Mom, I think I need a break from college."

I was stunned. He'd just completed his sophomore year, and I had no idea he was unhappy.

"Peter, what are you thinking?" I said, my voice rising. If he left now he might not return. I felt strongly he needed the degree. My own college experience had changed my life.

"I want to get to work, Mom. I just don't see that what I'm learning will help me get a job. I need some life experience."

His face was earnest. He meant it. I knew he was ambitious and impatient with many of his courses. He'd been working long hours at the Fess Restaurant waiting tables for some time, a hard but well-paying part-time job.

"I have a real feel for this, Mom. Maybe I'll learn to run a restaurant."

"Peter, I have no doubt you could, but what's the rush? I know you're entrepreneurial like me. There's so much you could do."

In fact, at only seven, he'd baked batches of chocolate chip cookies with my help and sold them on the street, out of a cardboard tray with a neck strap his dad made for him. A photographer from the local paper spotted him, and the next day a photo of Peter, dressed in jeans with a hole in the knee, blond bangs reaching his smiling eyes as he handed a packet of cookies to a customer, ran on the second page of the paper. In college, he and his best friend, Brian, had started a subscription newsletter for the arts community in Madison, the same year *The Onion* was launched there. It didn't have the same wild success, but it was an impressive achievement.

"Peter," I pleaded now, "I've never tried to dictate your decisions, but this is different. Not getting a degree will limit the work you can do, the choices you have. I want you to stay the course. Just two more years. And I'd like you to work part time at the Puzzlebox. That will give you a different kind of experience."

He looked uncertain. "I still think I need a break." We looked at each other, and then he spoke. "How about if I just take a semester off? I promise I'll go back."

I was just a mother acting on instinct when I insisted Peter get his degree. My own family had done well without one, but I thought the future might be different. Still, I had no idea how different it would be. By 2020, two-thirds of the country would not go beyond high school, and education would be the biggest economic divide in the country.

For now, Peter and I struck the deal, and I was relieved. But it didn't take long until he announced he was taking a motorcycle trip to California. I immediately started to worry about him traveling alone, but he was determined.

Later, I wondered at how both of my sons had struck out on their own on the verge of adulthood, as though intuitively knowing they needed some kind of rite to separate from their parents and childhood. With John, it had been the Army, and now Peter was headed west, on a motorcycle, alone. I'd always been fiercely protective of my boys' physical safety. Eventually, they had asserted their adult capability, and I had to let go.

Looking at my imminent empty nest, once again I was glad that I had Mike. And after a few more history courses at the University, I no longer had the solace of scholarship. I'd followed up my exciting foreign policy course with a graduate-level class on American Colonial History that gave me a bad feeling for the grind of graduate work. The professor who taught it was considerably drier than the charismatic professor in my first class. I did the reading, went to class dutifully, wrote two short papers on the period, and was glad when it was over. Then I took another graduate course on the Mexican Revolution, but it wasn't long until I saw I was going to have to memorize a lot of data to make the grade in the class. That did it, and I realized my dream of a PhD was not going to work.

That left me with the business as my mainstay, so it was lucky we'd gone for expansion. It would keep me busy for a few years until my managers took over completely. At that point, I was sure I would find another outside source of stimulation.

A FRONT-PAGE HEADLINE in the *Wisconsin State Journal* one Sunday ran across the whole masthead: *OPTIMISM PREVAILS IN REVIVING FADED SQUARE*. It was a story by Ron Seely on the history of retail on the Square, mapping the many empty storefronts left by the move to the suburbs. On the second page I found a large photo of myself with a quote underneath: *"The identity of the city is right down here. Call it the psyche, the soul."*

The story presented various strategies for reinventing downtown, including the Square's transition to a service and residential center. It was only after I read everything that I realized State Street had not even been mentioned. They seemed to assume it was just a quirky little street that served students.

State Street was booming and crowded with pedestrians seven days a week and evenings as well. By 1987, most of the storefronts left empty by older businesses had filled. New restaurants popped up regularly, with three or four new fast-food places on lower State. Another art gallery, Broden, had opened on the 100 block, adding weight to the arts district, and Vic's Popcorn began a long tenure close to us.

The city leaders, in dwelling on the sad condition of the Square, had missed the big story of State Street's transition to a major modern shopping destination. In fact, the street had everything that other cities were paying the Rouse Company millions of dollars to create. I would develop a theory later that most men weren't the kind of shoppers who understood the importance of small specialty stores. Most of the male lawyers, developers, and bankers I sat with on the Board of the Central Madison Council rarely ventured to State Street. They didn't seem to understand its importance to the economy of the city. In fact, although statistics weren't available until later, women made or influenced 70–80% of all purchases in the U.S., including cars and masculine items. But this fact was largely discounted by the power structure.

My depiction in this article as a community leader massaged my ego nicely. Once again, I thought I was ahead of the curve. The city's big shots were looking at the Square and had missed the big story on State Street.

The only wrinkle in the Puzzlebox fabric was the pattern of decline in the St. Louis store, which felt minimal. It didn't occur to me then that while I was looking at our success in Wisconsin, I was missing the big story in St. Louis Union Station.

TWENTY-SEVEN

I felt a little uneasy that the space we'd occupy in Bayshore Mall had no inherent physical beauty. Unlike our other three locations, Bayshore was standard issue construction, with mostly chain stores as occupants. It was simply the best site I could find in Milwaukee, located in an affluent family neighborhood with no toy stores nearby.

Luckily, James was eager to provide the missing beauty. He began drawing plans, repeating the stained wood motif, but this time in brighter primary colors to emphasize the children's toys. He designed a clever layered-wood, backlit framework for the storefront, with a large, lighted sign above it to draw attention to the conventional space. Jim and Sam's crew would again be our builders.

The store would open in October of 1987. I put Laura to work hiring a manager and staff, and Mary Ann began assembling the opening inventory. That left my own schedule light for the moment.

Which was lucky, because Mike was taking up quite a bit of my time and energy. He was unhappy at work, constantly complaining about his supervisor at the VA, who he called incompetent. He was actively looking for work in Milwaukee and was spending four nights a week in Madison now, which crowded me. I'd gotten very used to living alone by now. If he got an apartment in Milwaukee, it would give me some relief.

Mike was a good companion, and we'd developed our own comforting rituals. Our Sundays together were sweet. Late in the morning, we'd walk to the Fess Hotel, and if it was summer, eat creamy scrambled eggs and small, flaky pastries at one of the round tables in the flower-filled walled garden behind the building. The money jar had helped ease the friction between us.

One of the ways to my heart is through my pets, and Mike got there easily with his affection for Spike, my spunky black cat, who'd spent most of his life outdoors and felt confined in my second-floor apartment. One Saturday, Mike came home with a handsome, lightweight rattan cat carrier. People downtown soon got used to seeing us biking with Spike's carrier strapped on Mike's rear fender. We'd go for coffee at Victor's on King Street, with its marvelous view of the Capitol building, sitting at an outside table with Spike occupying a chair of his own, where he had a fine view of people passing, more than a few of whom stooped to admire him through the open weave of the rattan door.

Late that summer, Mike's two children, Andy and Kimmie, finally came for a week's stay. Mike hadn't seen them since he'd left Colorado, and I'd encouraged the visit. I knew it was the right thing to do, but I had mixed feelings. My relationship with Mike was based on the adult love and companionship I'd felt lacking in my marriage. I'd raised my kids and wasn't looking for a new batch.

But when I saw them walk in the door of the Puzzlebox on the day they arrived, I forgot all that. Andy at seven was a quiet, polite boy with straight blond hair and bright blue eyes, dressed neatly in shorts and a button-up shirt. He smiled widely when he met me, holding nothing back. Kimmie was just four, and looked a lot like her brother, with blonde hair braided into pigtails. She wore a red checkered blouse under a denim jumper, and her smile was shyer. I'd missed having a daughter, and I felt my heart open. Both kids were soon at the shelves, exploring the toys and stuffed animals.

As the week passed, I saw they were remarkably considerate children, fond of each other and happy to be reunited with their father. It was obvious they loved him, and despite the time he'd let pass, I had no doubt his love was true and deep.

Andy and Kimmi

IT WAS LATE OCTOBER of 1987, and I was just back from the Bayshore store opening. It had been a long week, made more difficult by a fight Mike and I had the night before I left for Milwaukee. He wanted to move in with me before he found a job in Milwaukee, and I'd initially resisted, afraid it could too easily become a permanent arrangement. I found I wasn't ready to give up my independence.

Jim and Sam had done their usual quality work producing the new fixtures for Bayshore, but doing the work out of town complicated the final steps. For me, the thrill of setting up was gone. Somewhere, it had turned into more work than fun. And in this mall, there was no Rouse presence to glamorize the process.

Given the ruckus with Mike and the stressful details of getting the store open, I had slept badly for a week and wasn't looking forward to the interview I'd scheduled with Jennifer Riddle from the *Wisconsin State Journal*. She was an excellent business reporter, and I'd have to be sharp.

We were in the conference room of the new offices above the store. The small, round freestanding room that James had dubbed the Temple of Wisdom and Discourse, had been constructed with fluted wood pillars painted in Mediterranean blues and greens. It was charming but windowless, and today I was finding the air a little close.

Jennifer had just asked me how it felt to have three stores, how it changed the business.

"It's a whole new phase," I said. "It was expensive and inefficient having just one store in three different cities. With two or more in the same location, we can share staff, combine shipments, split orders."

"Are you saying you'll add stores here in Madison and in St. Louis, too?"

"Here for sure," I said. "I'm looking at spaces on the west side now."

But the truth was, I was having a hard time finding another location in Madison. Hilldale Mall on the near-west side would be a good fit, but I'd have to pay percentage rent instead of a fixed rate. My experience with percentage rent in our two mall stores was discouraging—the harder you worked to build sales, the more you were penalized. Past a certain point, it was only fractionally more profitable.

I was also discovering that local developers were surprised when I asked about construction allowances. Rouse had been so generous in wooing me that I was spoiled.

Before I'd finished that thought, Jennifer led me on to the next question.

"You've been in business eight years now. What's the biggest change you've seen?"

I was tired and answered without thinking. "Competition." As soon as I said it, I was sorry. But she was on it, looking up sharply from her notebook.

"How do you deal with that?"

I knew I had to pivot to positive quickly. I didn't want to sound like I was whining about the big-box stores. "We're still the best buyers. I have excellent managers with great taste. Our company culture is special and affects the whole experience of shopping in our stores. Employees get management training and on-going learning and regular performance reviews."

Jennifer's probing questions were forcing me to remember my original goals. Maybe it was time to review just how well we were following them.

"I've always wanted customers to have a happy experience, whether they're a big spender, a little one, or just looking. I want them exposed to quality toys, to civility, to beauty even. And we won't sell toys that perpetuate sexual stereotypes, like Barbie."

Jennifer nodded. "You've never sold toy guns either, have you?"

"Never. And customers won't find vulgar or harmful toys here. I can swear with the best of them when I want to, but kids won't see ugliness or meanness in our books or toys."

"But surely with all these stores your own involvement has changed," she said. "You can't be on the floor that much anymore."

Her question took me by surprise. It was true I was in the stores less, and I didn't miss it.

"That's true," I said, "but I still show up every Saturday to work behind the counter, and the toys still reflect my taste. I do spend most of my time managing people now. That's my job. I've never had trouble delegating authority."

I didn't add that I wasn't sure how well I was delegating. With four stores, it took a lot of follow-through to make sure everything was done well. I'd been surprised a week ago to find that both Mary Ann and Laura were taking some Saturdays off, and one of them had even missed the annual inventory. I'd worked Saturdays in the store religiously for eight years, had only started taking them off recently, and I'd rarely missed inventory. But the effort to keep track of everyone was tedious.

"That's a big switch for you," Jennifer said, "with your inclination for hands-on action."

"Luckily, we have a great resource at UW to help with growing pains. I have a personal adviser from the Small Business Development Center. We've all taken classes from the center in personnel management and marketing. It's nice to have the SBDC to lean on."

Jennifer smiled, and we ended the interview. I was sure she'd write a positive story. One of my tenets in business was never to complain about sales. So, I hadn't mentioned that the weak sales in St. Louis had morphed into steady double-digit monthly declines, or that the fluctuations in Grand Avenue sales were worrisome. I was sure everything would turn around at Christmas.

A WEEK AFTER MY INTERVIEW with Jennifer, the stock market crashed, the largest one-day dip in history. Worried, I read everything I could find to explain it. Experts linked the crash to the bull market that began in 1982 as well as the hands-off business policies of the Reagan administration. Apparently, the last two years had been extraordinary. As I read, I thought about how business got glamorous somewhere around 1983 or 1984, how our sales jumped in that period, how people rushed to open retail stores to the extent that I had to worry about competition.

Suddenly my head hurt. Was the party over?

The next day, the market rebounded, and I breathed a sigh of relief. Analysts said the quickness of the recovery was a sign that it was just a correction, not the beginning of a recession. The crash had scared me enough that I took the sales book home for the night, to study it carefully. As of September 30, St. Louis was down another five points, almost 20% from the year before. It was a lot of money. Grand Avenue was down just 7%, but I wondered why it was down at all. Thank God for Madison, which held steady.

Before this year, none of the stores had had a monthly decline at all. Something was different, and I didn't know what. Why hadn't I paid more attention? I had to admit I'd felt so liberated by my new freedom from routine duties that I hadn't visited either Milwaukee or St. Louis in months. I'd always thought of myself as someone who saw things clearly, even when the truth was inconvenient, but now it seemed I'd missed something.

Still, our best sales months were ahead. The Christmas season—in fact, the last two weeks before the holiday itself—provided most of our profit for the year. We were a great toy store, and kids always got toys at Christmas, no matter the state of the economy.

Jennifer Riddle's story appeared a week later, along with a quarter-page color photo of Mary Ann, Laura, myself, and Jim Erickson holding up the large red cut-out Puzzlebox sign Jim and Sam had made for the Bayshore store.

It was a positive story, but it didn't change the fact that the timing of the sales decline and the market crash was really bad. First, I'd just given everyone raises, beginning with Mary Ann and Laura, then the assistant managers who took over their jobs, and the staff who replaced the assistants. The office construction had been expensive, and I hadn't budgeted enough for it. But mostly, we'd had to build Bay Shore without a construction allowance. Making something special out of that nondescript space was a lot more expensive than the Madison remodeling, where James had an existing beautiful space to work with.

But still. Christmas would pull us out of the slump. That, at least, was predictable and reliable.

ON THE FRIDAY after Thanksgiving, Mary Ann and I stood waiting for customers. They always came that weekend, but we never knew when or in what numbers. Sometimes it was as soon as we opened the door. But on a cold day, it could be 11:00, and then it would be wall-to-wall crowds until around 6:00 p.m. I'd decided not to share my apprehensions with Mary Ann. She had access to the sales book but hadn't brought up the declines. I wanted the staff to be happy, cheerful for customers, not tense. And I wanted badly to believe Santa would rescue us again this year.

By December 10, I knew we were in trouble. I still hadn't talked to anyone except Marty about my fears. It was easy to ignore the out-of-town managers, but I couldn't avoid Mary Ann. She finally brought up the disappointing numbers, but I was noncommittal. I couldn't explain exactly why I was so hesitant to confide in her. Instead, I told her this looked like a year with a last-minute surge.

I knew I was coming to work less cheerful than usual, less playful with customers. I couldn't help it. I had no idea what was happening and didn't want to alarm anyone until I had more information.

It was not unusual for our stores to do 40–50% of December sales in the last ten days before Christmas, so I had to wait until December 24 for the outcome.

State Street ended just even with last year, and that was a relief. But Grand Avenue had gone down 8%, and I could scarcely credit the drop in St. Louis, a crushing 18%. Between the two stores, we came up short $50,000 in cash sales.

I would keep the final totals to myself until after the Christmas party. The season was always physically exhausting, but there was a kind of triumph in that. Our Christmas parties were always happy celebrations, and I wouldn't spoil this one.

TWENTY-EIGHT

One Monday in early January of 1988, my ninth year in business, I woke with my bed sheets tangled after a night of restless sleep. I stared at the ceiling, remembering everything I'd tried to forget when I went to bed the night before. I knew I could no longer keep it to myself. The numbers didn't lie.

Usually, I liked January in Wisconsin. My friends and family groused about the frigid weather, the icy roads, the dark nights with no sparkling, colored Christmas lights to lift the gloom. But for me, the 25th of December meant liberation from physical and mental stress. January was like vacation to me, the hard work over and two winter trade shows scheduled for fun.

But not this year. Not with the balance sheet that wouldn't balance. Mike was away, so I'd been free last night to down a full bottle of wine, which only delivered a pounding head and a cotton-ball mouth this morning. Feeling stupid, I put on my clothes, drank a cup of coffee, then quickly picked up the phone to call Bill Pinkovitz before I postponed it once again. He was in his office, and I wasted no time asking to see him. He had a meeting on the Square at noon and said he could stop at my office at 11:00.

I hung up, relieved. I needed help badly.

Outside, I put a glove over my nose to ward off the damp, mean cold, and wondered why I hadn't dressed better for the short walk to work. I had to step carefully in my smooth-soled boots to avoid the scattering of ice on the sidewalk. When I got to the office, it was empty. Mary Ann was in Milwaukee, I remembered. Good. I walked into my corner room, small but choice, with its window overlooking State Street. I turned on the lights and made room on my desk for the sugar-crusted muffin I'd picked up at the Upstairs Downstairs Deli, anticipating the short-term comfort of fats and sweets.

When Bill walked in an hour later, I had papers strewn all over my desk. As usual, his tall, wiry body exuded nervous energy. He was a funny, irreverent man who didn't hold back his thoughts, and I needed that now. I respected his business acumen.

"So, Janice," he said, taking off his coat to reveal an argyle sweater over a white dress shirt and trousers, "it's been quite a while since we talked. How's your new empire?"

I squirmed in my chair, making a face. He sat down.

"Uh oh, what's going on?"

"Our Christmas was a disaster, Bill." I was eager to spill it out to someone who actually understood the ramifications.

"Sales were down drastically in both St. Louis and Grand Avenue. Even here they were flat, for the first time in our history."

"Whoa," he said, "slow down and tell me what happened."

"I wish I knew. St. Louis was down a few points every month last year, but I wrote it off as a readjustment after the fantastic sales the first year. Grand Avenue fell for a couple of months but then went up again, and I was sure Christmas would fix everything. Then the market crashed in October, and we've been down double-digits since."

The lines of his forehead furrowed. He leaned back and thought. "The crash was bad, but the market recovered quickly. It's hard to think that would explain everything."

"I know," I admitted. "The numbers are bad. St. Louis is down 18% for the year, Grand Avenue 8%. Between those two stores alone, we're down almost $200,000."

He whistled. I flinched. It had been a relief to tell him, but hard. Puzzlebox was a star in the Madison business firmament.

"Even this store's been sluggish," I said, "and you know this city has never been seriously affected by economic downturns."

"What does your new management team think? They've been in charge for a while now, right?"

I sighed. "Most of last year. Mary Ann goes to St. Louis regularly, and Laura's at Grand Avenue most of the time. Bayshore is too new to do much business; it'll be a slower build there. We've all discussed the weak sales, but no one rang an alarm."

I paused, looking out the window at the Civic Center across the street. "I've not been in the stores much this year, so I decided to put in a lot of hours on the floor here before Christmas."

"And?"

"I wasn't happy with some things. With our small space and the sheer volume of sales at Christmas, it's crucial to restock every hour. If best-sellers aren't on the shelves, they're likely lost sales. It can make a huge difference at the end of the day. I made a point of restocking myself and was shocked to find half a dozen of our best-sellers weren't even out, and it was the morning of a $10,000 day. Yikes. I talked to Mary Ann about it, but she was defensive. She assumed Cathy had the drill down. I guess she hasn't learned yet you can't teach something once and expect it to stick without regular reminders."

As soon as I said that I had a vague feeling of forgetting something important, but then it slipped away.

Bill had been listening intently. As I finished, he got up and walked to the window, looking down the street. He turned and eyed me, his face steely.

"Janice, your job is sales. If they're down, it's your job to get them up. You can't sit in the office and try to solve the problem. You need to go down to the stockroom and bring up the product yourself if that's what it takes, get it on the shelves, use your eyes to make sure it's there when it should be."

He wasn't finished. He came close and looked into my eyes.

"If it's necessary, you need to go into the stores and run them yourself. You may need to fire people. You're in charge of sales. It's that simple."

I felt the blood leave my face. Fire people? It wasn't that bad.

Before he left, Bill told me to direct Marty to prepare financial statements for the last calendar year and send them to him. He also shared the news that he'd been promoted, and I'd be getting a new adviser soon, Joan Gillman. I'd work with both her and Bill until he moved on. That made me uneasy. This was no time to lose a trusted adviser. Suddenly, way too much was changing.

A WEEK LATER, the Rouse Company sent two accountants to Madison to do a routine audit of the sales records from St. Louis. They'd done the same audit on the Grand Avenue store a year ago, so I knew it was no big deal. Both stores sent their daily sales reconciliation, along with cash register tapes, to our office regularly. I knew Rouse did the audits to make sure stores didn't underreport sales to avoid paying percentage rent, but that was no worry to us, straight arrows that we were.

I was surprised when the accountants found an irregularity. But it was Puzzlebox that had been cheated, as well as Rouse. The audit turned up a pattern of stealing by someone on the St. Louis staff who doctored the daily cash register receipts to show lower sales by a consistent $60 a day. It had been done through phony over-rings, by ringing up a sale that never happened. In this case, the sales had actually happened, but the employee faked a customer refund and pocketed the cash.

"Jesus, Mary Ann, how could this have happened," I said, my voice rising. "Checking the daily sales slips is rudimentary. They estimate this guy got away with close to $5,000 over a period of six months. Two over-rings a shift, three days a week."

"I know," she said, her voice low, her face grim. "Rose knew better. She should have been checking the daily deposits, but it's obvious she wasn't."

At least Rose was able to pinpoint the thief. The ring-ups had consistently been done during the shifts of a part-time male employee, and no other days. No one had suspected a thing. Rose would take no action until we decided what to do. In the meantime, she'd watch the receipts, and when the over-rings showed up, would quiz the guy as if there had been some other problem. That would call him off for a while.

THREE DAYS LATER LAURA, Mary Ann, Marty and I sat in our conference room, digesting the income statements Marty had prepared. It was time for me and my staff to face facts. I sat up straight and met everyone's eyes.

"The St. Louis theft is awful, but it's nothing compared to the lost sales. Between St. Louis and Grand Avenue, we're down $200,000. We've been working with a large cash cushion because of the huge sales from St. Louis the first year. How much of a cushion do we have left, Marty?"

She knew I wanted brutal honesty. Speaking carefully, she picked up a ledger full of her precise handwriting. She was an excellent bookkeeper but also had an unusual intuitive side I had rarely met in my dealings with numbers people.

"We've had big expenses this year, starting with Bay Shore, and then this office. Beyond that, the new salaries have added a big bump to the budget. Bay Shore won't make money for a while, so that's a deficit. We knew these expenses were coming and would have been fine if sales had held to projections."

"How could this have happened?" Mary Ann said, looking at me.

"I don't really understand everything yet," I said. "The market crash was a factor, but we just ignored the steady declines in both mall stores. And why weren't we up at Christmas here, Mary Ann? State Street has never had a year when December wasn't better than the year before, even when we had a blizzard."

She just shook her head.

Laura spoke up. "I've been asking other merchants at the Grand Avenue about their sales, but no one admits they're down, so I just don't know."

"My usual sources on State Street are reporting a normal Christmas," I said. "Chuck Bauer told me the Soap Opera was up." I paused, uneasy. "Still, that doesn't matter much. The big St. Louis drop is our real problem."

"I think it's got something to do with Rose," Laura said. "Maybe it's the southern thing. She had a hard time connecting with our culture. Whenever I flew in I'd talk to her about the way they weren't restocking properly, things like that, but when I'd come back in a few months, it was still going on."

I felt my face change. This was news to me. Why hadn't I been told?

"Rose is different from us," Mary Ann said. "She's calm, mellow, and slow. For sure her employees are not so good."

We all sat silent. Then I spoke. "Bill says my job is to get sales up. I haven't been paying enough attention, but now I am. I'm going back into the stores with you. Mary Ann, let's get a flight together to St. Louis right away. It's urgent we get sales up there." I smiled ironically. "At least we'll make sure the thief gets no more money."

She nodded grimly.

"Laura," I said, "I'll start going to Milwaukee every Wednesday again. We'll huddle with Janis and Jill, get a program going to stimulate sales."

"Good!" she said, energized.

"In the meantime, I need you both to get rid of the product that's left over—maybe a special promotion, maybe a small sale. We need cash for new product from the winter shows. New stuff is our best bet for a sales spike."

They knew I was desperate if I suggested a sale. Except for Maxwell Street Days, we felt sales cheapened our image. Marty and I sat for a while after Mary Ann and Laura left. Then she spoke, choosing her words carefully.

"It's going to take a lot of new sales to replace the money we've lost."

Her warning chilled me. I tamped down the panic I couldn't afford now. I felt my hands make fists.

"I know, but we just have to do it," I said. "I need you to draw up some alternative cash flows for the next year, the way you always do—best case sales, worst case sales, most likely scenario."

I desperately needed to get the business back on firm ground as quickly as possible. I told myself that the next morning when I faced myself in the mirror, blurry-eyed and pale. But deep down, I wasn't sure if I could do it.

TWENTY-NINE

I'd always hated the six a.m. flight to St. Louis. Leaving the house in the dark depressed me. Mary Ann and I would be coming back home on the seven p.m. flight that day, but even so I couldn't stop the thought that if she and Rose had done their jobs, I wouldn't have to be going at all.

On the plane, we both said little. She was no more a morning person than I, and the trip was too short for more than one cup of coffee.

The realization of how much I'd ignored the warning signs of sales declines was smarting. What had I been doing that I'd missed seeing this coming, missed seeing that the business had changed? I suddenly remembered how I'd answered Bill when he asked me what I thought had happened that the Madison staff hadn't restocked the store adequately at Christmas. Something about how you can't expect people to remember instructions if you only tell them once. I'd preached to my staff that a good supervisor constantly reinforced policy. Was it possible I'd been at fault as well, expecting Mary Ann and Laura to take on my work without my close supervision? I'd prided myself on being a good boss. It nagged at me.

Rose was there to open the door when we got to Union Station at eight, smiling tentatively. It had been a long time since I'd seen her. She was a slight woman, with a fragile, fine-featured beauty, and now the dark circles under her eyes were prominent. As we talked, I thought about how she'd been living for a year with sales declines every month, after the heady success of the first year. It must have been hard. And now, an embezzler she should have caught. I felt a pang I hadn't been here more.

In the course of the morning, she gave us a tour of the store, as was our usual routine, and my first impression was positive. The architecture of the store had held up well, with no visible wear and tear on the fixturing from the large crowds. But then I started noticing small things: old scotch tape on the front of the checkout counter where posters had been taken down. In the wind-up section, some of the baskets were full, but some had only a few toys in them. The baby section looked thin, sparse even. That happened after Christmas with some categories, but there were ways to shift things so the store didn't look understocked. On another shelf, stuffed animals had been crammed into too small a space. These were the little things that kept a store from excellence.

Worst of all, there was old gum on the carpet, in more than a few spots. We had a strict policy of cleaning gum up right away, before it was ground in permanently.

Since opening, we'd struggled to keep good part-time staff here. The mall was far from any university or even neighborhoods, where we usually found likely prospects. Rose had been short on staff at Christmas, and I guessed she'd probably covered many nights and Sundays to keep the long mall hours staffed. That might help explain her carelessness with the daily sales receipts, as well as the displays.

In Madison and Milwaukee, people liked the prestige of working at the Puzzlebox. In St. Louis, no one knew our reputation, so it was hard to invest staffers in customer service and attention to maintenance and cleaning. Rose was an easy-going manager, not one for confrontation. She'd never really adapted to our high-energy style, which tended to attract the same kind of high-energy staff. My guess was she'd burned out.

While Rose and Mary Ann huddled over some orders, I took over the sales counter. Most of the backstock was stored in a cubicle in a distant part of the mall, but at my request, the architect had provided wide, deep storage drawers below the shelving for best-sellers. I was surprised to find many of the drawers half empty, which didn't make sense. I knew we had plenty of stock left over from the poor Christmas sales. And the drawers hadn't been cleaned out for a long time, with bits of paper, cardboard and dust in the bottoms. In one drawer I found a small, handmade wooden fire truck, a perfect special Christmas gift, that wasn't out at all. When I asked Rose if something was wrong with it, she looked confused and said no, it was just an oversight.

At lunch, we talked over the police recommendation to deal with the thief. There was no direct evidence to prosecute. He'd have to be caught in the act. Rose had already talked to a detective who would be bringing in a colleague next week to discuss that.

I'd noticed Rose was subdued and not eating much, but I wrote it off to the depressing talk. Then she blurted out that she had accepted a good position with a local department store. She would give us three weeks' notice but needed to leave in February. She was nervous and apologetic, but there wasn't much to say about it. She'd had a very hard year, was facing the fact that she'd let an employee steal a great deal of money, and now had an out. I understood now that this job had been a bad fit. I wished her luck in her new endeavor, even as I acknowledged inwardly the depth of the hole that was opening up in front of me.

IN THE TAXI to the airport that afternoon, the stressful day caught up with me. I was angry and didn't hide it.

"The store is a mess, Mary Ann. Poorly maintained, badly stocked. The part-timers are clearly underperforming, for whatever reason. In no way is the store or staff up to our standards. You must have had a staff meeting to set some objectives and boundaries. Did that happen?"

"Of course," she said, turning to me sharply. "Rose had one just before Thanksgiving."

"What about performance reviews? Is Rose doing them for her staff? Have you given her one recently?" I wasn't letting her off the hook.

She'd been looking out the side of the cab window while I talked, and now turned to me, her eyes cold, her chin raised defiantly.

"No, I haven't," she said, "and you haven't given me one at all since I've been in my new position. And you haven't been to St. Louis in a year."

That stung. Had it really been a year? But why should I have come here? That was the point. I'd given her the power in exchange for leaving behind this kind of work. She'd run the Madison store for five years. Why hadn't she shown Rose how to do it?

I collapsed a little in my seat. "Mary Ann, the new cash flow Marty drew up looks bad. I don't know how we can recover. We're simply going to run out of money. There won't be enough to pay the bills and make the payroll."

She looked at me, unsmiling, unyielding, her face set. "You can fix it. You'll figure something out."

MARY ANN AND I sat silent in my office. On the street below, a city bus was idling at the stop light, its engine a steady drone that covered the tension in the small room.

Toy Fair had not been fun. To save money, just she and I had gone, for only two days. Laura and Janis would cover the Chicago Gift Show with me. During the days we'd spent together, I'd never complained again about Mary Ann's performance supervising St. Louis. The truth was, I still hadn't completely figured out the reason for the sharp sales drop.

St. Louis was a mess. The assistant manager there would step in when Rose left in a week, but we needed a real manager quick. I had run an ad in the St. Louis Dispatch, and we were looking through resumes now.

"None of them have enough experience to start building sales right away," I said. "We just don't have enough time."

I felt brittle. What I had to say, what I had to do, was hard. I looked up, meeting her eyes directly. "Mary Ann, you're the only one who can do it. You could run the store until we found somebody good."

She looked at me angrily, her mouth in a straight line. She must have known this was coming. "What?" she said. "You want me to go down and clean up that mess? What am I supposed to do, move there?"

"Just temporarily," I said. "You could rent a nice place, close to Union Station, fly home weekends."

"Live out of a suitcase? For how long? And why me? Laura knows the store as well. She's been going down every other month. Why should it fall on me?"

"Because you know the store operations better, and the staff. Being on the spot, you'll probably find a new manager quickly."

It was easier for me to talk now. The plan really was a good one, maybe the only feasible one. "The truth is, you're the only one who can do this job," I said.

She slumped in her chair, her mouth turned down. But I saw she was moving into acceptance. She was going to St. Louis. It would be lonely for her there, with no one at all except the staff she'd be supervising in an underperforming store. Her life would be work and stress, nothing more. My mouth felt like I'd eaten something sour. I didn't like doing this, but it was my job, after all.

She smiled ironically. "I guess it would be interesting to live in St. Louis for a while."

We talked more and finally agreed she'd leave as soon as possible. With Mary Ann covering St. Louis, coaxing the best possible sales out of it, I could concentrate on working with Cathy to get Madison on track again, and make weekly trips to Milwaukee to help Laura with the two stores there.

There were no hugs between us that day, or a week later when she left. There was too much unsaid and too much we didn't know for the tension to be resolved. And I was playing the strong boss mode, better late than never, I thought—cool, collected, logical.

Mary Ann was my first, most loyal and excellent employee, the closest thing to a partner I'd had in building the business. I could scarcely believe how quickly and bitterly our long, close relationship had come unraveled.

A CONFIDENT WOMAN around fifty smiled out from the cover of the new *Lears Magazine*. She was CEO of a rising communications company, featured in the cover story on entrepreneurship. As I read the story, some sentences struck a familiar chord.

"In business, there are two types of people: starters and maintainers. The entrepreneur is not a maintainer. Her primary interest is bringing new ideas to fruition.

"The entrepreneurial management style is like the structure of a tepee. Everyone reports to the boss. Entrepreneurs' reason for existence, what drives them, is their need to make a personal statement."

These words brought me back to the year I'd consulted Professor Filly before opening the Grand Avenue store. I'd known I had entrepreneurial impulses, and I knew I didn't do as well at management. I'd compensated for that by instituting the new non-hierarchical business structure. I thought I'd flattened the tepee by empowering my managers.

So why hadn't it worked? How else could a starter run a successful company? I didn't know it then, but it would take me ten years to find an answer to that question.

THIRTY

On an overcast morning a month after I sent Mary Ann to St. Louis, I riffled through my closet for something to wear for my meeting with Joan, my new adviser. When and why had clothes gotten so damned big? Skirts this season were voluminous and sweaters so roomy they had to be belted to show any shape at all.

I had the TV in my bedroom tuned to the the *Today* show, where an economist was explaining that Reagan's latest tax cuts had driven the national debt dangerously high. Or so some people thought. This cut included the personal income tax, which should help my sales. Certainly, the previous tax cuts had made a lot of companies happy. With all that money floating around, almost everyone in business was doing well. Which didn't explain why mine wasn't.

I pulled on a pair of loose black trousers and a purple sweater with shoulder pads. I'd put on a few extra pounds in the last few months from all the stress, so I skipped belting it. My recently permed hair, full and falling to my shoulders, balanced the outfit, but I wasn't crazy about what I saw in the mirror. The bright sweater did nothing to give color to my pallid complexion, which was never good in the sunless months. I hated the circles under my eyes. I'd slept badly again.

My mind returned to the news. It was like all the extra money in people's pockets had led to a general largesse. And what about all the new big-box stores, with items so inexpensive you could buy three sweaters instead of one? It made a kind of crazy sense, but it wasn't pretty. Thank God for State Street, still small, still local, still walkable and beautiful. No one could change that. Still, how was it possible that things had changed so much in just eight years? What was ahead that I couldn't see?

Three hours later, I sat sipping coffee in a booth in Nick's Bar and Grill, our neighbor on State Street. The bar was gloomy in the mid-morning light. A kitchen worker swished a mop back and forth on the black-and-white tile floor. Despite its fifties-style gaudy lights and black vinyl booths with squiggly gold patterning, Nick's was a hangout for the arts crowd, but the perversity of that was one of the reasons why I loved Madison, with its good share of people who went their own way.

I'd stuffed my red leather briefcase with my latest cash flow projections, and now I put them on the table. Joan arrived exactly on time, and as she approached, looking professional in a dark blue jacket and skirt, I smiled a nervous greeting. Her style was very different from Bill's. He was a voluble guy who loved to tell stories before he got down to business. Although Joan was some years younger than I, she carried herself with authority and didn't waste much time on niceties.

Apprehensive, I watched as she pulled out a pair of reading glasses and started absorbing the contents of my documents. This was the second meeting we'd had this month, so she understood my situation thoroughly.

"Janice, you have to face the fact that you need to reorganize the business. Your company is top heavy. With sales so far down and expenses way up, you're running out of cash quickly."

I felt my throat tighten. I swallowed hard. She went on, relentless.

"You've got to get rid of your administrative staff. You have to go back in and run the business yourself until it's repaired."

I stared at her, digesting. I knew I was in trouble, but her specifics shocked me.

"Let Mary Ann and Laura go? I can't do that."

Her face didn't change. "Not doing it could destroy your business."

Ten minutes after Joan's pronouncement, I walked out of Nick's into the chilling March air. I'd left her talking to a colleague she'd spotted at a table on our way out. My forehead felt clammy, and a wave of dizziness brought me to a halt. My denial was crashing down on me. I knew how bad things were, but I'd clung to the belief there'd be some recourse. Now Joan was telling me there wasn't.

I stood, uncertain as to my next move. The double doors of the Civic Center across the street opened to let out a chattering group of conventioneers. It was Tuesday, and the only other people on the street looked like tourists on their way to the Capitol building up the block. I had told the staff I wouldn't be back after my meeting with Joan, and now I started walking to my car.

As was the case lately, I'd been unable to stop at a prudent couple of glasses of wine at home the night before. But a lingering hangover didn't stop me from craving a drink right that minute. I needed to shut out the crushing reality of my position.

When I got to the car, I sat for a minute, too numb to put the key in the ignition. I was a mess, and I didn't know how I was going to handle this. My staff believed in me, trusted me, had bought the publicity that persisted in painting me a female forerunner, a marketing whiz with a big future. They would never understand.

Another bout of dizziness forced my head to the steering wheel. I'd taken a risk with the St. Louis store. I'd stepped out, and I'd failed. I had no doubt that Mary Ann and Laura would feel betrayed if I actually let them go. The two women were more than employees: they were friends, even daughters.

And now Joan was saying I would have to fix things without them. I hadn't been active in the stores for years. I'd cut my hours to three short days a week, mostly spent doing paperwork. When sales had started to fall, I dismissed it as temporary, taking no steps to counter my diminishing cash. Now I had to take responsibility

I thought about the wonderful run of luck I'd had, the promise of the early years, the pleasure of working with a team of talented people to create and run beautiful stores that people loved. Eight years later, everything had suddenly gone bad.

THE AIR IN THE SMALL conference room in the Puzzlebox office was stale. One of the fluorescent lights in the outer office flickered, emitting a low, grating hum. Mary Ann frowned, her eyebrows knitted together, her shoulders hunched as she read Marty's latest cash flow scenarios. Laura looked at me, smiling ruefully. It had been six weeks since I told them that we needed a drastic reorganization.

When Mary Ann had told me she'd be coming home from St. Louis for a few days, I'd asked Laura to drive over so the three of us could sit down together. I'd brought the meeting to order quickly, then waited quietly as they absorbed the cash flow report.

I couldn't accept Joan's simple solution of firing Laura and Mary Ann. The two women were an integral part of my story, of women's stories in our time. My own success had come unbidden but welcome. Elevated to a position I never expected, I'd elevated them in turn. So, I'd come up with an idea to save their jobs.

"You can see it would take a miracle to reverse the pattern we're in," I began. "If I don't change something quickly, I won't be able to pay suppliers, and by mid-summer it will be hard to make payroll. The only solution is to cut expenses."

"Couldn't we tighten up inventory to raise cash, sell what we have instead of ordering new stuff?" Laura, asked, her voice pitched high. "St. Louis has a lot of excess."

"We could, but it's not enough. And we need any cash we raise for new product in all the stores. You know that's the only real way to raise sales."

Mary Ann sat back in her chair and crossed her arms, lips pursed. "It's about our salaries isn't it? That's the only thing that makes a significant difference. They're the big new item in cash flow."

I had to say it. "Yes. It's the whole new administrative level, including this office."

Their faces were glum. I felt like shit.

"There is a solution," I said, "that would solve all our problems. We go back to what we had before, me as CEO, you two in your original positions as store managers. You could still take on more, but it would be my job to oversee things. The truth is, it worked beautifully that way, as long as I worked hard at being in charge."

I paused. "That does mean you'd have to take salary cuts. There'll be less money for everybody, at least for a while. But we'd be able to get the business we've built back on its feet, together."

The two women exchanged glances, and I had a feeling they'd anticipated this.

"That would mean Cathy and Janis would be demoted, back to

assistant managers," Mary Ann said, her voice low. "And the new assistant managers would lose their full-time jobs."

"Yes," I said. Denial was no longer an option.

We all sat, quiet, no one willing to speak.

"I don't see how we can go back," Laura finally said.

Mary Ann nodded. "It feels too much like failure. And it would hurt our staffs."

This was going way too fast. I tried to slow it down. "We've got some time. Just give it some thought for now."

We sat silent again. Mary Ann had turned away, face toward the door. Laura looked up, met my eyes, and shook her head sadly.

MIKE HAD FINALLY moved in with me after working his last day at the VA in Tomah. He'd stay with me while he looked for an apartment in Milwaukee. He and I were being very careful with each other.

Tonight, I'd planned to go over some orders for St. Louis after dinner, but when I went into the second bedroom, Mike had unloaded his briefcase on the desk. He looked up and asked quickly: "Is it OK for me to use the desk, sweetie? I have to read some patient histories before I meet with them tomorrow."

I smiled weakly. "That's fine, go ahead. I'll work in the kitchen."

WITHIN A WEEK, Mary Ann and Laura both announced they'd be leaving. I wasn't surprised. I didn't blame them. But it was bitter to accept what could only be called failure.

Mary Ann would stay in St. Louis until May 30, her last official day of employment with the Puzzlebox. I needed Laura a little longer to put Jill and Janis on a firm footing in the Milwaukee stores. She would exit at the end of June. I'd built in extra time to soften the blow of their income loss. I would buy back the Puzzlebox stock that I'd given each after their short-lived promotions. They should have that extra money, but the cash outlay at this particular moment was difficult.

As the weeks went on, I admitted to myself how angry I was with my two lieutenants. I knew I'd made mistakes, but I couldn't help but blame them. I'd left the tepee structure and handed them the power and control. They'd made a mess then left me to clean it up. Should I have fired them when it became obvious it wasn't going to work, rather than waiting so long?

In the moment, in the waning days of Mary Ann and Laura's tenures, mostly I just wanted them gone.

THIRTY-ONE

Few people in Madison had any idea that the business had faltered. The State Street store had recovered completely, showing modest increases every month, and I understood now how lucky I was to have a store on one of the best retail streets in the country.

I was grateful for the anonymity of my failure, but it still weighed heavily. I missed Mary Ann and Laura terribly, missed going to trade shows with them, talking business with them, but mostly I missed their companionship. My face might never show customers how things had changed, but inside I was a different person, less sure of myself, no longer happy just to be there.

A few months after Laura and Mary Ann left, I invited two of our best Madison student employees to lunch—Chip Mitchell, my favorite, and a more recent hire, John Fields, resident intellectual, PhD candidate in divinity, who came to staff parties in a professorial cardigan. No matter how much bravado I summoned on any given day, I increasingly felt the burden of rectifying the business failure by myself. To get to where we were before, I needed the whole staff with me. I needed a new vision, and I needed my people in it with me, with our old camaraderie. I thought Chip and John were my best bet.

Years had gone by since Chip came to work in pajamas. He was in campus radical mode now, his face fully bearded, his hair unruly and past shoulder length. I had a pang as I considered how our handsome young student now resembled Jesus.

"I've asked you here," I said, as we sat waiting for burgers at the Plaza, "because I need help. We've always had great teamwork at the Puzzlebox, but it's been hard since Mary Ann left. I know morale is down, and I want to build it back up."

"Well," Chip said, his face set in a scowl, "you did kind of disappear, didn't you?"

I listened in disbelief as he continued, his normally cheerful tone unrelenting. "Everything changed a couple of years ago. Mary Ann wasn't around much, and it just seemed like nobody cared about us part-timers."

John nodded in agreement, his face serious under its goatee. I knew that he had said some hurtful things to Mary Ann at one point about her frequent absences. That was one reason I'd set up this meeting. But it hadn't occurred to me that the underlying resentment might extend to me. I'd known that tempers were also frayed in Milwaukee. There'd been an outburst from a part-timer to Janis the last time I was there, but I hadn't realized Madison staff had been so affected.

"We used to feel we were important to the whole business," John said. "It wasn't the same going to staff meetings with just Cathy running them. It felt like you and Mary Ann didn't care much about this store anymore."

Chip added the final turn of the screw. "We're just angry that you moved from an egalitarian organization to an elitist one."

I sat silent and numb as they continued to voice complaints. This was not going to be easy. I'd get no help from them until I showed them things would be different.

I'D CAUGHT A BREAK when our assistant manager in Madison, Jackie White, offered to move to St. Louis to manage the store there. Young and ambitious, she welcomed the opportunity for valuable experience in a big city. For us, it was perfect. She was imbued with the company culture and knew how to run the store. In the meanwhile, Peter, who was back from his motorcycle trip and waiting for the fall semester, filled the gap until Jackie got there. When he came back, he began regular shifts at the store. I was grateful whenever he worked with me on Saturdays during that hard period. He had a way of raising everybody's spirits, especially mine.

My youngest son was a hugger. He lay hands on everyone he knew—my family when they came to visit, my friends, his parents, even his brother, who always resisted. His physical instinct was to get close to people, as if to shorten the space that kept us all apart. He leaned toward someone when he was listening to them, but never too close to invade territory. I loved it, and I thought it was a perfect retail approach. His body language said he was available—smiling, relaxed, non-hurried—but only if a customer wanted help.

His dark blond hair was cut close on the sides now and long and spiky on the top, giving him a jaunty look. He came to work in clean jeans and a checkered sport shirt, often with a quirky, skinny red tie that hung below his belt. He loved working the counter and practiced a favorite maneuver of approaching customers with a perfectly serious demeanor while wearing a rubber pig nose.

I was grateful for our work time together because my boys hardly needed me anymore, except to cook an occasional dinner, or more likely, buy them one at Gino's. Peter had gone back to school as promised. John was still finding his way with various computer-related jobs, happy to immerse himself in the gaming world in his free time. Both boys shared apartments with friends, and both saw their father regularly. My ex-husband lived on the first floor of the triplex unit he'd bought

My boys and I

on the near-east side. He spent much of his time in a county south of Madison doing contract consulting work with a social services agency. We'd all made our adjustments.

That winter, Mike finally found an apartment in Milwaukee, and we fell into a two-city arrangement that worked well for my business and for our personal relationship. He spent weekends in Madison, and every Wednesday I packed a bag, put Spike in his carrier, and drove to Milwaukee. I stayed two weeknights at his place there, giving me a full day and a half to work in the stores. Both Janis at Grand Avenue and Jill at Bayshore welcomed the attention, and sales improved almost immediately.

FOR THE NEXT SIX MONTHS I worked in the stores almost every day. Our lovely new offices were deserted, except for Marty, who would stay on until the finances were sorted out. She had projected cash flow for July, when the big salaries would be gone, and I was enormously relieved to see that if we increased sales just a little and held other expenses down, we could come into the black within six months. Cash was still tight, but I got the bank to increase my line of credit so I could pay bills due urgently. If our sales held up for the next year, we'd squeak through to positive cash flow.

Finally, I felt operations were under control. The managers had picked up much of the ordering, which I was coordinating. I'd put an ad campaign in place and trimmed the bloated budget. Sales were still poor, but I was doing all I could to increase them through better buying, promotion, and advertising. The computerized inventory system made the bulk of the ordering easy. For the rest, I'd started to turn more work over to the new store managers. And this time, I met with them weekly to follow up. And I made sure I was at every store-wide staff meeting.

In the course of that difficult year of reconstruction, I thought again sometimes what a relief it would be to just let go of the business. But then I'd get a pang, thinking about how my personal identity was so tied to the Puzzlebox.

Often, I found myself going into the past, out of my need to reconcile that magical era with the tarnished present. I remembered with perfect clarity a lovely day in June two months after we opened in 1979. I was walking up State to the door of the Puzzlebox. As I put the key into the lock, looking through the panes of glass to the toys on the shelves, I said aloud, with fervor and delight, "There is no place on earth I'd rather be."

Another time, a few days before Halloween, I laughed at Mary Ann's costume, especially the fat plastic cheeks she'd put on as some cult character I'd never heard of. I told her she looked like a chipmunk, and we laughed in delight at our silliness.

And then I'd start thinking of all the windows Anne and I put together, me the willing dupe on a stepladder risking throwing out my back to hang a B.B. Bear just right, so his chunky, furry legs would make a ballet plié, then looking down and seeing people on the sidewalk watching us work, big smiles on their faces, thumbs up in encouragement.

Oh, what fun!

I knew that magic hour would never return. But what I could do was work to restore our early principles of excellent, unique products, great customer service, and always, always, fun for all ages.

THIRTY-TWO

I felt enormous relief when at the end of the next year, 1988, Christmas sales actually increased. Finally, the heat was off. It had been an exhausting effort, and I took a few days off to recharge. But soon enough when I came back in and inspected the stockroom, it was clear we were still left with too much inventory. And clues began to appear that explained how our buying had gone wrong.

A thorough stock count in all stores revealed stacks of imported toys that used to sell steadily, but didn't that Christmas, especially in our mall stores.

It took weeks to piece it all together, but after I met with the Milwaukee managers and consulted several sales reps who worked our accounts, I began to understand what had happened. One day when Peter was working, I took him to the stockroom, eager to share what I'd learned.

"Peter, we totally underestimated the competition from the national chains, the big ones that now sell a lot of our lines."

He looked puzzled. "Which toys are you talking about?"

"The imported ones," I said, pointing to a stack of preschool wood cut-out puzzles, formerly dependable sellers. "I knew a lot of the big stores had picked them up, but I assumed most of our customers would rather buy them from us."

"So what changed?" he asked.

"Price! The sheer size and buying clout of the nationals gave them a huge advantage. We ordered in dozens, but they ordered in grosses for a deep discount, which let them charge much less than we could. You can't blame people for liking that."

To make it worse, I now discovered we had dropped many small vendors in favor of the large importers, abandoning the unique lines that made us different. This felt devastating and then calming. Knowing what had happened, I could now act.

Free trade and globalism were hitting us hard, but it would be many more years until the full effect of it on small retailers would be evident.

It was clear to me that we simply couldn't compete with the low prices of the chains and big-box stores, but I knew we could do better on quality and originality. We needed to make our niche clear. And if we decided to sell some of the same toys, we'd have to mark them up less and take the loss, so at least our price came close.

That spring, I instructed managers in all stores to mark down old inventory, then mark it down again until it sold. Then I began to restructure the buying, setting strict budgets. I watched the mix carefully and made up a hot list of best-sellers we should never run out of. I made sure the stores reordered the new products I'd worked hard to find at the winter shows, and they also reordered from many of the small companies we'd neglected. We could still get a good markup on them because the big stores didn't carry them. In fact, it was to our advantage that small companies simply couldn't make enough quantity to fill a big chain's orders.

I now accepted the reality that I had forgotten our origins. For the past few years, we'd put sales before product, favoring items that made more money. From the first year, the quality of the toys had been paramount to me. How could I have so quickly forgot how crucial it was to carry unusual, interesting toys even if they didn't make a lot of money?

In fact, we'd been seduced by the computer spread sheets that so clearly showed where the profits were. Our reorder choices could add a lot of cash to the bottom line. I had a hard time accepting this, that greed was a factor in our decision-making. I didn't think it was so much for the cash, but for the win. It became very praiseworthy in the eighties to be a smart money-manager, and we were not immune.

With the added stores, we'd concentrated on the money-makers to finance the expanded business. In our zeal to do well, we failed to make room for the quirky, lovely products people had always expected from us.

Luckily, the unpleasant truth that emerged motivated me to buy better and pass that on as an objective for store managers. With that, and by cutting administrative costs, we stopped the sales slide and made the company profitable again by summer of 1989. Both Madison and Milwaukee were able to reverse the poor sales of 1987. In St. Louis, we slowed the decline, but the store never fully recovered. The mall there would be a canary in a coal mine. If we only could have seen it earlier. The beautiful Union Station would never recover.

BUT I COULDN'T BLAME globalization and monopolies for everything. I'd opted to grow the company and desert it at the same time. Instead of starting my day in silence in the store, I'd gone to the office or to history class. Before, I'd often worked fifty hours a week. In the early years, we'd all pushed boundaries, paid no attention to hours, eagerly worked nights to create fabulous windows.

I'd wanted to carry the best products I could find, toys that were safe, non-violent, and good-looking. Everyone who walked in the store should feel welcome, no matter how poor or rich they were. I would hire staff that shared my vision, and I would be a good boss.

Our toys were still fun, safe, and gender-neutral, but the other values I was less sure about. With success, the store culture had changed, at first subtly. Our parties and softball games were fun, but it all got out of hand. The pursuit of pleasure became routine rather than a reward for good work. At trade shows, we stayed out late at night, walking the miles of show aisles the next day with diminished energy. We took our eye off customers and turned it to our own wants. We thought we were so excellent that we could quit working harder than anybody else, could get by on our reputation, on our many awards for best toy store, our shiny new mall stores, our good press.

The Puzzlebox culture that had taken us so far had been diluted. The expansion had killed the magic. We were not all in it together anymore.

And I wasn't seeing yet, in early 1988, the difference between the city of Madison and the two larger cities of Milwaukee and St. Louis. Madison was my physical and spiritual home, and I thought I knew it like a loving relative. In truth, it was an atypical American city, with an unusually stable government and non-profit economy, and the superior performance of our store there would obscure the truth of what was happening in the country for some time to come.

Eventually, the anger I had felt when Mary Ann and Laura left dissipated as the complexity of my business failure emerged, and I started to admit my own mistakes. My relatively sudden success had made me overconfident in my abilities, and in those of my young managers as well. Later, I would understand how lucky my timing had been. When I opened the first store, shopping was on an upswing, and I assumed it would stay that way. I couldn't foresee the future, how quickly the new economic era would skew everything.

It had all happened too fast. My decision to expand as an absentee CEO was simply a mistake. I was a little like the country then, in its own rabid business expansion, walking on water, deluding myself that the success which had come so easily would continue. Sooner or later, everything changes. Be they finance, tech, or housing, the bubbles burst.

It would be decades before Mary Ann, Laura, and I would meet again, to talk about the business. We kept in touch casually after the harshness of the last months we were together in Madison began to fade. In 2018, I invited them to spend time with me in Madison, after sending them copies of what I had written about our time together. Sitting in my apartment, we finally talked honestly about the past, as I took responsibility for neglecting the business and my supervision of them during the period before everything fell apart.

Both women built successful careers after they left the Puzzlebox. In Milwaukee, Laura returned to making art, specifically scarves, table linens, and fabrics from her original designs, silk-screened in her own studio, counting stores as prestigious as Neiman Marcus among her customers. Mary Anne moved to California, where she became a sales rep to specialty toy stores, demonstrating and selling many of the same lines she'd sold at the Puzzlebox. She was so good at it she ended up with the best territory in Southern California, later starting a sales repping company of her own, even publishing a toy catalog for store owners.

There was never any question in my mind as to their contribution to the success of the store and to those wonderful first few years I call the Magic Hour.

THIRTY-THREE

Bill Pinkovitz sat across from me in a booth at Gino's, working on a plate of spaghetti and meatballs. It was two years after the 1987 stock market crash. I was in full confessional mode.

"I made a lot of mistakes, Bill. The old model that worked so well for Puzzlebox broke down with the new model. I thought I could run the company a couple of days a week, and I couldn't."

Bill jumped in, his voice matter-of-fact, his face untroubled. "Janice, Puzzlebox was classic—the promotional organization that went administrative and didn't make it. It was easier for you to start something successful than to do the work to keep it that way."

"But Bill, I knew what those terms meant. We took the classes, I flattened the power structure, went horizontal instead of everyone reporting to the top. How could I have gotten it so wrong?"

He looked up, still chewing. "Why? You can read all you can, but you still live it." He sat back and smiled dourly. "Being an entrepreneur is like joining a revolution. Sales keep increasing, finance the growth. If sales slow down or decrease, you run out of money. Depending on growth to keep a company solvent is dangerous."

I thought about that. "St. Louis changed everything for us. All that money pouring in made me think our store would do well in any location."

"On the other hand," he said, "your growing pains were no worse than anyone else's. You got through it." He was pulling on his ear as he talked. "Janice, you were a classic example of a woman in business over-nurturing employees, but in particular, giving power without adequate controls."

OUCH. That was hard to hear. But it was at least partially true. It was entirely possible that by not holding my people to the highest standards, I had cost them their jobs.

Years later, when women in positions of authority had greatly multiplied, I would recall this conversation. And I wondered if, in fact, Bill was just being chauvinistic. Certainly, men had their old boys' clubs, which worked well to protect the group, including the weaker members. Was that different? Then I wondered, if Bill was right, and women did over-nurture employees, if it was because we were simply kinder, better at caretaking, mothers at heart, in fact? In the end, I would come to believe that just about anyone, male or female, was capable of acting badly when handed power or wealth.

While Bill's assessment of my company that day in 1989 was fair, there were forces at work bigger than my missteps. How could we know then that a little-known rereading of the Sherman Anti-Trust Act by a few academic economists in the seventies would result in such runaway growth of monopolies in the next thirty years that many small businesses would die?

This transformation of the American economy began at the climax of what has been called the American Century, at the end of the seventies when manufacturing was at its height, and the economy had been strong for so long that no one could be faulted for thinking it would go on forever. In 1979, equality of class was at its height in our country. We had reason to be proud of our democratic society. And who would have imagined that forty years later, a yawning new income gap would expose an inequality of wealth and class that rewarded only the top 20% of Americans.

Years later, when the pandemic started to uncover the devastating effects of the new economy on the working class, Michael Sandel would trace it, pointing out that from 1946 to the 1970s, when my dad worked for Northern States Power, it was possible for those without a college degree to find good work, support a family, and lead a pleasant middle-class life. But when jobs started moving overseas to cheap labor, the number of manufacturing jobs in the U.S. fell by over seven million. Blue-collar workers struggled to find a decent job, leaving them with first-time mortgages they couldn't pay and a loss of self-respect. And by 2014, CEOs of major American companies made 300 times more than the average worker.

WHEN I EXPANDED the Puzzlebox in 1985, the American Century was at its height, and it felt like we could go anywhere with our store concept and succeed, that everyone would always want our toys. That had all changed so quickly, but at least I could mend and save my business. But I would find the two hard years of reconstruction took its toll on my body as well as my spirit. One Sunday in January of 1989, I stared in dismay at the photo the State Journal had run next to their weekly *Know Your Madisonian* feature. My face was puffy, my forehead lined, there were dark pockets under my eyes. My hair was a curly mass covering half my forehead and my cheeks. I seemed to be drowning in my stylishly oversized suit jacket with big shoulder pads. I smiled weakly out at the readers, hardly the picture of the successful woman the article described.

Unfortunately, my habit of salving my wounds alone at night with drink had intensified. I would walk home from work telling myself I wouldn't drink that night, couldn't afford another hangover in the morning. But then I'd open the door to the apartment, turn left to the kitchen, and take the bottle of wine out of the fridge. I had just enough nights alone in Madison to drown my sorrows way too much. No wonder I looked so tired all the time. I remember vividly one morning a few months after the story ran waking so physically ill that I dressed with difficulty, too sick to eat breakfast. But I had a meeting I couldn't miss, so I pulled on my heavy winter coat and walked out the door. Trudging along, my thoughts were so grim that I suddenly stopped in the middle of a block and silently screamed, "God, I can't go on like this!" I hit my bottom that day, even though I continued drinking for several more weeks.

I almost always drank alone, careful to be moderate in public, but it was getting harder to control that. One night that winter, I got so drunk at a Puzzlebox staff party that I barely staggered into the house, supported by Mike. The next morning, I couldn't get out of bed. Mike was the most indulgent of creatures, but now even he judged me harshly. Before he left for Milwaukee, he told me bluntly that I had to fix my drinking problem. I'd been so clever in the past by drinking in private that no one had ever called me on it. Now I felt so disgusted with myself that it was easy to go on the wagon for the next few days, a few days that would turn into a lifetime.

I flew to St. Louis that week, and at the end of the day when I got to the airport to fly home, my flight was delayed four hours. Bored, I browsed the bookstore and saw a book called *Any Woman's Blues*, by Erica Jong. Coincidentally, I'd seen her interviewed on the *Today* show a week before, when she'd described her book's protagonist as a woman artist who at the age of 55 found herself at an Alcoholics Anonymous meeting. In the past, I'd only identified AA with gutter drunks. Nobody like me. Jong's book gave me the courage to be open to a program for myself. I read it in two days and immediately called a friend who had told me years before that she didn't drink because her ex-husband was an alcoholic. It would turn out that she was a recovering alcoholic herself and took me to my first meeting at 501 N. Carroll Street, which just happened to be around the corner from my apartment.

By the end of the week, I'd gone to four different meetings. I soon learned that Madison was full of them, and I started a lifetime habit of attending regularly. It was a whole month later that I realized with a start that the day I hit bottom on my way to work, I'd been standing in front of the AA clubhouse near my apartment.

It was an enormous relief to stop drinking. I'd wanted to, many times, but could never string more than a few days together. It seemed miraculous to me that after a few months in AA, the urge to drink disappeared completely.

IN THOSE EARLY months of 1990, serendipity, luck, timing, and surely a modicum of grace created a series of events that put me on a new, unexpected path. One day in late January, I was shocked to see a For Sale sign in the window of *K-Sera*, the accessory store on our block that I'd patronized happily for years. I went inside, where Kay Miller, the owner, confessed she was burned out and was quitting retail. I loved her store and went away saddened by State Street's loss.

I'd recently accepted an offer from a buyer who would take the St. Louis store off my hands for the cost of inventory. Our Madison and Milwaukee stores were on an even keel, but sales in St. Louis had continued to fall. The store still brought in some cash, which helped cover our administrative costs. But if the pattern continued, it would lose money soon. In fact, although it wasn't obvious yet, the once-brilliant mall was in a general decline after only four years.

In February, I made a last trip to St. Louis. The day after I came back, I made an intuitive move that seemed crazy in the moment. I woke, up, drank two cups of coffee, and thought about the fact that no one had made Kay Miller an offer for K-Sera. It was a beautiful space, just the right size for a specialty store, on one of the best blocks on what I now understood was one of the top retail streets in the country. Al Goldstein, a veteran retail owner on the Capitol Square, had drilled into me years ago the wisdom of the mantra: *location, location, location*. It made sense to have two stores on the same block, and I had an idea for a new kind of store that had been cooking in my head for months. I called it Little Luxuries. I didn't run the decision by anyone. I knew this was what I wanted to do, and I just couldn't let the opportunity slip away.

I got dressed, walked to K-Sera, and told Kay I wanted to buy her business. Three months later, I reopened with my new concept, keeping costs ultra-low by using the fixtures already in place and selling off the inventory I didn't want, using the cash to buy new products. The money from the sale of the St. Louis store helped finance the start-up costs.

Three days after Kay accepted my offer to buy her business, I asked my sons to meet me at Gino's for dinner. I explained my new move, and without a beat invited them into the business with me. They were both excited but wary. John spoke first, peering uncertainly over the top of his glasses.

"I see where Peter would fit in, Mom, but I don't think I'm very good at sales."

"I don't need that from you, John, I need your tech skills, behind the scenes with me. I'm overwhelmed with office stuff. We need a new inventory system. You know how to put that together, and you can learn to do the monthly financials. You'll be the boss of the office. I spend too much time on the phone with the Milwaukee managers, just holding their hands, answering questions you could handle. You could be a big help there."

He nodded, digesting it, and I knew it would work. I looked at Peter, who had been listening intently. "How would you like to run the new store?" I said.

He laughed, but when my face stayed serious, his changed. "You think I'm ready for that?"

"I do. You're comfortable with women customers. They like you and so does the staff." He smiled, knowing it was true. "You're a real presence in the store, and you're great at customer service. I'll teach you how to do the rest."

In Business 1987

I looked at both of them closely. "The truth is, it's been a hard two years working alone. I'd love to have you with me." I paused. "I think it would be a way to keep our family together."

They both nodded at that, not speaking. We all smiled then, and for the first time in a long time, I felt that life was getting better.

MIKE AND I GOT MARRIED a month after Little Luxuries opened. I was in the pink cloud phase of early recovery, when newly sober alcoholics think all their troubles will disappear with the liquor. In fact, it did feel that way. I had my kids with me in the business, which was finally on firm ground. I had a brand-new store to play with, and I was newly married to a man I loved who loved me.

The idea for Little Luxuries had come to me on a dark night of the soul. Mike and I had quarreled one morning before he'd left for Milwaukee. I was still in the hard work of reorganizing the business. I'd made so many harsh decisions that I yearned for softness, and now the warmth was even leaving my relationship. That week, the *New York*

Times Magazine had run an illustrated article called "Little Luxuries" that celebrated small, inexpensive pleasures, with a photo of a breakfast tray on a pretty bed, set with flowered china, a carefully folded white napkin, and a fresh rose in a pretty vase. My eyes filled with tears as I looked at it. I realized then how starved I was for the comfort of beauty.

The idle thought came to me of a store that spoke to the need of women in my era for things in their lives that softened the hard effects of their new, challenging work. Some of the professional women I knew liked a day at the spa, or a massage, or just a long soaking bath. I needed something beautiful, in nature, art or design. In my early courtship days with Mike, I'd loved the flowers he brought me routinely, and even now the beautifully packaged gifts he gave me at Christmas.

Of course, had I any idea of the dubious future of small retail stores, I might have thought twice about starting another new concept store. I think my faith in State Street was so strong that I never considered it a risk. I'd learned a lot about the street, about the people who shopped there, where they came from, where they worked, what they liked. And I'd learned a lot about how not to run a store. It was time to make some lemonade out of my lemons. With this new venture, I would give it my all, be completely present, be a great buyer, a good manager, and a good boss.

I'd learned with Puzzlebox that the product came first, and for this street it needed to be special and not too expensive. And yet, it had to be somewhat unusual, maybe something that changed with the seasons, like scarves, hats, gloves, hair ornaments. A good buyer who worked hard at it could always put together a special collection and be competitive with anyone.

In the end, I felt I could create a special mix for women of my time. The Puzzlebox had met its customers' needs for play after the harshness of the Vietnam period. Now, Little Luxuries would reflect my own need for beauty in the face of difficult work. Hopefully, it would translate to women customers as well.

THIRTY-FOUR

I stood in front of Little Luxuries wondering where the customers were. Up the street toward the Capitol building, there was no one on the sidewalks at all. Turning toward campus, I saw a few stragglers looking in the window of the Puzzlebox. That end of our block was a natural stopping point for tourists, with only a few stores on upper State in 1990 to draw pedestrians in our direction. I fought panic sometimes, afraid my decision to open the new store had been rash.

But spring came in a few months, and state workers came from the Square for lunch and discovered us. We lured summer tourists on their way to the Capitol with lush window displays—polished silver jewelry laid out on deep green velvet, floral hatboxes overflowing with pretty spring scarves. On Saturdays, locals who headed down State after visiting the Farmers' Market made us a stop on their route.

Little Luxuries 1990

The slower pace of business gave me time with Peter, who took to his duties with the ease of a natural manager. He caught on quickly, working well with our small staff. I started spending Saturdays with him at Little Luxuries rather than at the Puzzlebox, schooling him in the business as we worked, taking pleasure in his company, appreciating the camaraderie he built with staff and customers.

In the office, John bloomed. I'd known his computer skills would be an asset, but his telephone relationships with the two Milwaukee managers was a revelation. My girl-shy, loner son, who was often short-tempered with his family, took on a new persona. Walking into the office just about any time of day, I'd find him on the phone at the central console, explaining complex computer changes to Janis or Jill or assuring them their order for bags and boxes had been placed, his voice patient and reassuring. When I visited the Milwaukee stores, the two managers praised him enthusiastically. He was invaluable in keeping them connected to the central office in Madison.

By 1991, the State Street Puzzlebox had recovered the losses from 1987, with improved sales every year. The Milwaukee Bay Shore store hadn't been open when the market fell so precipitously, but its sales had risen yearly thanks to its solid neighborhood base. Only Grand Avenue had faltered, struggling to come back from its reversals. That store did twice the sales of Bay Shore, so our bottom line was dependent on the cash it brought in. Altogether, it felt like we were back on firm footing.

AFTER A YEAR AT Little Luxuries, Peter had demonstrated leadership skills and a strong bent for business. He was eager for advancement, and I made a decision to send him to Milwaukee to take over the Grand Avenue store. It needed new energy to reverse the losses, and Peter had plenty of that. The store also looked tired after nine years. Luckily, my favorite architect was available to do a physical make-over. As usual, James produced a fresh, unique design, in rich shades of green with a ceiling of curvy golden panels.

Even so, Grand Avenue sales dipped 9% that year before they began to reverse in the fall. Undeterred by the volatility, Peter surprised me by proposing to buy both Milwaukee stores on a five-year payout. I was impressed by the detailed financial projections he'd done showing the plan's feasibility. I could see no reason to delay, especially since I would be around to advise him. The Madison store was having a good run again, and I assumed it would just be a matter of time until Grand Avenue did the same. I felt sure things were going back to normal. The business had held so steady for me since the overhaul that I felt secure in leaving it to others now.

MIKE'S RECURRING PROBLEMS with money had reached a crisis point, casting a deepening shadow over our marriage. By now, I was more comfortable and honest in my AA program, and I began to confront him. We fought in closer and closer cycles. At my insistence, we started an intense course of counseling with a married couple. I found support there, but Mike was resistant to the changes the counselors recommended. We were at stalemate, and I finally admitted our future was shaky.

The sale went through in October of 1991. And suddenly, after ten years in business, I was ready to let go of the Puzzlebox. It made sense now to sell the Madison store to Cathy Sullivan, its manager, on a land contract similar to the one I had with Peter. The two of them got on well and could cooperate on joint projects. I would then be free to focus on building sales at Little Luxuries.

The only downside, but a big one, was that the changes had no room for John. There simply wasn't enough work to justify his position or keep our expensive offices open. When the deals were struck, things would change for the three of us. I would move from being Peter's supervisor to his banker, leaving him sole owner of the Milwaukee stores. With his experience at the Puzzlebox added to his resume, John landed a good job in the computer division of the local energy utility. He'd had a dream since childhood to become a pilot, and that Christmas, I gave him flying lessons at a local airport. He was thrilled and soon became an avid amateur pilot.

When my life settled down after these changes, I realized I'd finally had enough of concessions with Mike. I decided to hold my ground, and in turn, he decided to end our counseling sessions. Despite that, I was taken by surprise when he upped the ante by abruptly moving to an apartment in Milwaukee. Initially, I held out hope he'd come back to counseling and our marriage.

I still loved Mike, but after more time apart and a last-minute attempt at reconciliation, I had a powerful feeling of having saved my life.

We would divorce a year later. Mike would eventually remarry and move back to California, to a Veterans' hospital not far from his parents' home. I would never regret the marriage, remembering the many gifts, both concrete and psychological, he had given me, among them support for my recovery program. I had reaped wonderful benefits from saying goodbye to alcohol. I was healthier physically than I'd been since my youth, my brain was clear, my self-esteem high.

ONE WEDNESDAY AFTERNOON almost a year after Peter bought the Milwaukee stores, I drove away from the Grand Avenue, my mind a jumble of uneasy thoughts. It was past 5:00 when I got back to Madison, but I called Joan Gillman anyway. She'd been my business adviser for five years now, and I had critical need of her judgment. She was at home and told me to come over in an hour.

I found her in her kitchen with an apron around her waist, folding flour into an electric mixer filled with batter. Brushing a lock of hair from her face, she explained she was making a cake for a fundraiser that night.

Watching anxiously from my perch on a stool, I struggled to relax. She finished, turned the machine off, wiping her hands on a towel as she looked at me. "So what's going on?"

"It's Peter. He was late in sending his monthly income statement, and when it finally came I saw his inventory levels are way too low. I knew he was trying to trim fat, but I had no idea how much."

She stood leaning against the counter. "He hadn't told you about it?"

"No! He only admitted it when I pressed him, on the phone." I looked at her, stricken. "He thinks I shouldn't question any of his decisions."

She said nothing. I went on, calmer now that I'd said it out loud.

"Today I got assertive. The store looks scant. It doesn't look awful, but it just looks ... mediocre! Not special. It should look chock full of wonderful toys, and it doesn't. And when I told him that he denied he'd even cut back. He said he was just being more efficient so he'd have a better cash reserve. I told him starving the inventory was a sure way to lose sales and hurt the business, but he just brushed it off."

I felt defeated. "This is not like Peter. He's always respected my judgment."

Joan was silent, then moved closer to me, crossed her arms, and spoke firmly. "Janice, you've got to tell him if he doesn't listen to you, you'll take the business back."

I was surprised. How could I say those words to Peter, after all we had been through together, after all the hard work he'd done to take over the stores?

But if I had learned one thing after the business almost crashed, it was to listen to my business advisers. So, Joan and I sat at the kitchen table and drew up a plan of action. I would write a letter to Peter outlining my specific concerns, with a list of actions he needed to take. She sat with me and dictated the opening line: "I regret to say that, as your banker, I find it necessary to reassess the terms of our agreement of your purchase of the two Puzzlebox stores in Milwaukee."

A week later Joan, Peter, and I sat at a round table in the public area outside the store at the Grand Avenue. At 8:00 a.m., it was eerily quiet there. On the table were three cups of coffee Peter had brought, plus financial reports on each store.

My personable son had met us smiling, as always, dressed neatly in pressed pants and blue-and-white striped sport shirt, but the tension in his slender frame signaled otherwise. When he picked up his coffee, I saw that his fingernails were bitten to the point of pain.

Joan got right to it. "I'd like to tell you both a story. A man who owned a grocery store hired his son to work in the produce department, not as a manager, just a regular worker. Because he was the boss's son, he felt he didn't have to take the produce manager's orders and ignored most of them. The manager kept after him, but the son continued the behavior. Frustrated, the manager finally went to the owner and told him he felt he had to quit.

"But the owner quickly said, 'No, no need to quit. I'll fire the boy.' And he called his son in and fired him.

"At home that night the father sat down with his son and said: 'Son, I hear that son-of-a-bitch fired you today.'"

Joan sat quietly while we absorbed her story, then spoke. "When you have a family business, you need to be clear who you're talking to." She looked at Peter. "You're confused about when Janice is your mom or when she's your banker. The roles are confusing, and it's common to have trouble with them."

Then she pulled four paper hats out of a bag. With a magic marker she wrote SON on one, OWNER on the other, and gave them to Peter. The ones she handed me were MOTHER and BANKER. Then she had us play our parts.

With my mom hat on, I said to my son, "Peter, I am so sorry you're struggling with the business. I know how much you want this, how hard you're working at it. I just don't want you to get hurt."

And my son replied, "Mom, I know you're the one person I should listen to, but I haven't wanted to. I wanted to figure it out on my own."

When Peter put his owner hat on, he confessed that he'd been squirreling away money because the cost of goods had proved higher than he'd projected in the business plan. His voice was desperate. "I'm worried because I have less cash than I should. I'm afraid I won't be able to pay bills or make the loan payments."

His words went straight to my heart, but it was a relief to hear them. With my banker hat on I said, "I understand, Peter, but there are other ways to deal with this problem, and I can help you with them."

In fact, working together after this, we would find a solution to his cash flow problems and allay a good part of his uncertainty and fears.

But there was far more wrong at the Grand Avenue than Peter's shorting the inventory. That could be fixed, and his stores should have recovered and prospered. Peter was a careful, smart administrator. Except for this recent experience, he had kept the stores looking good, empowering people who excelled at display and merchandising. The hardest part of a store manager's job was managing people, but that was Peter's strength. He delegated well, and staff liked and respected him.

Joan had saved the day for us this time, but there was no protection against the changes that had begun to erode hundreds of small retail businesses, eventually emptying main streets in small towns and shopping districts in cities around the country.

Trade between the U.S. and China would go from four billion dollars to six-hundred billion in thirty years. At first the imports were low-cost, labor-intensive products—dishes, toys, clothes—but then changed to more expensive things, many of them tech products—phones, car electronics, and even furniture. Eventually there would be a 6-1 ratio of trade, in China's favor.

In the beginning, our stores had benefited from globalization and the cheaper goods it brought. We bought inexpensive toys made in

Asia—wind-ups and plastic dinosaurs and pint-sized baby dolls—in large quantities and filled our plastic bins to overflowing. And people loved it and bought a lot.

But in the nineties, customers began to change their shopping patterns, with middle and upper-middle-class people frequenting big-box stores, formerly the province of the working class. Suddenly, it was downright chic to shop cheap, and small stores that couldn't compete started to disappear.

When I started expanding, I expected all our stores would do as well as the original one, not fully understanding the special nature of State Street, with its recession-proof market of government workers, university staff and students, and continual tourists. But from his perch in Milwaukee, Peter had no protection from direct competition from the big chains. As it increased, he came up with a prospective solution, a bigger, hybrid store he would call the Puzzlebox Emporium, set in a new location with lower rent. It was the right idea and could have worked, but once again, timing was everything. The malls declined more quickly than we could have imagined. When the sales slide accelerated at the Grand Avenue, Peter knew there would be no way to finance the larger store, which would have required a million dollars to capitalize.

When the Grand Avenue lease was up, Peter would have the achingly hard job of closing the Puzzlebox, one of the last of the local stores in the center. With his plans shot, he sold the Bay Shore store for the cost of the inventory to Cathy Sullivan. But even the State Street store was feeling the competition now, too. With the economy of scale she gained with another store, Cathy would be able to make the business work, but just for a few years more.

Peter moved to Minneapolis for a fresh start to work as a financial adviser with Piper Jaffray, an excellent local company. His new profession would better reward his talents. Due to his intelligent, personable approach, he would go on to retain an impressive base of clients. It was a happy ending when a year after he moved, he married Julie Cureton, a Minnesota native who as a fellow college student had waited tables alongside him at the Fess Hotel restaurant in Madison.

The changes in retail accelerated with astonishing speed, compounded by the astounding growth of monopolies that eliminated most competition. The brilliant Rouse malls in Milwaukee and St. Louis lost many tenants in that period. Both would soon deteriorate and eventually be adapted for other purposes. Then within a year, a large toy chain store moved into Bay Shore Mall. The competition was so overwhelming that Cathy would close the store when the lease was up. And finally, the Puzzlebox on State Street closed in 1997, eighteen years after it opened.

THIRTY-FIVE

Despite the global changes, most of State Street would remain remarkably stable through the end of the century. Many of the stores that began in the post-Vietnam era still operated, many under the original owners; others were passed to employees or new owners. How lucky I had been and still was to have Little Luxuries there.

In 2004, the twenty-four-year-old Civic Center was replaced by the Overture Center, funded by an extremely large private donation. The new complex was bigger and grander than the old Civic Center. Its need for space had taken away several beloved restaurants—Dotty Dumplings Dowry, Radical Rye, and Miller's Grocery with its tasty homemade soups—that had brought many state workers from the Square to State Street for lunch. Even as our noontime business at Little Luxuries fell off, we expanded evening hours for the theater and bar crowd. Upper State was changing again, this time into an entertainment center.

Main Streets everywhere had been emptied out by suburban malls in the mid-twentieth century. Now the malls, already threatened by the Walmarts, Targets, and Costcos, were under attack by internet sales. State Street was still so strong, so local, so compact, that it would take longer for the change, but it would happen there, too. There would always be competition from national chains, but the smaller local stores that survived learned to buy products that appealed to people coming downtown for entertainment. And the flood of new tech workers to downtown apartments would lead to a new demand for good food and drink.

The Little Luxuries concept turned out to be a model that survived. Unlike the Puzzlebox, with its narrow range of products, the new store could take advantage of trends, buying from companies too small to supply big companies. Selling accessories was fun and profitable, with the styles changing with the seasons, guaranteeing new product regularly, and these things sold well to tourists and people coming to Overture performances. I continued to observe that people were willing to pay more for something special they didn't see elsewhere.

BY 2008, the store felt stable. We had survived the two years it took to demolish the Civic Center, build the Overture Center, and redo the adjacent streets. An unfortunate side effect of the new performance center was a sharp rise in property values on the blocks nearby, triggering higher rents. When my lease at Little Luxuries was up for renewal that year, my landlord presented me with a large rent increase. We had just endured two years of construction losses, and it rankled.

I was mulling this over one day as I walked down the block and stopped to look into the window of the former Puzzlebox space, scene of many B.B. Bear widows. After Cathy Sullivan closed the Puzzlebox, the Garvers had rented the space to a Chinese importer. Now the display window was a jumble of inexpensive jewelry, bamboo tables, and bric-a-brac.

"Janice, I need a new tenant," a familiar voice said over my shoulder.

I turned and smiled at the craggy, aging face of John Garver. I was always glad to see him. I'd come to appreciate his ethics in business, especially in contrast to other landlords who invariably put their bottom lines first.

"What happened?" I said. "Is your tenant leaving?"

"Next month," John growled. "The street construction took him out. I need a new tenant." Now he looked at me slyly. "How about you? You're good at stores. Don't you have a new one you can start here?"

I laughed.

But I started thinking about what great landlords the Garvers had been. In a way, they had been more like partners. Fanny had invited me into the space when I was an unknown quantity. I still remembered the original one-page lease John drew up for me, remarkably fair and simple.

The Garvers had a vested interest in their own business and building, but they also loved the street and the city. They were local landowners in the best possible way. My current landlord was also local, but his interest was strictly financial.

It was this understanding of the value of a great landlord that gave me the impetus to move Little Luxuries down the street. When I asked John what the rent would be, he quoted a figure that was a little lower than the one I was currently paying, and a lot lower than my proposed raised rent.

A month later, I gave notice and signed a five-year lease with Fanny and John Garver. It would be expensive to relocate, but the lower rent gave me an incentive. I never doubted the soundness of the investment.

The promoter in me was thrilled. I had a new project! But I needed help. The space had deteriorated badly. The shelving was worn, the carpeting dirty and bare, the lovely colors painted over. But much of the woodwork remained intact, and happily, the clouds were still there.

As fate would have it, James was available to give the store a new look. The walls became a new, softer blue and green. He designed a series of low glass tables that led the eye all the way to the back window, a visual line reinforced by the repainted clouds in the space above them. The new fixtures created perfect platforms for the orderly placement of perfumes, bowls, and scarves. In another spot of luck and timing, Sam Breidenbach and his crew came back to build it out, and Anne Boyle designed a lovely new logo to paint on the window, use in ads, and print on new stationery.

When the store reopened after the remodeling, it was beautiful twice over, and I ruminated on how I had come full circle. I'd first sold toys in this space to war-weary customers looking for fun. Now, in the hard-edged technological era, I offered lovely, sensual objects—filmy silk scarves, soft leather purses, glittering hair ornaments, scented soaps and lotions—that answered the need for touch, pleasure, and beauty.

And the new store had come about with the help of my old team, Madison people who continued to love what they did. And so, I ended my retail career back where I started, a small business owner at the top of the pyramid.

With Little Luxuries, I had finally found a business model that worked for me, for my staff, and my customers. With just one store, I was able to honor my original vision of selling high-quality, good-looking products displayed with taste and verve. In this second incarnation. I would try to be a better boss, pay more attention to employees, do regular performance reviews, and provide opportunities for growth. I would hire the best people I could find and stay close to them and to customers.

Despite the difficult period of overexpansion and recovery, I felt grateful for my business. It allowed me to leave a life I wanted out of and move into a life with richer experiences. If I stayed small and kept an oversized foot in the store, I could spread my entrepreneurial wings in other directions.

In the last years of my retail career, Little Luxuries would provide me an income while giving me the freedom to do what I did best—start new projects. While keeping a close watch on the business, I pursued a new passion, documentary filmmaking. In the next decade, I produced several documentaries, notably *The Gee Whiz Kid*, the story of a pitchman I met at my hometown fair that screened at the first Wisconsin Film Festival. In some kind of ironic twist, the pitchman Jack Nyberg would eventually negotiate volume discounts with my vendors that enriched my business and my own skill set, resulting in the most profitable period of my retail career.

But even the skilled itinerant pitchman would be felled by globalization after 2000, as it became impossible for him to buy products at low-enough prices to match online and big-box competition.

THIRTY-SIX

When I walked into the living room with a tray of drinks, Peter and Julie were standing at the bay window. It was a late autumn Saturday in 2018, and the lights on the Capitol building had just switched on. The tall, graceful white dome glowed in the darkening sky.

My son stood tall, his once white-blond hair dark now, cut short, shot with gray. His body was still trim and youthful, despite his 51 years. Julie stood close to him, her long, brown hair moving as she turned to me, smiling. She had enjoyed a successful career in commercial banking before their marriage. After the children came, she'd quit working until they reached school age, then turned to a field she loved, design, becoming an expert at the renovation of old houses.

"This view never disappoints, Janice," she said.

"No, it doesn't," I agreed, bending to place the tray on the coffee table.

My apartment was the first floor of a hundred-year-old house in a historic neighborhood called Mansion Hill, just three blocks up from the Capitol Square. The room was one long space with ten-foot ceilings, used as both dining and living room. I'd arranged comfortable chairs around the white fireplace, flanked on two sides by built-in shelves filled with my favorite books and family photos.

The house was old, as was I now, and much of what I loved was in this room. My parents' formal wedding portrait, an old beauty in an oval frame with beveled glass, shared wall space with antique textiles under glass that dated from my tenure at the Elvehjem Art Center.

The high ceilings left plenty of space for the art I'd acquired over thirty years from the Garver Gallery. It ranged from my very first purchase, a small lithograph of a nineteenth-century dome house shaded by tall oaks, to a black and white print of a girl taking aim as she leaned over a pool table, her long blonde hair highlighted by a nearby window.

My life was on these walls. The etching of the house with many rooms and the print of the girl shooting pool spoke to my quest for a life with many experiences. The horizontal lines in two prints by Frances Myers—one of a Frank Lloyd Wright building and another the vertical facade of an art deco theater—reflected my love of architecture, form, and beauty. The pieces on my walls spoke to the comfort of art and the sheer experience of being alive.

When I'd sold Little Luxuries and retired, I'd started writing about the business, knowing I'd lived through a historic era, and my boys had been swept into it with me. Now I wanted to share what I'd learned with Peter, who'd seen his ambitions for the Milwaukee stores dashed in a national retail reordering.

Johnny

I speak only of Peter, now, not Johnny. On April 25, 2002, our lives had come to a stop with his sudden, stunning death. I'd been happy when my girl-shy son had found Gaye, a girl from Texas, whom he adored and who adored him. I loved having them near me for the short year they lived in Madison. When John found a new job with a Dell start-up in Austin, they'd moved to Texas.

Sadly, his promising job disappeared when the company dissolved only months after he'd started, a casualty of the dotcom bubble collapse of 2000. They moved again, to be near Gaye's parents. John had been working at a bank in a small town in east Texas when he took ill. He'd not yet been diagnosed with a mysterious malady that had lasted for months. Then, during a routine medical workup, his heart simply stopped. Six agonizing months later, an autopsy revealed the cause of death, a rare disease called amyloidosis that had stealthily spread through the organs of his body, eventually shutting it down. As a sign of its regard for John, the bank where he worked closed on the day of his funeral.

We all flew there to help bury him in a small family cemetery ringed with pine trees that could have been in Wisconsin, a group including his father, Peter, Julie, and their three-year-old daughter, Giselle. I was in and out of shock for a year. Life went on, sometimes unbearably, and eventually I came to accept the reality of the lasting grief of his passing.

It would help that my ex-husband John and I had established a new friendship throughout the years. As he neared retirement, he'd begun writing seriously, a return to the passion that drove him when we first met as students. He went on to publish a number of books, mostly non-fiction, including my favorite, *Behind Enemy Lines*, a richly detailed, vivid memoir of growing up in small-town northern Wisconsin, including life with the polio he contracted as a small boy.

After our grandchildren were born, John and I began to share holidays with Peter and Julie and the children. Peter would say his divorced parents' joint presence was unusual and interesting, but I only know it felt good, important, and natural to come together as the family we had become.

JULIE AND PETER'S beautiful family, first Giselle, then Ellis and Stuart, lightened the shadow of John's death. As the youngest of eight, I never knew my grandparents, and now I got to invent the role for myself. My memories of their visits to me during their growing years are vivid: Giselle at eight sitting on a stool at Little Luxuries, avidly unpacking the tiny rubber take-apart toys she'd urged me to carry; at seventeen, in the lead role in her high school production of *Up the Down Staircase*, startling me with her luminous, self-assured performance.

Ellis at six counted inventory with my staff, spreading hundreds of the now-best-selling take-apart toys on the floor, delighting us all. And then there he was at sixteen, tall, rangy, and graceful, helping me fix a setting on my iPhone.

Stuart, the youngest, was usually first to lift the top off the blue glass camel dish on my coffee table to see what candy was there, and invariably made his way to the basement to fetch his favorite Lincoln Logs, petting my cat Scarlet on the way.

TODAY, AS JULIE, PETER, and I settled into chairs, Ellis and Stuart were busy on their devices in the guest room downstairs. Giselle was far away, a theatre student at a college in Los Angeles. I looked around, loving the graceful proportions of my apartment, out of fashion now as modernism ruled, and antique stores went broke. The changes in the country and culture were on my mind.

As the decades had passed, I had sometimes paused, wondering what had happened that everything had gotten so big. Really big houses, with bulky furniture made to fit the enormous rooms. We didn't just have cars and station wagons anymore, we had SUVs and pickups crowding the narrow Madison streets. At the movies, soft drink cups were the size of milk cartons, difficult to hold in one hand. In restaurants, food portions were more than enough for two. And then a lot of us got obese. After all, we'd become the best market in the world, the best consumers ever, so much so that in 2017, author Yuval Noah Harari would write in his book, Homo Deus, that more people died in our time from eating too much than eating too little. In fact, he said, "In the early twenty-first century, the average human is far more likely to die from binging at McDonald's than from drought, Ebola, or an Al-Qaeda attack."

And then there were the huge corporations, so oversized that no human answered the phone anymore, and no one expected them to. The bigger a corporation the more impersonal. With no competition, they didn't have to care. People asked for refunds through an arduous process and got them twelve months later. How many of us left messages never returned, hung up in frustration after half an hour of wait time, kept a bad product just because it was too difficult to return?

The major trust busting cases to curb monopolies that began with Teddy Roosevelt at the turn of the century, after the Sherman Anti-Trust Act was passed, had ended abruptly in the 1980s. By 1985, a new Gilded Age began, with 2,274 manufacturing firms merging to 157 corporations in just ten years. Most had a monopoly in their fields, producing enormous wealth that went mostly to a small percent at the top.

According to *Business Insider*, by 2017, ten corporations controlled everything we ate, seven owned most beauty brands, ten dominated clothing, and a single beer corporation captured most of the world's beer sales.

My home state was not immune to the fever. In 1947, Wisconsin had 47,700 dairy farms. In 2018, there were about 7,000, and the number continues to decline while milk production rises with the growth of farms with thousands of cows and automated milking assembly lines that never pause.

A few years later, it would be clear that the really big losers in all this were factory workers, when the powerful combination of monopoly growth and globalism eliminated their jobs, including benefits and pensions. Despite retraining programs, most blue-collar workers ended up in lower-paying jobs. The great promise of America for its middle-class workers had simply collapsed in several decades.

In 2020, a book called *Deaths of Despair and the Future of Capitalism* would delineate in painful detail how unfair the last economic era was for many people, but most particularly, the working class. The authors, economists Anne Case and Angus Deaton, wrote of the huge increase between 1990 and 2017 of deaths by suicide, drug overdose, heart disease, and liver disease from alcoholism, especially frequent among white adults in middle age, most without a college degree, struggling to make their way in a meritocratic society with no credentials.

Reading that, I would think of my own father, who with only a seventh-grade education enjoyed a long, successful life of good work with a company that provided him with a middle-class wage, health insurance, a pension, and, most important, respect from both his employer and his peers.

SITTING ACROSS from Peter and Julie, I shifted in my chair, thinking of a recent visit to Milwaukee. I told them how I'd stopped at the Grand Avenue and had been shocked at the physical deterioration of the lovely old Plankington Building where our store had opened twenty-five years ago. The mall currently housed mostly national discount chains, and now, as I described plaster peeling off the once elegant columns, Peter shook his head.

"Mom, that mall was so beautiful when we had the Puzzlebox there. It was just sad how quickly it went downhill."

I nodded. "There was so much we didn't understand then. Nobody understood how globalization was devastating small businesses."

I continued, thinking it through. "The free-trade agreements Bill Clinton signed in the nineties were meant to be good for everybody, but they were equally deadly to blue-collar workers and small retail stores."

I turned to Peter. "That was when you took over Grand Avenue and Bayshore. With no tariffs on their goods, China flooded the U.S. with cheap products. And those early nineties were the time the retail giants were growing into monopolies. No small store could compete. I don't think anyone could have stopped the decline of the big malls. But that wasn't so clear then." I paused, thinking.

"It took me years to see that the Madison store blinded us to reality. The Puzzlebox lasted longer there because of the city's stable economy. Besides, we had constant tourist traffic and later on an influx of tech workers. The Puzzlebox might have survived with major changes, but the State Street space, so perfect for the era before, was never big enough for the new model."

Peter nodded. "I still think my idea for an emporium in Milwaukee was the only way we could have competed with the big boxes. But it was impossible to pull the money together fast enough."

I nodded. "Even Grand Avenue couldn't turn business around after people shifted their buying habits. You were one of the last independents to leave. That was something, to last that long."

"It was just a bad time," he said.

"It was a bad time, all right," I said, "but no one could have predicted it. I was supposed to be a retail guru, and yet I couldn't imagine the Puzzlebox wouldn't survive. It's easy to see now that the new economy killed off a lot of small stores, but why it happened so quickly very few people understand."

They both looked at me. "What do you mean?" Peter asked.

"That's what I've been reading about in this book." I held up a slim paperback, *The Curse of Bigness* by Tim Wu, a professor at Columbia Law School.

"In the sixties, a handful of academic lawyers convinced the courts that the Sherman Anti-Trust Act had been misinterpreted for decades, and that many unfair judgments had been made against monopolies. They argued that the main intent of the law had been to protect consumer pricing, not prevent monopolies, and a lot of state judges believed them."

Julie sat forward, putting her cup down on the coffee table. "Wasn't the Sherman Act passed at the end of the last century?"

"1890. It's still on the books, but it's hardly been enforced for almost forty years."

"So what changed?" Peter said.

"The original act was meant to break up the monopolies that had stifled competition. But the authors back then also believed communities were hurt by the loss of small businesses. It was only in the 1980s that courts ruled that companies could get as big as they wanted unless the government could show their increased size-raised prices. They made it just about the money."

"That's a huge change," Peter said, his forehead wrinkling. "How could it have happened without everybody noticing?"

"Because most monopoly cases are tried in small state courts, which don't get much press. They tend to be complicated and messy. Judges loved the simplified new interpretation, and most ruled on it. After that, there was nothing to stop growth."

Peter was looking out the window, where the Capitol still glowed. He shook his head. "I remember the year I realized the big-box stores had huge inventories I couldn't match, and they were carrying our toys at much lower prices."

It was easy to see in hindsight, but Peter had lived it in real time, before it was so obvious that all the Puzzlebox stores would fade and die.

Julie had been listening closely. "We've gotten used to the changes now, haven't we? Everybody likes a deal. Maybe it was inevitable."

"I don't think it had to be so drastic," I said. "Why eliminate all tariffs? We don't think about how it changed things, how many factories closed, and how many jobs were lost when so many small stores closed—the employees, the owners, even the sales reps that worked with them and gave personal service."

We talked then about how the mergers had increased, the buy-outs, the consolidation. And then the internet came, and Amazon put the nail in the coffin. Three huge national corporations—Walmart, Costco, and Amazon—dominated retail sales.

"So we were in on the start of all that," Peter said.

"Smack in the middle of it!" I remembered how excited Peter had been when he took over the Milwaukee stores. He'd worked with unstinting energy and joy, as though he'd found his future

"Peter," I said, "you cleaned up a mess that should have been mine. I wish I could have been smart enough then to make it easier for you."

He looked at me, his face serious, and then it cleared, and he laughed. "Well, the way I look at it now, Mom, I figure I got a master's degree in business, in real time."

I leaned back in my chair and smiled. "I guess we both did."

THIRTY-SEVEN

June 2020

I was slicing mushrooms for a stir-fry dinner when I heard shouts and honking horns. Looking out the kitchen window, I saw a dozen people congregating on bicycles in the middle of Gilman Street. I quickly walked to the large window at the front of the house to get a better view.

The four-way intersection of Wisconsin Avenue was filled with another large group of bikers. I looked closely, surprised to see they were all young women. A tall girl stood in front of a row of stopped cars, one foot on her bike pedal, one hand high, palm out, in a command position. The first stalled driver was out of his car, yelling at her. The rest were honking their horns.

"What the hell!" I said. I'd seen plenty of protestors go by my house on their way to the Capitol Square, but none like this. I went back to the kitchen and out my back door, walking to the nearest cyclist, who looked about eighteen.

"Hey, what's going on?" I said.

Her eyes were wide, excited. "A cop beat up a Black activist on State Street. We're protesting his arrest."

I took that in, saying nothing. I'd been listening to the news in the kitchen and knew a Black Lives Matter protest had shut things down that day. But the report I'd heard said a crowd had pulled down a bronze statue in front of the Capitol building, and that later a protester had been arrested for entering a nearby restaurant with a baseball bat on his shoulder, demanding free food. But I didn't tell the girl that. In fact, she and the others all had their heads down, peering at their phones. Suddenly, the ringleader got on her bike and gestured to the cyclists, who geared up and followed her as she headed out, freeing up the captive traffic. My new friend climbed on her bike, smiled at me over her shoulder, and shouted "Join us!" as she rode away.

THAT WAS MY PERSONAL INTRODUCTION to the Woke movement, which propelled many of the social justice demonstrations that year, often in the heart of American cities. In Madison, they took place mostly on the Square and upper State Street. The next day the protests continued, and in the afternoon, to get closer to the action, I walked a few blocks from home and ran into Sue Springman, my long-ago boss at the Central Madison Council, who was standing outside her office building looking toward the street. I told her about the crowd by my house the night before, and in turn, she said she'd been at a meeting with the police that morning. There'd been looting and window breaking on State Street, and the company she worked for was worried about the buildings they owned on the Capitol Square.

Critical race theory, or CRT as it came to be called, had been simmering on some back burners for decades, but it found a new home and national focus in the culture wars that split the country in the new era, just as the Vietnam war protests had in the 60s and 70s. In the 2020 model, before the year was over, half a dozen social justice protests would pass by my house. One night I watched as a horizontal street-wide line of helmeted police pushed the crowds up and away from State Street and the Square. The next morning I found a neat pile of sharp-edged stones nestled in my front lawn. Another night, when the crowd had been successfully driven to Langdon Street, a small band came back and lit fires in two large dumpsters, sending them careening wildly down Wisconsin Avenue.

I remembered then how in the late 1960s the general public had supported the anti-war demonstrations as long as they were peaceful, but they began to oppose them when they got violent. In 1968, Richard

Nixon handily won the Presidency on a clearly stated law and order platform. Two years later, the Sterling Hall bombing on the UW campus killed Robert Fassnacht, a physics researcher with three small children, who was working late in the building. This incident, which severely shocked the Madison community, marked the end of the street protests here.

The demonstrations on State Street in 2020 resulted in blocks of boarded-up store windows, even as the reality of COVID-19 set in. The pandemic, which would expose how much our country had changed in forty years, was a catalyst for me. As the spread of the virus began to expose the fractures in our economy and social system, I began to examine and understand how my 35 years on State Street had been affected by the changes in the country. Over the next year, I would see State Street fade into a shadow of itself, as stores closed their doors one by one, leaving only a handful of original retailers behind.

In 1979, when I opened the Puzzlebox, America was more equal than ever in its history. I had no idea then how special that was. Some people were rich, a lot more were poor, but a sizable proportion of us led comfortable middle-class lives. As the youngest child in a farm family, I'd been lucky to go to college, along with my next older brother, but my six other siblings did well without degrees, mostly by working for small companies or starting businesses themselves—one brother patiently acquired rental properties, another worked in advertising, yet another started an industrial battery factory. One sister owned a tack shop for horse owners, another reviewed restaurants for Minneapolis's *Star Tribune*, and my oldest sibling, Freddie, published a novel when she was 92.

But by 2021, a new class system was in place. With the combination of technology, globalization, and the growth of monopolies, wealth had shifted dramatically. Extreme economic concentration yields gross inequity. The Pew Research Center reported in 2018 that the upper class held 79% of all wealth compared to 60% in 1970. The lower class fell from 7% to 4%. Notably, the middle class, formerly so solid, fell the farthest—from 32% in 1970 to 17% in 2018.

These stunning statistics reflected a changing economy that mostly rewarded college graduates, just 24% of the population by 2022. The changes had been good for the upper middle and upper classes but disastrous for working class people. That wasn't clear in Madison for many years, in large part because state government, the university, and a major medical establishment guaranteed stable jobs and incomes. The city had one big manufacturing plant, Oscar Mayer, which held on longer than most, but its closure in 2017 left a hole in the city's north side. Behind the counter on State Street, I had hardly noticed these changes, maybe because by then the new tech companies had settled in and brought their excellent salaries with them.

Most of Madison would do very well in the new economy. By August of 2017, *Wired* put Madison at the top of a list of next hot cities for highly-paid tech workers to move to, advising its readers that if they wanted to move to where the other cool kids were going, Madison was the best. Houses there were still increasing in value, unlike cities like San Francisco (bottom of the list), which were now played out.

Throughout its history, State Street has reflected what's happening in the country, and in this new era it still does, as the city settles into its fortunate new role as a prosperous urban center with many businesses grounded in technology. The phenomenal success of Epic Systems, a medical software company located near Madison, was an economic boom for State Street. Its well-paid young workers loved the downtown scene. They moved into new city apartment buildings and came to State Street to eat, drink, and shop.

When I walked the street at night in that time, well-dressed young men would spill out of the restaurants and bars that lined the street, even as townspeople had left it. I missed the eclectic mix of my early years on the street, but I was grateful to see people patronizing the stores and restaurants. Unfortunately, the combination of the unrest on the street and the COVID-19 outbreak emptied State Street of customers for more than a year, as the young tech workers left the street for the safer edges of the Capitol Square and the near-east side for food and entertainment.

When I came back to Madison from the east coast in 1969, my kids and I ran into tear gas on Library Mall and broken windows on State Street, which was undergoing a sea change as one era ended and another began. Rents were low then, which allowed low-budget entrepreneurs like myself to get a foothold. Now another era has begun, its outcome unknown.

In his book *The Tyranny of Merit*, Michael Sandel writes of the lack of public spaces in our country that gather people of different classes, races, and religions together. Four decades of globalization has brought unequal incomes and wealth so extreme they lead us into separate ways of life, and that has happened here as in other cities. Affluent people and those with less money rarely encounter each other in daily life in our time.

Sandel believed that citizens need to meet in public spaces face to face in order to negotiate our differences. In fact, common spaces help to create and reinforce the common good. In their absence, identity politics threaten to divide us.

We're lucky in Madison to have a downtown that, despite recent history, still functions as the heart of the city, a place where people of wildly different ilk are free to come to express their beliefs and hear those of others. It's still a marketplace where people buy and sell goods, the essential human transaction.

And it's still the place where our two political parties have met for over a hundred and fifty years—to air our differences, argue them out, and, at our best, unite for the common good.

With its small spaces and relatively low rents, State Street excels at reinventing itself, especially in troubled times, and in 2022, I see that happening again. Many of the stores on upper State are still there, classics in their fields that will lead the transition to what is to come. They have talented, hard-working owners with admirable survival skills, starting with Ian's Pizza and Teddywedgers at the top of the street. On the 200 block, Little Luxuries, now owned and managed adeptly by Amy Moore, has survived and thrived in the original Puzzlebox space. Next door in the space formerly the Garver Gallery, Anthology, a popular paper and crafts store with devoted customers, belongs to Sachi and Laura Komai, former managers of Little Luxuries. At 214 State, where I first opened Little Luxuries in 1990, an imaginative new store called Singlestitch sells vintage jackets, T-shirts and whatnots, and feels a great fit for the street.

One block away, The Soap Opera abides, with new owners carrying on the tradition of Beck and Bauer. Sassafrass, where I bought stylish clothes through the decades, regrettably closed its doors early in the pandemic, as Dan and Karen Fix took early retirement. But their action opened the door for Paul Strong of Jazzman to expand from his small space across the street. Flexing entrepreneurial wings in the middle of the pandemic, Paul exhibited the kind of careful risk-taking State Street has always rewarded.

These stores and others down the length of this extraordinary city street reflect the best of local talent. In an age of look-alike chain stores, State Street remains stubbornly unique. I am heartened to see it starting to renew itself once again, with original concepts and plenty of space for the next entrepreneur with a good idea and the grit to develop it.

THE LAST CHAPTER

I came to the world of work late in life, in an era with extraordinary waves of change. The Vietnam War was shuddering to a close, the second feminist revolution firing up, a bright new retail era on the cusp of invention.

I opened The Puzzlebox in 1979 because it was the best job I could find. I had no notion then that it would turn into my life's work. Happily, it would be a venture that would let me test and trust my own judgments and put me in charge of my life. What I initially feared was a narrow path would lead to a life of many experiences. And my timing was inadvertently perfect. I couldn't have picked a better time or place to open a toy store.

Other catalysts worked in my favor. In the early eighties, the Rouse Company successfully wooed me into expansion. My association with that excellent developer would complicate my life for good and ill for the next ten years.

The subsequent failure of my expansion and the necessity of scaling down and firing employees was a mind-numbing experience, but with the help of advisers, I survived and even thrived by restructuring my business and learning to be a better boss.

It was a privilege and a pleasure to be part of the post-Vietnam-War retail surge on State Street, with its burst of ingenuity and creativity, when so many people channeled their alienation from government into unique businesses that reflected their personal values. The success of the Puzzlebox didn't have to do with profits or high mark-ups or cut-throat competition. It had to do with love and joy and trust in people, with pleasure in first-rate products and the many customers who appreciated and bought them.

State Street has had its fans and its detractors. Mayors have loved it or hated it. One even advocated building an overpass so people could avoid going downtown at all. The street has been maimed by violence, avoided by suburban shoppers, embraced by students, traversed in pleasure by bikers, downtown workers, and tourists.

In the end, State Street is a wonder, with six compressed retail blocks of variety, color, ingenuity and vitality, a ten-minute walk end to end, linking the State Capitol and the University of Wisconsin. No wonder a senior editor at *Governing*, a magazine devoted to news of local and state government, called it "one of the great streets in America."

Maybe one day all brick-and-mortar stores will be gone. Maybe the need to see and touch and hold a polished bowl, smell a fragrance, or try on a velvet beret will disappear. Maybe globalization and the internet have changed everything. But the truth is that nobody knows what will happen. When we're in the middle of something, we always think it will stay that way.

After all, it took a pandemic to reveal the momentous changes in the nation during the 35-year period that spanned my small business career. It took more than half a million people dying before the damage that the new economy had wrought became clear. And it took me more than three decades to see clearly how my small business was related to all that.

LOOKING BACK, I still feel my best work was in the first five years of the Puzzlebox, the years that comprised what I call the Magic Hour, with modest beginnings and low expectations. I loved the infectious joy and creativity in those early years, and it was gratifying to have people respond with such enthusiasm to the store.

And even after it all changed, after I got too big for my britches, after we all succumbed to the self-indulgence of the eighties, even after the pain of losing employees and friends, after all that, I have no regrets.

I was privileged to have been a part of those early years, the beginning of a new era that was to change everything. Even as I have written here of the painful years, I saw how it was all a whole, the good and the bad of it, in fact, the full life experience I'd wanted since a young age.

Perhaps the highest accolade I received as a store owner came to me anonymously one day in 2008 soon after Little Luxuries reopened in the old Puzzlebox space on State Street. I got to the store early that day and put on my favorite Stevie Wonder tape. It was a glorious spring morning, so I propped open the back door to get a breeze through from State Street. I stopped for a minute, enjoying the sweet, cool air on my cheeks and bare arms as Stevie purred, *"You are the sunshine of my life."* I walked through the space, pleased with the display of silky scarves spilling from a rack onto the glass-topped table by the front door.

My excellent assistant Amy Moore, who would take over the store when I retired, walked in a few minutes before the first customers from the Farmers' Market arrived, carrying their baskets of broccoli and bags of springy cheese curds. We took our places behind the counter, enjoying the mix of ages and sexes. A young couple stood, trying on the swanky new sunglasses that had just arrived. A pretty woman with gray hair brought a scarf to the counter, and I wrapped it for her, the soft chiffon tumbling into the tissue paper like a heap of rose petals. As she left, a middle-aged man in jeans and a T-shirt walked up to the counter, put down an armful of jigsaw puzzles, looked at me and smiled.

"You know, this shop is as much fun as the toy store that used to be here!"

JOHN

In 2020, at the age of 84, John Durand died, unexpectedly but peacefully, at his southern Wisconsin home in Elkhorn. He is greatly missed, but never forgotten, at all our family gatherings now.

I am grateful for the twenty-one-year period of co-grandparenting John and I enjoyed, traveling from our respective cities to Peter and Julie's home in Minneapolis for birthdays and holidays. It was a special gift to the two of us to have our family together again, with mutual respect and affection, on those happy occasions.

ACKNOWLEDGMENTS

Many thanks to Michelle Wildgen, author and editor, for guiding me patiently through writing classes and multiple revisions of my manuscript. Thanks as well to her partner at Madison Writers Studio, Susanna Daniel, who gave the book a last look.

I am happy that many of the friends who appear in this book are still active in my life—Doreen Adamany, Joan Gillman, Gail Selk, James McFadden—good friends who let me fill their ears with my notions. Anne Boyle, intrepid window designer, helped me out with finishing details, and Susanne Voeltz lent an expert hand at promotion. A special shout-out to John Ribble, who created the cover design, just as he gamely produced the Puzzlebox full-color calendars at Christmas year after year.

Members of my writing group critiqued many chapters. Thank you Nancy Jesse, Keesia Hyzer, Willa Schmidt, Alice D'Alessio, and Nancy Kendrick for your help and encouragement.

I'm grateful to my long-time book club members, Mary Trewatha, Carol Doeppers, Gail Shea, Judith Thompson, Sally Schrag and Barbara Klein for years of monthly exposure to new writers and ideas.

Finally, I want to thank my son Peter for his good grace in allowing me to write about his key role at The Puzzlebox. Peter, Julie, and their children Giselle, Ellis and Stuart remain the emotional foundation of my life.

BOOKS THAT WERE HELPFUL IN WRITING *THE MAGIC HOUR*

Wu, Tim. (2018). *The Curse of Bigness: Antitrust in the New Gilded Age*. Columbia Global Reports, New York.

Case, Anne & Deaton, Angus. (2020). *Deaths of Despair and the Future of Capitalism*. Princeton University Press.

Haidt, Jonathan. (2012). *The Righteous Mind: Why Good People Are Divided by Politics and Religion*. Vintage Books, New York.

Sandel, Michael J. (2020). *The Tyranny of Merit: What's Become of the Common Good?* Farrar, Straus and Giroux, New York.

Stockman, Farah. (2021). *American Made: What Happens to People When Work Disappears*. Random House, N.Y.

Cramer, Katherine J. (2016). *The Politics of Resentment: Rural Consciousness in Wisconsin and the Rise of Scott Walker*. University of Chicago Press.

Printed in the United States
by Baker & Taylor Publisher Services